CW00607383

The Economic Impacts of Population Ageing in Japan

ESRI STUDIES SERIES ON AGEING

In April 2000 the Japanese government launched a series of comprehensive, interdisciplinary and international research projects called 'the Millennium Projects' and as part of this initiative the Economic and Social Research Institute (ESRI) of the Cabinet Office of Japan initiated a two year project entitled 'A Study on Sustainable Economic and Social Structures in the 21st Century', which focuses on ageing and environmental problems in the Japanese and international context.

The *ESRI Studies Series on Ageing* provides a forum for the publication of a limited number of books, which are the result of this international collaboration, on the three main issues of macroeconomics, pension and social security reform, and the labour market The series is invaluable to students and scholars of public economics and public finance as well as policymakers and consultants.

The Economic Impacts of Population Ageing in Japan

Landis MacKellar

*International Institute of Applied Systems Analysis (IIASA),
Vienna, Austria, Vienna Institute of Demography, Austria, and
City Health Economics Centre, City University, London, UK*

Tatiana Ermolieva

*International Institute for Applied Systems Analysis (IIASA),
Vienna, Austria*

David Horlacher

*Department of Economics, Middlebury College
Vermont, USA*

Leslie Mayhew

*Faculty of Actuarial Science and Statistics,
Cass Business School, City University, London, UK*

ESRI STUDIES SERIES ON AGEING

In Association with the International Institute for Applied Systems
Analysis (IIASA)

Edward Elgar
Cheltenham, UK • Northampton, MA, USA

Published by
Edward Elgar Publishing Limited
Glensanda House
Montpellier Parade
Cheltenham
Glos GL50 1UA
UK

Edward Elgar Publishing, Inc.
136 West Street
Suite 202
Northampton
Massachusetts 01060
USA

A catalogue record for this book
is available from the British Library

Library of Congress Cataloguing in Publication Data
The economic impacts of population ageing in Japan / Landis MacKellar ... [et al.].
    p. cm. — (ESRI studies series on ageing)
    "In association with the International Institute for Applied Systems Analysis (IIASA)."
    Includes bibliographical references.
    1. Japan—Population—Economic aspects. 2. Aging—Economic aspects—Japan—Mathematical models. 3. Age distribution (Demography)—Economic aspects—Japan—Mathematical models. 4. Population forecasting—Japan. 5. Economic forecasting—Japan. I. Title: Economic impacts of population aging in Japan. II. Title: Population ageing in Japan. III. Title: Population aging in Japan. IV. MacKellar, Landis. V. Economic and Social Research Institute. VI. International Institute for Applied Systems Analysis. VII. Series.

    HB3651.E25 2004
    330.952—dc22   2004047066

ISBN 1 84376 360 5

Printed and bound in Great Britain by MPG Books Ltd, Bodmin, Cornwall

The International Institute for Applied Systems Analysis

is an interdisciplinary, nongovernmental research institution founded in 1972 by leading scientific organizations in 12 countries. Situated near Vienna, in the center of Europe, IIASA has been producing valuable scientific research on economic, technological, and environmental issues for nearly three decades.

IIASA was one of the first international institutes to systematically study global issues of environment, technology, and development. IIASA's Governing Council states that the Institute's goal is: *to conduct international and interdisciplinary scientific studies to provide timely and relevant information and options, addressing critical issues of global environmental, economic, and social change, for the benefit of the public, the scientific community, and national and international institutions.* Research is organized around three central themes:

- Energy and Technology;
- Environment and Natural Resources;
- Population and Society.

The Institute now has National Member Organizations in the following countries:

Austria
The Austrian Academy of Sciences

China
National Natural Science Foundation of China

Czech Republic
The Academy of Sciences of the Czech Republic

Egypt
Academy of Scientific Research and Technology (ASRT)

Estonia
Estonian Association for Systems Analysis

Finland
The Finnish Committee for IIASA

Germany
The Association for the Advancement of IIASA

Hungary
The Hungarian Committee for Applied Systems Analysis

Japan
The Japan Committee for IIASA

Netherlands
The Netherlands Organization for Scientific Research (NWO)

Norway
The Research Council of Norway

Poland
The Polish Academy of Sciences

Russian Federation
The Russian Academy of Sciences

Sweden
The Swedish Research Council for Environment, Agricultural Sciences and Spatial Planning (FORMAS)

Ukraine
The Ukrainian Academy of Sciences

United States of America
The National Academy of Sciences

Contents

Series Preface

The Millennium Project

At the beginning of the 21st century, the world must place a high priority on constructing a sustainable socioeconomic system that can cope with two global transformations: the rapid ageing of populations in developed countries and growing global environmental problems.

At first glance, the problems of ageing and the environment may seem to be quite separate issues. However, they share a common feature: they both deal with intergenerational problems. The essence of the ageing challenge is how to find effective ways for a smaller working generation to support a larger non-working generation. The essence of the environmental problem is to find a feasible way to bequeath adequate environmental resources to future generations.

These concerns are especially acute in Japan, a country with a rapidly ageing population and a very modest natural resource/energy base. This volume, the companion volumes in the ESRI Studies Series on Ageing, and the volumes appearing in the associated Studies Series on the Environment testify to the fact that the Japanese government has recognized the vital importance of these two problems. In April 2000, former Prime Minister Keizo Obuchi launched a set of comprehensive and interdisciplinary research projects known collectively as the "Millennium Project." The Millennium Project had two tracks, population ageing and environmental sustainability. As part of the Millennium Project, in the same month, the Economic and Social Research Institute (ESRI), Cabinet Office, Government of Japan, initiated a two-year project entitled "A Study on Sustainable Economic and Social Structure in the Twenty-first Century." Like the Millennium Project, this study had two tracks, one dealing with ageing and the other with the environment. While the Millennium Project covered a wide range of topics and disciplines, including natural sciences and engineering, ESRI's contribution placed the primary emphasis on social sciences. The aim was to identify socioeconomic structures that can cope with the pressure of an ageing population and environmental constraints by identifying the necessary policy tools to attain stable and sustainable growth.

As befits a project dealing with global challenges, the project was international in design, featuring close collaboration among Japanese and foreign scholars, and research institutes. Participating institutions came from Japan, the United States, the United Kingdom, Norway, Austria, Italy, Australia, Korea, and Thailand. In total, the ESRI study involved 10 countries and 30 working groups. Twice a year, all the members of the project, along with selected participants, met to discuss the results of the research, in addition to which participants organized a number of side meetings with ESRI's support.

Population Ageing

The Japanese population is graying rapidly, and the elderly are expected to account for a quarter of the nation's total population in 2020. There is widespread recognition that Japan must reform its social security system, pension management schemes, financial and capital markets, and labor markets if it hopes to create a better and sustainable future society. The macroeconomic context is not favorable, as Japan must also cope with large fiscal deficits, bad-loan problems, and long-term structural weaknesses. The clock is ticking and the time to act is short, but our problems are not insurmountable. Pessimism is not our rallying call. Rather, we are optimistic and encouraged by the European example. In Europe, countries have successfully improved fiscal conditions and reformed social security systems at the same time.

Studies on the economics of ageing populations can be divided roughly into three categories: (i) analyses of macroeconomic problems related to the decline in the workforce due to ageing; (ii) analyses of social security systems, with many of the studies looking at pension systems; and (iii) labor market studies, many focusing on employment of the elderly, competition with younger workers, the female workforce, and immigrant workers.

Many people are pessimistic about the effect of ageing on the macro-economy. By contrast, a number of participants in the ESRI project reasoned that the negative impacts of ageing on economic growth can be overcome by policies to stimulate technological progress, as well as other policy measures. However, the current economic and social system requires reform to achieve the flexibility required for these policies to be effective. The transition period will not be without its costs and distress. Only by coping with current economic problems and returning to a comparatively high rate of economic growth can the conditions necessary for coping with population ageing be put in place.

Luckily, the steps necessary to escape the current macroeconomic situation are closely related to longer-term reforms necessary to cope with an ageing society. Solving the bad-loan crisis and putting in place an efficient financial and capital market will not only make it possible for enterprises to raise their funds more efficiently, but will also improve portfolio diversification, thus improving pension asset management. The labor market reforms that reduce costly inefficiencies today will, in the long run, accommodate a variety of employment arrangements that will encourage labor force participation of the aged and women.

Study participants placed emphasis on the need to carefully define the public and private roles in social security and ensuring that an adequate social safety net is maintained. Attention has to be paid to equity issues relating to the social security system and employment of the aged, since these will affect fair sharing of the pension burden between the young and the old in addition to affecting the sustainability of the system.

Natural Resources and the Environment

Studies on natural resources and environmental problems fall, roughly speaking, into four large classes: (i) studies on the management of waste and residuals; (ii) studies on sustainability and technological innovation related to natural resources and energy; (iii) studies on policies for addressing climate change; and (iv) studies on the relationship between environmental policies and the economy, including impacts on employment.

Long-term global environmental sustainability will require public sector involvement in setting standards and encouraging technological innovation. There is a high possibility that emergent technology will lead to a new cycle of sustainable rapid economic growth by creating new products, stimulating demand, and leading to the development of new high-productivity industries. Under this scenario, 21st century technology will contribute to attaining the goal of the "closed-loop" economy/society by enhancing the efficiency with which natural resources are used and encouraging recycling and proper disposal of waste. In particular, technologies for the 21st century must use renewable energy resources efficiently and on a large scale. Paradoxically, past experience suggests that regulations and restrictions imposed on economic activities actually stimulate new technological developments as firms seek to minimize the impact of the restrictions.

Today, environmental issues encompass a very wide range of problems, from local waste disposal to global environmental change. Study participants pointed out that a similarly wide range of policy responses, including regulatory and economic instruments, voluntary agreements, and international emissions trading, is needed for coping with these issues. It is important that policies skillfully use incentives, taking advantage where possible of market mechanisms. Japan is one of the most advanced countries in environment-related technology in the world. However, further technological breakthroughs will be called for in the future, and study participants pointed out that use of both market incentives and public support is essential in areas where long-term risks are uncertain.

It has been suggested that change in the behavior of individual consumers is the key to attaining the closed-loop economy/society. Such change in the behavior of individuals occurs as a consequence of the diffusion of environmental values. An example is the widespread adoption of the precautionary principle (enshrined in the European Union's approach to the environment) to deal with areas characterized by high uncertainty.

Attaining the closed-loop economy/society is especially important for Japan, which is endowed with little in the way of energy or natural resources. There has already been some progress. Study participants have pointed out that, given climatic and topographical conditions and population density, the waste management system in larger cities of Japan can be a model for Asia and that Japan can play an important role in the Asian area in coping with global environment issues.

Common Themes

All of the issues dealt with in this project are closely related to one another, and they will require simultaneous decision making. Among the common themes that cut across ageing and the environment are the role of the market and the role of technology.

We should, of course, take advantage of market forces in trying to attain goals related to both ageing populations and the environment: health care and pensions, employment of the aged, labor force participation of women, climate change, pollution and waste disposal, etc. However, we should not lose sight of the fact that many of the problems encountered in these areas come about precisely because market mechanisms have failed. Externalities need to be dealt with and the perennial questions of efficiency versus equity and the role of the public versus private sectors need to be addressed.

In both population ageing and the environment, research undertaken by ESRI project participants has highlighted the important role played by technology. Looking back on human history, we find reasons for optimism; restrictive conditions have often given birth to technological innovation that presented a way out of the difficulties faced. Perhaps, when we consider the range of challenges faced in the 21st century—scarcity of natural resources and energy, climate change, declining labor force and population—we should conclude optimistically that the new century offers all the conditions for stimulating major technological innovation. A richer economy and society might be the result.

Population ageing and the environment are directly linked through consumption. The slowing of population growth that goes along with population ageing may serve to retard consumption, easing stress on the environment. However, especially in the short term, countries with ageing populations and shrinking labor forces may adapt by substituting energy for labor, that is, consume more energy without any thought to the long-term impact of their consumption patterns and economic activity. This tendency must be offset by imbuing consumers with a new sense of sustainability, one that looks to the future, one that thrives on improved resource/energy efficiencies, one based on eco-friendly waste disposal and new eco-friendly technologies.

Without lowering living standards, we must solve global environmental problems and overcome the constraints of limited energy resources. Failure to attain the closed-loop economy/society may spell the end to our way of life in the not-so-distant future.

Closing Thoughts

In ESRI's contribution to the Millennium Project, we explored optimal solutions to social problems in two broad areas, population ageing and the environment. After taking into account the political and social constraints we face, and after alignment and coordination with the results of the studies, we will sketch out an ideal design and examine the possible direction of future research.

The Millennium Project came to an end in March 2002. It contributed to a better understanding of many theoretical and empirical issues, but has created new debates. In view of the size and scope of the enterprise, it is not possible to publish all the papers and other manuscripts produced in the context of the project. However, thanks to the diligent work of two editorial boards, it has been possible to make a selection of the work done available to policy makers, academics, and businesspeople in two ESRI study series, one on population ageing and the other on the environment.

In the near future, we strongly hope we will have a chance to discuss the research once more from a common standpoint.

In closing, let me acknowledge the ceaseless efforts of the members of ESRI's staff, especially members of the Department of Administration Affairs, throughout the project period. We would also like to express our gratitude to Dymphna Evans, Matthew Pitman, and Karen McCarthy from Edward Elgar Publishing.

Yutaka Kosai, President, ESRI

Preface

For two years, the Social Security Reform (SSR) Project at the International Institute for Applied Systems Analysis (IIASA), outside Vienna, conducted a multidisciplinary study of population ageing in Japan. This study was made possible by financial support from the Economic and Social Research Institute of the Japanese Cabinet Office as part of its Millennium Project. That project brought together research institutions from around the world to carry out studies falling into two areas of particular importance for the new millennium: population ageing and environmental sustainability.

Overview

The comparative advantage of IIASA was in demography and the economics of population, so it will not be surprising that this book focuses on population, economic impacts of demographic trends and structures, and associated uncertainties.

The first chapter, a general synthesis of the economics of population ageing, emphasizes that societies do not go crashing blindly into a wall of population ageing. Even without taking into account institutional and social change, the traditional static neoclassical model of the economy suggests that there is a wealth of possibilities for adapting to the challenge of ageing. Just as a neoclassical view holds that rapid population growth need not mire developing countries in poverty, so it suggests that population ageing need not, as some have suggested, bankrupt the advanced industrial economies of the world. However, shifting factor prices and the rising cost of pension and health systems will give rise to intergenerational distributional pressures that will need to be worked out through the political process. Some combination of higher payroll taxes, longer working lives, lower pension payments, and higher patient co-payments for health and long-term care is to be expected. At the aggregate level, capital may become less productive as labor grows scarce, and saving rates may decline as the ratio of dissavers to savers increases.

The second chapter focuses on Japan, summarizing the demographic outlook and reviewing the results of major studies. One of the main conclusions from

Chapter 2 is that the Japanese demographic prospect is indeed daunting. While rapidly declining mortality at older ages is one important factor, the main force driving population ageing in Japan is the sustained decline in fertility. Available evidence gives no reason to believe that fertility will increase any time soon; indeed, if experience is a guide, current official forecasts for fertility may be too high. Reinforcing the problem, current forecasts for longevity may be too low. Even under a scenario in which labor force participation rates of the elderly are increased and discouraged workers, mostly women, are brought into the workplace, the labor force will still start to decline around 2025. Holding labor force participation rates constant, the decline has already started.

We are particularly interested in assessing the sensitivity of the Japanese economic outlook to changes in demographic parameters. IIASA has developed an economic–demographic simulation model to answer questions like this in a globally consistent macroeconomic framework. The model is described in Chapter 3, and its analytic structure is presented in detail in Annex 3.1. Initialization assumptions—that is, the values of model parameters and exogenous variables—are presented in Annex 3.2, and the resulting baseline solution for the period 2000–2050 is described in the main body of the chapter. The general long-term picture painted by the IIASA model is one of slowing per capita economic growth, a declining national saving rate, downward pressure on capital productivity, rising payroll tax rates (assuming no change in labor force participation rates or benefit calculation rules), and a reduction in net foreign assets. While we do not devote much attention to the international picture, one striking fact is that this scenario applies, grosso modo, to all the developed, rapidly ageing regions of the world. Japan may be leading the way, but other countries must surely follow. In Annex 3.3, these baseline projection results are compared with the results of other studies. While there are some broad similarities, the models cannot be said to speak with one voice. Model structure, demographic assumptions, and definition of variables significantly affect conclusions.

How sensitive is the baseline scenario to changes in demographic assumptions? In Chapter 4, we present two alternative scenarios featuring lower fertility and greater longevity. To compare these alternative scenarios with the baseline, we decompose the total difference between baseline and alternative scenarios into components attributable to differences in population size holding age structure constant and differences in population age structure holding size constant. The broad conclusion of Chapter 4 is that even quite significant changes in demographic assumptions do not change the economic outlook qualitatively.

In an afterword, we attempt to distill a few general conclusions. Whatever the level of government involvement in pensions and health, population ageing is sure to have pervasive impacts. Political pressures are inevitable. However, rising long-term prosperity for *both* young and old is possible (albeit at the price of steadily increasing transfers from young to old). Japan surmounted the Malthusian challenge of the twentieth century. We have no doubt that it will cope successfully with ageing and population decline in the twenty-first century.

Study Team

This book is the result of a team effort spanning several disciplines. Landis MacKellar, an economist, was responsible for the overall design and coordination of the project as well as the writing of the initial draft manuscript of this book. The algebraic structure of the IIASA model is essentially due to him. Tatiana Ermolieva, a mathematician, handled programming and mathematical aspects of the model. David Horlacher, a population economist, produced an extended literature review of Japan, which is summarized in Chapter 2. He was also responsible for Annex 3.3 and took the lead in revising the manuscript in response to reviewers' comments. Les Mayhew, an expert in the application of operations research approaches to forecasting social sector expenditures, designed the health and long-term care modules of the IIASA model and performed an in-depth analysis of mortality trends in Japan. The section dealing with health care in Chapter 1 is due to him. Akiko Tsuji of Waseda University, Japan, and Martin Spielauer of IIASA made incidental contributions.

Acknowledgments

We are grateful to Ingrid Teply-Baubinder for overall project support and to the IIASA Office of Sponsored Research for handling external administrative matters. We wish to express our thanks to the staff of the Economic and Social Research Institute for arranging international meetings at which these findings could be shared with other institutions participating in the Millennium Project and to the discussants who provided comments on our work at those meetings. We were exceptionally lucky in the choice of anonymous reviewers, whose comments have contributed tangibly to the finished product.

Finally, the impetus for a project dealing with social security and population ageing at IIASA came from the Institute's former Director Gordon MacDonald. Gordon died in May 2002, a few months after reading the first draft of this manuscript. We miss him, his wonderful intellect, and his unforgettable warm human qualities.

Chapter 1

The Economics of Population Ageing

1.1 Introduction

The problem of population ageing is complicated, and policy dialogue in the area has been characterized by too much blind extrapolation and tub-thumping. "There's an iceberg dead ahead. It's called global ageing, and it threatens to bankrupt the great powers," reads the blurb for one fairly recent book (Peterson, 1999). These sorts of analogies—like the wall of natural resource depletion that some writers in the 1970s argued the global economy was going to crash into—invite overreaction and costly policy mistakes. There are many adjustment mechanisms and safety valves built into the socioeconomic system. Some of these are market responses set in motion by changing supply and demand conditions. Others amount to the state reneging on promises made by previous generations of policy makers; but voters are accustomed to that.[1]

In this chapter we review what is known and, more importantly, what is not known about the economic impacts of population ageing. We concentrate on the industrialized countries, where ageing is most pronounced. One purpose of the chapter is to show that, from a modeling perspective, ageing is baroque and one model cannot be all things to all people. Another purpose is to focus on practical policy options. Therefore, throughout the chapter we return to the question, what

Portions of this chapter appeared in MacKellar, F.L. The predicament of population aging: A review essay. *Population and Development Review*, **26**(2), June 2000, 365–397.

can policy makers do? After finishing this survey, we proceed, in Chapter 2, to focus on population ageing in Japan.

1.2   Global Demographic Trends

If "population ageing" is defined as an increase in the average age of the population, all populations are ageing. However, when a more conventional approach is taken and "population ageing" is defined as the transition from a high support ratio (population aged 15–59 divided by population aged 60 and older; the inverse is the so-called old-age dependency ratio) to a low support ratio, then the populations of the world fall into two groups. In the first, the North, consisting of populations in Europe, the European regions of the former Soviet Union, North America, Japan, Australia, and New Zealand, the support ratio is declining rapidly from an already low base. In the second group, the South, consisting of populations in Africa, Asia, and Latin America, the support ratio is also declining, but it will not reach levels currently seen in the first group of countries until the middle of this century (Kinsella, 2000).

Two salient demographic aspects should be highlighted:

- First, populations in the North will age "from the middle" of the age pyramid as persons in the large baby-boom cohort become elderly in approximately 2010. Populations in the South, by contrast, are ageing "from the bottom," meaning that as today's young persons move into their working years, they are being replaced by a much smaller cohort of children (due to rapid recent fertility decline). Therefore, prospective demographic changes imply divergent trends in labor force growth across the two regions. Assuming that age- and sex-specific labor force participation rates (LFPRs) remain unchanged, labor force growth rates will decline rapidly in the North and turn negative for the region as a whole after 2010. In contrast, age-distribution changes are increasing the labor force in the South, where the support ratio will remain roughly constant over the next 50 years despite a rapid increase in the elderly population.
- Second, according to some economists, the proportion of the adult (aged 15 and older) population that is in the prime saving years (40–59) should be an index as relevant as the more often cited support ratio. As the baby-boom generation moves through the peak years of asset accumulation, this ratio, like the support ratio, will rise until approximately 2010 in the North and then commence an extended decline. In the South, too, this ratio will rise until 2010; however, in contrast, it will remain roughly constant thereafter.

The United States, which accounts for about 40 percent of the industrial world in economic terms, is a somewhat special case. Because the United States never experienced the extremely low fertility of Europe (post-1960s) or the rapid fertility decline of Japan (post-World War II), the support ratio, already falling in other major industrial countries, will rise in the United States through 2010 before it starts to decline. Thereafter, the United States will resemble other countries in the rapidly ageing group, although ageing in the United States is not projected to be as extreme as in Europe and Japan. Japan is also distinctive because the "baby boom" there lasted only a few years. Rather than the ageing of a large cohort, it is extremely rapid fertility decline and the persistence of radically sub-replacement fertility that are driving population ageing in Japan.

1.3   Ageing and the Labor Force

At the level of the individual, "ageing" amounts to an increase in the proportion of the life span spent in the state of being elderly. The post-World War II decline in age at exit from the labor force is often contrasted with rising life expectancy, as though the coincidence of the two tendencies were unnatural or somehow morally repugnant (e.g., Peterson, 1999, pp. 137–139). But while increased longevity (and better health, a major determinant of older workers' labor supply) causes workers to wish to work longer (Dohm, 2000), rising income causes them to wish to retire earlier (Costa, 1995). As impressive as were the gains in life expectancy during the twentieth century, the gains in income per capita were greater still, so the tendency for earlier withdrawal from the labor force is not surprising. However, this tendency has been accentuated by the expansion of public and private old-age pension arrangements (Wise, 1997; Clark *et al.*, 1999).[2] If the coming years see downward pressure on public social security benefits and stagnation (or even further erosion) of the annuity value of accumulated assets, as many economists forecast, then rising longevity and reduced disability and incidence of chronic conditions (Fogle and Costa, 1997) will assert themselves in prolonged labor force participation. The reform of social security systems might also encourage workers to stay in the workplace longer. Probably the most important variable over a time scale of decades, however, is the rate of productivity growth, which is practically impossible to project. If economic growth continues to increase the demand for leisure, public authorities will be hard-pressed to stop the trend toward earlier withdrawal from the labor force.

At the level of the labor force, "ageing" consists of an increase in the number of older workers relative to the number of young ones. At the same time, the slowdown in labor force growth linked to ageing is reducing the supply of all workers.

Projections show that, holding participation rates constant, the labor force in Organisation for Economic Co-operation and Development (OECD) countries will begin a slow decline about 2010. It is the combination of labor force ageing and shrinkage that is important for the economy, not ageing per se.

In a smoothly functioning labor market, slower aggregate labor force growth would increase the average wage relative to the rate of return to capital and lead firms to substitute capital for labor. At the same time, labor force ageing would cause the wages of older workers to fall relative to the wages of younger workers. There would be no impact on unemployment of workers at any age.

The problem is that firm-level policies impede the smooth absorption of the "bulge" cohort of older workers into the workplace. In order to discourage shirking and encourage firm loyalty, firms pay younger workers less than their marginal product and older workers more than their marginal product. The reason that firms do not shed money-losing older workers is to maintain the credibility of this institutional arrangement in the eyes of younger workers. Under such circumstances, firms with an ageing workforce face rising unit labor costs. Arguably the most sensible option is to free up the internal labor market so as to flatten (rotate clockwise) the age-earnings profile, keeping older workers on the job while containing costs (Jackson, 1998, pp. 104–107). But firms fear alienating younger workers, who will correctly perceive that there is no reward for firm loyalty. Nor is the problem simply one of changing pay schedules. The structure of benefit programs, such as defined-benefit (DB) pension plans and health insurance programs, dramatically raises the price of older workers (Peterson, 1999, pp. 134–135). Finally, some of the rigidities discouraging employment of the elderly may be there for a reason. Part-time work, which many older workers desire, decreases the number of hours over which fixed costs can be spread and may stand in the way of teamwork.

One way out of this predicament is "pensioning off," which rids firms of expensive older workers while preserving the appearance of having honored commitments. The typical firm sharply reduces pension accrual rates after an arbitrary fixed age (Wise, 1997, pp. 86–87).[3] The result is to reduce the net wage to a fraction of the nominal wage (Hurd, 1990, p. 594). Not surprisingly, many workers choose to leave the firm.

If the costs of exit were entirely internal to the firm through the operation of a pension scheme, the early retirement option would raise social contribution rates[4] by increasing the number of beneficiaries and reducing the number of contributors (van Dalen, 1996, p. 180). This would hurt younger workers and encourage an even greater number of older workers to retire.[5] But in the modern welfare state, a significant portion of the firm-level costs of an ageing labor force can be foisted onto an accommodating public social insurance system. In all industrial countries, public pension arrangements encourage older workers to leave the workplace (Hurd,

1990; Wise, 1997; Gruber and Wise, 1999; Friedburg, 1999; Favreault *et al.*, 1999; Blundell *et al.*, 2002). This is especially the case in Continental Europe, where the main policy response to the structural unemployment problems of the past quarter century has been early retirement (van Solinge *et al.*, 1998, pp. 20–22), generous disability pensions (*ibid.*, pp. 32–35), and favorable treatment of the older unemployed (extended benefits, relaxation of job-search requirements, etc.). Such measures reflect the "lump of labor" fallacy—that there are a fixed number of hours to be worked in the economy, and excluding one group from the labor market will mean more employment for other groups. The effect of these policies has been to keep the labor force artificially young, but this has only put off the day of reckoning. Eventually, fiscal pressures will force policy makers to scale back the social insurance programs that have encouraged workers to leave the labor force at a relatively young age. Whether the trend toward earlier labor force exit actually ceases (or is reversed) as a result remains to be seen.

Evidence on ageing and productivity is mixed. There exists evidence suggesting that elderly workers can be as productive as younger ones (Clark *et al.*, 1978, pp. 927–929; Warr, 1994, pp. 497–504; Disney, 1996, pp. 182–188; Jackson, 1998, pp. 95–100).[6] What older workers lack in dynamism, they make up for in experience. They have lower rates of absenteeism, are less likely to move to another employer, and require less supervision than younger workers. They have been sorted and matched to the tasks for which they are best suited, a process not yet completed for younger workers. Admittedly, the evidence that older workers are as productive as younger ones comes in large part from studies of job performance in mechanical tasks, like sorting letters, or from supervisory ratings.

Several recent research projects that use matched employer-employee data sets find that productivity does, in fact, decline with age (e.g., Hægeland and Klette, 1999; Crépon *et al.*, 2002; for a review, see Skirbekk, 2002). In an age of rapid technological change, general skills (punctuality, for example) may become less important than specialized skills. The latter are gained by flexibility, mobility, and adaptability, all of which are characteristics that the older worker may lack. Above all, however, they are gained by training. The ability of the old to acquire new skills is generally underestimated (a brief review is given in Maddox, 1987, p. 380). Although they have fewer expected years on the job, older workers have lower inter-firm mobility as well, so the rate of return on training older workers compares more favorably with the rate of return on training young workers than might be thought. Assuming rapid technological change, older workers will be in the strongest position when skills are quickly acquired and quickly depreciate, because they can keep their productivity high by staccato episodes of short-term training (moreover, under such circumstances, young workers' skills are also being constantly eroded). The greatest threat for older workers is the introduction of an entirely new class of technology—like digital technology—which requires a long period of training to acquire what is an essentially a new mode of thought. However, if older workers can clear the digital hurdle, the move toward a knowledge-based economy may prove to be the greatest boon since the invention of eyeglasses.

Moving from the level of the individual to that of the labor force as a whole, the possible impacts of ageing on productivity become very complicated. When labor force growth is slow, incentives to innovate and use existing resources efficiently will be high (Habakkuk, 1962), an argument that found rather casual empirical support at the aggregate level from Cutler *et al.* (1990).[7] Another argument is that, as population ageing increases the real wage rate, it will lead to a reallocation of investment away from physical capital toward human capital, with positive long-term implications for economic growth (Fougère and Mérette, 1999). This might happen, for example, if forward-looking young persons were to anticipate that the rate of return to education would be especially high for members of a small cohort (Disney, 1996, pp. 174–178). However, young persons might also respond to higher wages by forgoing human capital formation in order to enter the labor market immediately.

What Can Policy Makers Do?

The policy objective is not to force people to work longer, but to encourage them to make time-consistent labor supply decisions (i.e., ones they will not regret later) that are broadly in line with social costs and benefits. Pension reforms can be implemented to achieve a level playing field. Researchers at the OECD (Blöndal and Scarpetta, 1999, Table V.6) estimated that achieving actuarial neutrality (i.e., a situation in which, at each age, the payroll contribution made if the worker stays in the labor force equals the present value of additional benefits received) in such countries as the United States, Germany, France, and Japan would have the effect of raising the LFPR of males aged 55–65 by about 3–4 percentage points.[8] Such a shift would represent a return to approximately the situation prevailing in the early 1970s. Van Dalen and Henkens (2002) report that the Netherlands may experience a substantial delay in retirement now that it has moved to financing retirement benefits on a more actuarially neutral basis.

One way to achieve actuarial neutrality is to move to a Chilean-style capital-reserve financed defined-contribution (DC) pension system.[9] This is no place to recap the heated debate over the pros and cons of the Chilean pension reform; however, let it suffice to say that the reaction has been mixed.[10] What is certain is that, as we discuss below, such reforms must overcome formidable political obstacles. To put it simply, unless the cost of transition is substantially financed by debt, it will fall on current workers, who are therefore likely to oppose reform (Miles and Timmerman, 1999). However, actuarial neutrality can be achieved (or at least approached) more simply by eliminating perverse incentives in existing DB systems (Belan and Pestieau, 1999). In fact, since early retirement at a reduced pension is a standard feature in private DC pension plans, it might be argued that Chilean-style social security systems encourage early retirement (Venti and Wise, 1989). The real problem is that, according to all indications, today's workers desire and fully expect to retire young. An option that may offer the best of both worlds is the notional DC approach (introduced in Sweden and some East European countries), which improves transparency by calculating pension benefits as if the system were DC, but avoids transition problems by continuing to finance benefits on a pay-as-you-go (PAYG) basis. The notional DC approach is not, however, without its critics. Valdes-Prieto (2000) warns that it is not possible to achieve automatic short-run financial equilibrium by adopting notional accounts and choosing appropriate adjustment rules.

If such options, and others, are available, why are policy makers slow to eliminate distortions that encourage workers to retire early? The "lump of labor" fallacy mentioned earlier is one reason. Collusion with the private sector for reasons discussed above is another. Excessive concern with hard-luck cases—coal miners and the like, whose strenuous occupations make delayed retirement a real hardship—is another. Stated differently, the problem is that actuarial neutrality in the absence of individual tailoring means forgoing redistribution. One person's efficiency gain is another person's inequity, and the wide political appeal of the redistribution taking place within PAYG systems is not to be underestimated (Conesa and Krueger, 1999).

Even if policy makers act, there are limits to what they can accomplish on their own. Changing the behavior of firms and unions is likely to be more important than changing public pension rules. Most models attribute only a relatively small portion of the observed decline in LFPRs of older workers to public social security arrangements (Hurd, 1990, p. 605; Magnussen, 1994, p. 48). Wise (1997, pp. 92–93) estimated that, for a hypothetical American worker covered by both the public social security pension scheme and a typical private DB pension plan, eliminating penalties implicit in the firm's pension arrangements would increase labor supply much more than eliminating social security early retirement provisions. Lumsdaine *et al.* (1997) also found for the United States that eliminating penalties implicit in firms' pension policies would increase labor supply much more than raising the social security retirement age. However, for workers who do not participate in a firm-provided pension scheme, social security retirement rules are crucial. One reason for the political acceptability of mandated increases in the normal retirement age is that it is those at the low end of the labor market who, having no wealth but their entitlement to public pensions, will be most seriously affected.[11] Early retirement is characteristic of low-paid, low-skilled workers, whose health is often poor, whose life expectancy is short as a result, and for whom the opportunity costs of leisure (i.e., forgone wages) are low, as is the amenity value of the workplace.

Finally, it is not just the labor supply of *older* workers that needs to be rationalized. The difference between the rate of return on social security contributions and the rate of return on personal savings can be interpreted as a tax, and as payroll taxes rise in an ageing society, the deadweight costs of this tax—forgone output and tax revenue because workers choose to work less—will increase (Forni and Giordano, 2001). Losses to official gross domestic product (GDP) and fiscal revenues would be especially high in countries where escape to the informal sector is easy and tax evasion is an honored social tradition.[12]   Kotlikoff (1996), who estimates substantial efficiency gains from social security reform in the United States, attributes most of these to eliminating distortions in the labor market. Liu *et al.* (2000) also found that the most important source of efficiency gains from social security "privatization" was eliminating the payroll tax.

Conclusion

The individual retirement decision reflects mainly life expectancy, arrangements concerning pensions and health insurance, and income. Trends in the first two will probably slow or reverse the tendency to retire early, while trends in the last are essentially unpredictable. While the behavior of firms and unions is more important than that of the state, existing public pension arrangements give rise to substantial inefficiencies in the form of early retirement. Means exist to reduce such distortions, but they are politically difficult to implement. Contributions to support social insurance programs also discourage labor supply at all ages, exacerbating the problem of adapting to population ageing.

The early-retirement bias of public pension systems is not accidental—it has evolved in line with firms' desire to rid themselves of expensive older workers while preserving a wage profile steeply rising with age. Fiscal pressures and the increasing number of older workers make it unlikely that this can continue. There is no overwhelming reason to believe, however, that an ageing labor force need be a lower-productivity one.

1.4   Ageing, Saving, and Investment

A priori, age structure should affect both the supply of savings and the demand for investment (Lindh, 1999; Miles, 1999). Regarding the first of these, age structure should affect both the income streams out of which savings are drawn and the saving rate, that is, the ratio of savings to income. Note that not all consumption is financed by income, as sales of assets also generate resources that can be converted into consumption.

Most projections that population ageing will put downward pressure on household saving are based one way or another on the life-cycle hypothesis (LCH) of consumption, according to which individuals save while young in order to maintain consumption after they cease to receive labor income in old age.[13] Life-cycle models are greatly complicated if one adds to the picture possible bequest motives, liquidity constraints (inability to borrow against future labor income and pension wealth; the necessity to accumulate down payments for purchases of housing and consumer durables), precautionary motives translating into saving against adverse contingencies such as ill health (Palumbo, 1999), and uncertainty (Browning and Lusardi, 1996). Only in recent years have the data, computational power, and econometric methods needed to test the LCH rigorously become available. Results have been mixed, with studies based on time-series data supporting the LCH more strongly than within-country studies based on cross-sectional data.[14] When Bernheim *et al.* (2001) tested the rationality assumptions concerning life-cycle saving behavior, they found little support for them. Nevertheless, Browning and Crossley (2001) claim that life-cycle models have more empirical successes than failures; this roughly echoes the finding of a previous review (Hurd, 1990), which found that the bulk of evidence supported some weakened form of the LCH.

The implication of the LCH, if accepted, is that "ageing from the middle," as in developed countries, will put downward pressure on household savings by shifting population out of the prime saving years into the years when accumulated assets are converted into consumption while income from wages is low.[15] The view is not universally supported, though. Börsch-Supan (1996) argues that private savings in OECD countries will grow for three reasons: the elderly are saving in defiance of the LCH, economic growth raises the young's share in total income, and the baby-boom cohorts are relatively high-saving cohorts. According to Deaton and Paxson (2000), studies that track the saving behavior of household heads over time yielded age-saving profiles that are too flat to have much effect on the aggregate saving rate.

There is, however, no disagreement that when government balances in industrial countries are projected extrapolating current public pension and health programs, the result is invariably a flood of red ink. Roseveare *et al.* (1996) looked at public pension and health systems in 20 OECD countries and estimated that, for the OECD as a whole, government deficits could drive the aggregate saving from 7.4 percent in 1995 to almost nil, or even negative, by 2030. Franco and Munzi (1997) performed a similar analysis for the European Union and reached equally pessimistic conclusions. Börsch-Supan (1996) projected that, without higher taxes or reduced age-related public expenditure, widening government deficits would more than wipe out the private savings increases alluded to above, with a large gap emerging after 2015 between *ex ante* savings and demand for investment.

When presented with dire predictions based on extrapolation, one should keep in mind that they will never come to pass. If social insurance systems are time inconsistent (i.e., policy makers make promises on which they are later forced to renege), then it is a fallacy to analyze them as though they are not (van Dalen, 1996, p. 159). Pension systems can be reformed, health care finances can be tightened up, labor markets can be made more flexible, and so on.[16]

However, in fairness, even models that incorporate a fair degree of economic behavior (including, naturally, the LCH) also project that aggregate saving rates are likely to decline. In the U.S. case, three models reviewed by Auerbach *et al.* (1991) all predicted a demographically driven decline in the U.S. national saving rate beginning during the first decade of the twenty-first century, with each model predicting negative national savings by 2030–2040. Auerbach and Kotlikoff (1987) also predicted a decline in the U.S. national saving rate, and Auerbach *et al.* (1989) came to the same conclusion for the United States, Japan, Germany, and Sweden. In the next chapter, we review a number of studies for Japan, all of which project declining saving rates.

Would lower savings necessarily be a bad thing? A change in the population age structure (holding population size constant) might affect the composition of investment demand—more hospitals, fewer factories—but there is not much reason to think it would affect the *level* of investment demand. The little work that exists on the relationship between the old-age dependency ratio and investment suggests that population ageing would tend to reduce investment. What is indisputable is that slower population growth (holding age structure constant) will reduce investment demand because a given path of per capita output growth can be maintained with less investment; that is, a given per capita consumption path can be sustained with lower saving. Stating the same thing differently, if the saving rate remains constant as labor force growth slows, then in a closed economy the result will be a rising capital-labor ratio and a lower real rate of return to capital (in combination with a higher real wage rate). One way of looking at this is to consider that, just as inadequate endowment with capital reduces the productivity of labor, so rising scarcity of labor might reduce the productivity of capital. The most often cited simulation exercise in this area is that of Cutler *et al.* (1990), who showed that, in a dynamic optimization framework, the proper response to projected changes in the U.S. population is a *reduction*, not the often called-for increase, in the national saving rate.[17] More recently, Elmendorf and Sheiner (2000) found that if the United States were a small open economy that desired to smooth consumption as the population aged, it should increase saving today; in a closed economy, however, it is not clear whether it would be better for saving to increase or decrease.[18]

In the voluminous literature on social security and savings, it is conventionally assumed that the capital-output ratio in the presence of a PAYG-financed pension system will be below its optimal value. Thus, for example, Auerbach and Kotlikoff (1987) suggest that the welfare loss associated with lower capital formation due to the presence of a PAYG-financed pension system characterized by a 60 percent replacement rate amounts to about 6 percent. However, in a model calibration that they claim better reproduces existing income-wealth ratios, Imrohoroglu *et al.* (1995) find that the presence of a PAYG-financed social security system *increases* welfare by *reducing* capital formation.

The main alternative to this neoclassical story is the body of economics basing itself on learning by doing, increasing returns to scale, and other such nonlinearities. Taken together, these can be boiled down to the proposition that the rate of technological progress is an endogenous variable (Romer, 1990), in which case there can be no such thing as overinvestment. Anything that reduces investment, as slowing labor force growth is likely to do, reduces the welfare of future generations (Marchand *et al.*, 1996, pp. 34–35). Slower growth in the capital stock will increase its average age, a distinct disadvantage in a time of rapid technological change (Lee and Skinner, 1999). Similarly, one might argue that only young workers use new, superior technology, so an older labor force will be dependent on old technology. With a smaller labor force, fixed costs of invention and innovation will be spread over fewer workers.

What Can Policy Makers Do?

The population-ageing policy debate has been in large part framed in terms of the need to mobilize greater savings through pension reform. Yet, assuming that there really is a need for greater savings in anticipation of ageing, it is doubtful that changing pension arrangements can mobilize these savings.

Consider a closed economy in long-term steady state. There are only three possible strategies to finance the consumption of the non-working elderly:

- One is for current workers to transfer income to the current non-working elderly, either directly at the level of the family or indirectly through a PAYG-financed public pension system. Assuming that the non-working elderly consume all of their income (i.e., transfers) and that workers save at least some of theirs, the impact of population ageing will be to reduce the aggregate saving rate on compositional grounds (Deaton and Paxson, 1997, p. 97).[19]
- A second strategy is for the state to borrow in order to finance the consumption of the non-working elderly through the public pension system while leaving payroll taxes unchanged. In this case, population ageing will increase the public sector deficit and again reduce the aggregate saving rate. Examples are the

partial financing of public pension system deficits through general revenue, as in Europe, or the use of pension system surpluses to relax fiscal constraints elsewhere in the budget, as in the United States.

• The remaining strategy, which can be implemented only over time, is for to-day's workers to save, whether privately or through a capital-reserve financed public pension system, in order to finance their own retirement. In this case, projected age-structure trends in developed countries will increase the saving rate as members of the baby-boom cohort move through their peak saving years. Starting about 2010, however, retiring baby boomers will begin to sell off the assets they have accumulated (to younger persons who are accumulating as-sets to finance their own retirement) and convert the proceeds into consumption (Schieber and Shoven, 1997).[20]

The first strategy transfers income, and thus claims on real resources, from the current young to the current elderly; the second transfers claims on real resources from the future young (i.e., taxpayers) to the current elderly; and the third trans-fers financial claims on real resources from the current young to the future elderly. Whichever approach is followed, the goods consumed by the elderly still come out of the stock of goods currently produced, and thus offset potential savings one for one. All else being equal, an older society will save less.

The often-postulated advantage of the accumulation-based social security strat-egy is that higher saving in the medium term will translate into higher capital accumulation, which will result in higher output in the long term.[21] Since the future young also benefit, in the form of more capital per worker and hence higher wages, the accumulation-based strategy offers some equity advantages in an ageing society.[22] There might also be beneficial effects from financial deepening, which would stimulate the growth of a financial sector well suited to allocating capital (James, 1998).

There is an elegant theoretical literature on whether the institution of a PAYG-financed pension scheme will discourage saving, as well as a huge empirical literature growing out of it that tests whether social security wealth is inversely related to savings. Magnussen (1994, p. 40) was unable to elicit any conclusion one way or the other from his review of some two dozen articles. According to Samwick (2000), countries with PAYG public pension systems tend to have lower saving rates; however, correlation does not prove causation. Studies reviewed by the OECD suggested that public pensions in member countries have reduced the volume of private savings by 10–30 percent (Kohl and O'Brian, 1998, p. 11). A weakness of this literature, in addition to the fact that it is inconclusive, is that the impacts of creating a PAYG-financed system from scratch may not tell us very much about the impacts of moving from an existing PAYG-financed system to a capital-reserve financed one (Orszag and Stiglitz, 2001).

The problem is what to do about the transition cohorts, who face the prospect of paying twice—once to honor commitments under the existing PAYG-financed system and once to accumulate the capital reserve that will finance the new pension system.[23] The blow can be cushioned by debt finance,[24] but absent Ricardian equivalence (i.e., households' perception that government savings really belong to them), debt-financed transition defeats the purpose. In the limit, a transition financed entirely by debt simply replaces one form of obligation (payroll taxes to support the PAYG-financed social security system) with another (taxes to pay interest on the public debt). One interpretation of such a reform is that it just replaces implicit debt with explicit debt. Some economists think this is a good thing. Others argue that people (and financial markets) are not deceived; they know exactly how much debt exists. Debt-financed transition is especially unattractive when the real interest rate is greater than the rate of population growth, in which case the real per capita value of government debt rises over time (Disney, 1996, p. 56). But high real interest rates combined with low population growth pose a problem for *all* debt, not only debt incurred as part of the transition process but also debt taken on to meet unrealistic pension promises, so we are back where we started. Tax-financed transition has the disadvantage that tax increases discourage efficiency gains in the labor market. This leaves reductions in government consumption as a source of finance, but these are everywhere politically difficult to achieve.

The draconian prescription is to impose mandatory saving for old age, accepting that the transition cohorts will have to pay for two retirements, their parents' and their own. But households may be ingenious in thwarting policy makers' stern intentions. If accumulation were required through the public pension system or mandatory occupational schemes imposed on employers, then households might simply save less (or, equivalently, if they are not liquidity constrained, borrow more) elsewhere in their budgets (Disney, 1996, p. 42).[25] Evidence relating to private pension plans indicates that households offset increases in pension wealth with decreases in other forms of wealth, although there is disagreement on the size of the offset (Gale, 1995; Poterba *et al.*, 1997).[26] The OECD concluded from a review of studies that about half of an increase in private pension wealth is offset by reduced savings in other forms (Kohl and O' Brian, 1998, p. 11). On the other hand, Bailliu and Reisen (2000) found that the buildup of pension assets exerted a statistically significant positive effect on aggregate savings in OECD countries. Feldstein (1996, p. 8) believes that about half of each additional dollar in a U.S. household's retirement savings account translates into higher individual savings.[27]

If retirement saving behavior cannot be compelled, can it not at least be encouraged? Probably not. First, tax exemptions, the most common tool, have both

substitution effects (the price of current consumption increases relative to the price
of later consumption, so households save more) and income effects (after-tax income is higher than it would have been had it not benefited from the tax exemption, so households consume more). There is typically a ceiling on the amount of
retirement savings that can be deducted from taxable income. Low- and moderate-
income households, who would be saving less than the ceiling before the exemption
was instituted, experience both income and substitution effects and may save more
or less, depending on the relative magnitudes of the effects. High-income households, who would have been saving more than the ceiling before the exemption
was instituted, experience only the income effect and unambiguously save less.[28]
Second, government also unambiguously saves less: not only has household taxable income been reduced, but some capital gains that would previously have been
taxable are now being earned on assets held in tax-favored accounts. The best ways
to maximize the impact of schemes to encourage saving are to (i) make saving
mandatory, not voluntary, (ii) make it impossible to borrow against retirement assets, and (iii) tax capital gains in the saving scheme like capital gains anywhere else
(Bailliu and Reisen, 1997, p. 30). None of these three alternatives is likely to be
politically popular.

The empirical evidence is mixed. Most national case studies have found the
impact of private tax-favored retirement saving schemes on national saving rates to
be positive but modest (an exception is Poterba *et al.*, 1997, for the United States).
Recently, Attanasio and DeLire (2002) found that only 9 percent of individual retirement account (IRA) contributions represented net additions to national saving
in the United States. Studies reviewed by the OECD (Kohl and O'Brian, 1998)
suggest that tax incentives raise private savings by 20–25 percent, with the impact
on national savings being less because of the fiscal offset. In international cross-
section, however, there is a significant positive relationship between pension system
assets and the aggregate saving rate (Bailliu and Reisen, 1997).

A common fallacy is that because of the individual-level link between contributions and benefits, capital-reserve financed pension arrangements have only
to adjust to individual ageing (i.e., longevity extension), not to population ageing
(i.e., change in population age structure). However, this ignores the link between
demography and the rate of return to capital (Reisen and Fischer, 1994, p. 10). As
the labor force grows more slowly, the capital-labor ratio rises, placing downward
pressure on the rate of return to capital or, equivalently, asset prices. Members of
the baby-boom generation, it might be argued, are buying dear as they save and
will be forced to sell into a glut when they desire to dissave or annuitize (Schieber
and Shoven, 1997).[29] Diamond (1999, 2000) would interpret the bursting of the
equity-market bubble in 2000–2002 as a dramatic return to the long-run growth
path justified by the fundamentals, demography being one of them. Abel (2001)

foresees continued high demand for assets by members of the baby-boom generation who wish to make bequests; however, he predicts that this will not attenuate
the fall in asset prices.[30] Brooks (2000a, 2002) has argued that members of the
baby-boom generation will receive substantially lower returns than earlier generations, even when markets are rational and forward looking. One of the few long-
term asset-market bulls is Poterba (2001), who maintains that there will not be a
sharp decline in asset demand after the retirement of members of the baby-boom
generation. Time-series analysis, he argues, reveals no consistent relationship between age structure and rates of return on various asset classes. But this comes as
no surprise, because asset returns are volatile while population age structure is not.

Even if policy makers are unable to elicit added savings, they might still achieve
an efficiency gain if existing savings were to be reallocated from government (i.e.,
the social security system) to households' personal retirement saving accounts.
This would occur if households, through their financial agents, were more efficient
than the state at allocating savings across investment projects (James, 1998, p. 276).
One of the most popular proposed changes in social security in the United States is
the allocation of a portion of contributions to the equity market. Investing part of the
U.S. Social Security Administration's "trust fund" in equities would improve the
system's expected returns while entailing greater risk; however, this risk could be
mitigated with an insurance scheme (Miles and Timmerman, 1999). In any event,
the magnitude of the risk falls substantially over a 75-year period (Harris *et al.*,
2001). However, the ultimate macroeconomic impact of allocating social security
contributions to the equity market is difficult to discern. The impact on household
portfolios will be nil—households will acquire equities through the social security
system but reduce their non-social-security equity positions in order to purchase
treasury obligations that would previously have been bought by the Social Security
Administration! Whether the Treasury borrows directly from households via the
capital markets or indirectly via the Social Security Administration's purchase of
government securities should have only a minor effect on the real economy.[31]

Conclusion

Projections of the impact of ageing on private savings are in large part dependent on
the LCH, which has lost some of its erstwhile authority. Most economists probably
believe that population ageing will put downward pressure on private savings, but
the view is not universal. There is, by contrast, universal agreement that ageing
will put downward pressure on government balances. Nonetheless, fiscal gloom
and doom predictions deserve to be taken with a grain of salt. They are meant
to be not predictions, but hortatory exercises illustrating the grim consequences of
political inaction.

The purpose of economic policy is not to encourage high saving rates any more than it is to promote hard work. Saving is warranted only if the present value of the expected increase in future consumption is worth forgoing current consumption. Neoclassical theory suggests that population ageing represents a golden opportunity to support the same consumption path with lower investment and hence savings. This view is, however, not popular in orthodox policy circles, where the implicit assumption is that there are external benefits to higher investment.

An older society will likely have a lower saving rate than a younger one because the ratio of consumers to producers is higher. This will be equally true whether the pension system is PAYG or capital-reserve financed, whether it is defined benefit or defined contribution, and whether it is public or private. If policy makers could increase savings during the transition to an older society, however, the economic pie might be enlarged and the difficulties of supporting a larger elderly population would be diminished. Unfortunately, the evidence that they can do so is not particularly strong. Transition from PAYG financing to capital-reserve financing (whether a public pension system or individual retirement saving accounts) is likely to increase national savings only if it the transition cohorts are forced to finance both their parents' retirement and their own, which is easier said than done. Measures to mandate private retirement savings can have some effect, but there are substantial offsets elsewhere on the household balance sheet. Measures to encourage private saving are also subject to offsetting behavior at the level of the household, in addition to which, the impact on national savings is modest once account is taken of forgone fiscal revenues.

1.5   Ageing, the Distribution of Income, and Transfer Programs

The impact of ageing on intergenerational distribution will be determined by the fact that the young live on labor income while the old live on wage-based transfers from the young and income derived from accumulated assets and the proceeds of selling such assets to young savers who are accumulating for their own retirement. Assume, first, that there are no transfers. Then, population ageing would improve the welfare of the young by raising the wage rate relative to the rate of return to capital (and hence depressing the price of assets). The same change would reduce the welfare of the elderly, who are sellers of capital and purchasers of labor services. Within cohorts, population ageing would reduce inequality because the poor depend on labor income while the rich earn rents. The story is likely to be complicated, however, to the extent that workers of different ages are imperfect substitutes (Disney, 1996, pp. 156–174). When age-structure change is imposed on a labor force of a given aggregate size, the wages of young skilled workers may rise relative to those of old skilled workers, because the two are poor substitutes (think of computer programmers). The wages of young unskilled workers, by contrast, might remain unchanged relative to the wages of old unskilled workers, because they are close substitutes (think of taxi drivers). The impact might be to widen income inequality (between skilled and unskilled workers) in the young age group while reducing it in the old age group.

Both theory (the LCH) and empirical evidence show that inequality in the distribution of income rises linearly with age (Deaton and Paxson, 1997) and that inequality in the distribution of wealth follows a U-shaped curve with a minimum around age 40. Thus, population ageing redistributes people from low-inequality age groups to high-inequality age groups. Population-wide indices of inequality might rise as a result, but it is not clear why this purely compositional effect should be a source of concern.

These inferences have the advantage of being straightforward; however, it is a gross oversimplification to assume away transfers. The role of PAYG-financed public pension systems for the elderly as a whole can hardly be overemphasized, and for the elderly poor, intergenerational public transfers are a matter of life and death.[32] Most of the population ageing debate is really about the need to prevent such transfers from overexpanding while preventing the return of old-age poverty.

At least five striking insights have emerged from research on the role of intergenerational transfers. The first of these has to do with the welfare impacts of ageing. Neoclassical theory asserts that a decline in aggregate population growth leads to an increase in the equilibrium level of per capita output (Solow, 1956). However, when population is disaggregated by age and a system of intergenerational income transfers is put in place, this increase in aggregate output may not be advantageous from the standpoint of a representative individual who is interested in his or her lifetime consumption. The population ageing associated with slower population growth widens the "spread," now typically three to seven years, between the average age of production and the average age of consumption. The effect, for given income transfer rates, is to reduce the net transfer income received by the average individual over a lifetime (Arthur and McNicoll, 1977, 1978). This is the Ponzi-scheme aspect of PAYG-financed pension schemes in reverse (van Dalen, 1996, p. 172). Whether the negative impact on per capita consumption of this reduction in transfer income is greater or less than the positive impact of greater output per capita is an empirical question (Ermisch, 1989). Lee and Lapkoff (1988, pp. 643–644) conclude that the average individual in a slow-growing, old population will be materially better off than the average individual in a fast-growing, young one (whether he or she is better off in a welfare sense would depend on the substitutability between children and consumption in the utility function). But this result is by no means assured, and it breaks down entirely if the system of intergenerational income transfers becomes dysfunctional.

A second insight has to do with understanding the conditions under which intergenerational transfers become unsustainable. Assume that the old receive (and consume) their income in the form of transfers from the young, who consume whatever is left over. If the goal of policy is to maintain a basic fixed income for the elderly, then the higher transfers required when the old-age dependency ratio rises can be paid out of productivity growth. The share of output that the young transfer to the old need not rise over time and, if productivity growth is sufficient, may decline. However, if the goal of policy is to make the income of the elderly proportional to the income of the young, then even with productivity growth, the share of output that the young transfer to the old must continually rise in an ageing society.[33] Blake and Orszag (1998) show that, among the major OECD economies, not a single PAYG pension system is actuarially viable if pensions rise at the rate of productivity growth (i.e., if pensions are fully indexed to wages), but all are viable if pensions are frozen at current real levels.[34] Thus, attempts to maintain parity between young and old relying purely on intergenerational transfers are a political time bomb in an ageing society, even when productivity growth is adequate. With this in mind, the danger of the coming decades is that the baby-boom generation will use its ballot-box power to force transfers that encumber the young (keeping in mind, however, that real wages are likely to be higher). Does intergenerational warfare lie ahead?

The third striking insight is that there are some reasons to be pessimistic in answering the question just posed. Public choice models going back to Browning (1975) suggest that collusion between old and middle-aged voters will lead to the overexpansion of intergenerational transfer programs.[35] The empirical proof lies in generational accounts (although these suffer from the defects of fiscal extrapolation exercises discussed above), which show sharply rising net tax rates for tomorrow's young. Gokhale *et al.* (1996) document huge historical increases in elderly consumption in the United States, to the point that the total (i.e., including health spending) consumption of 60-year-olds is now almost as high as that of 40-year-olds (Gokhale *et al.*, 1996). These authors ascribe the increase in elderly consumption to the provision of a lifetime inflation-indexed annuity through the social security system and of third-party financed, in-kind medical services through the Medicare program. The market failures addressed are real (Friedman and Warshawsky, 1990, for the annuity market; Barr, 1992, for the health insurance market), but the generosity of the policy response seems excessive. It has long been known (e.g., Heller *et al.*, 1986, Tables 4 and 5) that the problems of PAYG pension systems in industrial countries can be mostly ascribed to rising replacement rates, not to growth in the number of pensioners.

When considering the intergenerational transfer question, one should not take for granted that parents are altruistic toward their children. If they were, one would expect them to make transfers of income and wealth to those children who are in greatest need, rather than transferring even-handedly.[36] The evidence is mixed (McGarry and Schoeni, 1995; Laferrère, 1999). Altonji *et al.* (1997) strongly reject the hypothesis of altruism in inter vivos transfers. Stark and Zhang (2002) go further, maintaining that parents tend to transfer more to children whose earnings are higher. U.S. panel data on the decumulation of wealth by age show that parents dissave at the same rate as non-parents (Hurd, 1990), which casts doubt on the existence of any bequest motive (i.e., observed bequests may be accidental). It is extremely difficult to ascertain whether bequests represent a joy-of-giving gift or a strategic purchase of support and affection in old age. Perhaps it does not matter: Zhang and Zhang (2001) found that altruistic and exchange motives for bequests yield equivalent outcomes with regard to saving.

The fourth insight has to do with the value for money of contributions into capital-reserve financed as opposed to PAYG-financed pension systems. One factor driving the pension reform debate is that members of the baby-boom generation and their children are receiving a much lower implicit rate of return on pension contributions than did earlier cohorts. In the United States, depending on household structure, a head of household who turned 65 in 1970 could expect to earn a rate of return in the range of 6–9 percent per year; a typical member of the baby-boom generation turning 65 in 2020 may expect to earn 2–3 percent. This decline is mostly due to the maturing of the system, which eliminates the windfall gains received by early participants. There is not much that policy makers can do to combat the maturing of pension systems (they often try, by extending coverage so as to bring in new participants, but the well has just about run dry). Since early participants received much more than they paid in, it is unavoidable that latecomers will pay more into the system than they take out; anything else would amount to a perpetual-motion machine. Moreover, talk of the "rate of return" to social security, while deeply entrenched in the debate, is somewhat misplaced: social security contributions are not investments in the traditional sense and cannot, strictly speaking, be evaluated according to an internal rate of return (Mulligan, 2000).

Even in an ageing society, however, ways may be found to improve the rate of return of a mature pension system. Samuelson (1958) and Aaron (1966) showed that slow labor force growth and slow productivity growth reduce the rate of return to contributions to a PAYG-financed system (equal, assuming the contribution rate is fixed, to the rate of growth of the wage bill). In doing so, they increase the attractiveness of capital-reserve financing. Aaron's law (Aaron, 1966, p. 472) states that institution of a PAYG-financed pension scheme can increase the welfare of each generation if the sum of the rates of growth of population and the real wage rate exceeds the financial rate of return. Conversely, if this condition is not met, a generation that institutes a PAYG-financed instead of a capital-reserve financed pension system harms future generations.[37] A corollary to Aaron's law, the "paradox of social insurance," states that, provided the condition above is met, an individual will receive better value for money by participating in a PAYG-financed pension scheme than he or she will by saving (or participating in a fully funded capital-reserve financed pension scheme). Intuitively, in a capital-reserve financed system, a generation of size N_1 is financing the retirement of a generation (itself) of size N_1, whereas in a PAYG scheme, it is financing the retirement of a generation of size $N_0 < N_1$. The paradox disappears when population growth slows or turns negative, when the financial rate of return rises, or when there is negative growth in the real wage rate.[38]

A mixture of PAYG-financed and fully funded pensions (i.e., holding claims on labor productivity as well as capital assets) is a desirable diversification of the retirement portfolio (Boldrin *et al.*, 1999; Dutta *et al.*, 2000). In the same spirit, Sinn (2000) favors a partial transition to a funded pension scheme because it replaces missing human capital with real capital and helps smooth taxes and child-rearing costs across generations.

Finally, a fifth insight is noteworthy. Demographers are accustomed to concentrating more on fertility than mortality when discussing age distributions. In the pension context, however, it is a mistake to underestimate the impact of increasing longevity. In the case of fertility decline, the number of workers is reduced with a 20-year time lag while the number of retirees remains the same (vis-à-vis a scenario in which fertility does not decline) for some 60 years. Fewer workers must support the same number of retirees, and either wage-based tax rates must rise or there must be an equivalent reduction in benefits (whether directly or by means of an increase in the statutory retirement age) or an increase in the effective retirement age. However, the reduction in the number of workers will increase the real wage rate, so the payroll tax rate will not have to increase nearly as much as would be predicted by a partial equilibrium model (Auerbach *et al.*, 1989; Auerbach and Kotlikoff, 1990). In the case of longevity extension, by contrast, the number of non-working elderly increases immediately (for fixed effective retirement age) owing to enhanced survival while the number of workers remains the same (for fixed LFPRs). The same number of workers must support a larger number of elderly, so the payroll tax rate must again increase.[39] This time, however, since factor availabilities are unchanged, the real wage rate is unaffected. Thus, whereas fertility decline sets in motion forces limiting the required increase in wage-based tax rates (which, anyway, is some 20 years in the future), longevity extension translates directly, and immediately, into higher demands on workers.

What Can Policy Makers Do?

An apocryphal story has it that President Franklin D. Roosevelt once remarked, "The way this thing [the newly instituted U.S. social security system] is put together, those bastards on Capitol Hill [the legislative branch] will *never* be able to take it apart." If true, it was a prescient remark. In an ageing society, pension financing should, almost without question, switch from PAYG to capital-reserve financing. The problem is that Samuelson–Aaron logic, so crisp when the blackboard is blank, is not nearly as useful when it is already marked up (Orszag and Stiglitz, 2001).

When there is a transition from PAYG to capital-reserve financing, three adjustments must be made to the projected rate of return on contributions into the new system. The first reflects the fact that a higher capital-labor ratio implies a lower rate of return, but let us assume that this offset is modest. The next is that the financial rate of return must be adjusted for investment risk (i.e., risk of retiring during a bear market); but let us also assume that this adjustment is modest.[40] After all, investment risk in a capital-reserve financed system must be balanced against the near certainty that governments will fail to make good on the promises of current PAYG-financed pension schemes. The third and really significant adjustment is that transition costs must be taken into account by adjusting the financial rate of return down to reflect the taxes necessary to meet the obligations of the existing pension system when it is dismantled (Mitchell and Zeldes, 1996, p. 366). When this adjustment is made, proposals to reform social security finance look far less attractive. For example, Burtless and Bosworth (1998, pp. 10–12) present calculations made by the Office of the Actuary of the U.S. Social Security Administration comparing the rate of return in a business-as-usual scenario (including rising payroll taxes) with the rate of return under a partial "privatization" plan presented as an option by the President's Advisory Council on Social Security.[41] Under this proposal, payroll taxes would be immediately raised by 1.5 percent (to cover liabilities of the pre-reform system) and 5 percent of all contributions would be allocated to individual investment accounts. The findings of the Actuary demonstrate clearly that there is no benefit for those born before 1970. It is difficult to understand how a reform that essentially bypasses those over age 30 will attract much political support. Voters under 30 appear fatalistic and unborn generations have no voice at all (Breyer and Stolte, 2001), save indirectly through their parents-to-be whose altruism, we have noted, is much to be doubted.

Whatever the means of financing, population ageing is certain to prompt intergenerational conflict and debate. Under a PAYG-based regime, the debate will be over rising payroll taxes and shrinking pension benefits.[42] Under capital-reserve financing (whether through the public pension system or private retirement saving accounts), the debate will be over the declining purchasing power of pensioners' assets vis-à-vis the real wage. It is not clear that the second type of political debate will be more constructive than the first; indeed, the opposite could be very effectively argued.

Political problems also affect what have come to be called "parametric" reforms—adjusting the levers of the social security system rather than fundamentally changing its structure. Leimer and Petri (1981), in one of the most thorough and straightforward model-based assessments, examined the implications of such reforms on various cohorts for the United States. From the viewpoint of older cohorts, whose retirement is in sight, the most favorable approach to strengthening the system's finances is to raise payroll taxes. From the viewpoint of younger cohorts, the most favorable approach is to cut pension benefits, on the assumption that forward-looking members of the middle-aged cohorts will begin to save in anticipation of lower pension benefits. Remove the forward-looking assumption, and young cohorts will be indifferent between tax increases and benefit cuts: in either case, they will end up supporting their parents, in the second case through private transfers.

If there is less than meets the eye to changes in social security system financing, then policy makers will have to cobble together a strategy from a number of measures, each of which is less than fully effective. Changes in public pension retirement ages, as mentioned above, can have only a limited impact. Means testing, an often-proposed measure to improve equity given limited public pension resources, is slippery. When asset tests are imposed, households adapt their lifetime saving and labor supply strategies in order to benefit from transfers in old age (Fenge and von Weisacker, 2001), or they engage in devious behavior such as transferring assets to children. "Earnings tests," which reduce benefits when the recipient earns income, are self-defeating because they discourage labor supply of older workers. This leads to losses all around—pensioners lose a chance to augment their incomes, government loses tax revenues, and firms lose potentially productive workers. Even breaking the link between pensions and wages, a cost-saver that policy makers around the world have discovered, has its downside. Indexing pensions to wages addresses the market failure implicit in the fact that children cannot transfer their human capital to their parents, as a result of which parents might underinvest in their children's education.

Current-income transfers from children to aged parents, while the norm in Asia, are rare in the West (see Kotlikoff and Morris, 1989, for the U.S. case) and always have been (Willmore, 1998). Any move to reduce public pension benefits will, however, likely lead to greater private transfers (offsetting again any potential impact on savings). Leimer and Petri (1981, p. 14) cited findings to the effect that every dollar reduction in public transfers might lead to a 50-cent increase in private transfers. This is fine as a cost-saving measure, but the welfare implications are unclear. The purpose of public policy is not to promote close family ties but to make people happy. Some families may derive utility when direct personal transfers are substituted for indirect, impersonal ones through the social security system; others may derive disutility. The laws of contract governing public transfers are black-and-white; those governing private ones are complex and may involve efficiency loss (Bernheim and Stark, 1988). On the other hand, there is better information at the family level (i.e., children understand their parents' needs better than the government does).

Conclusion

Most households do not spontaneously save for their retirement, and if they do, they do not save nearly enough to achieve lifetime consumption smoothing (Disney, 2000a; Mitchell and Moore, 1998). Some of this is due to myopia, some is due to free riding (consuming freely while young in anticipation of forcing a humanitarian transfer when aged), and some of it to the fact that many households simply do not have enough money to save. Therefore, the certain result of a laissez-faire approach to income in old age would be that a large proportion of the elderly population would live in destitution or be at the mercy of private charity. This is not acceptable.

The currently prevailing form of providing income in old age, PAYG-financed public pensions, is poorly suited to an ageing population. The benefits of moving to a better-suited capital-reserve financed system, however, will not materialize in the near future. Unless older voters, including the baby-boom generation, can be persuaded to put their personal interests aside, the politics of pensions will probably ensure that the bulk of income in old age will continue to come from pension systems that greatly resemble those of today. The reforms that can be foreseen are incremental, parametric corrections designed to curb social security systems' innate tendency to overextend themselves (MacKellar and McGreevey, 1999). One way of looking at this is to observe that social security lies at the very core of the welfare state, and the different forms assumed by the welfare state, in turn, reflect differing social attitudes toward risk. The sweeping World Bank–sponsored social security reforms in Latin America and the formerly socialist countries of Eastern Europe have occurred because the countries have undergone a fundamental ideological and political shift; in Europe, the United States, and Japan, reform is likely to be modest because there has been no such shift.

If this forecast is correct, then the coming decades will see non-stop bickering between the generations as governments steer a course between rising pension costs and a return to widespread old-age poverty. Because of the simple mathematics of intergenerational transfers, it appears certain that social security will revert to a role much closer to the original Beveridgean ideal of providing a basic income.[43] This may be less painful than might be thought, because, on average, members of the baby-boom generation are doing well economically (Easterlin, *et al.*, 1993; Macunovich, 1999). However, poor baby boomers, having done no better and in many cases worse than their parents, will be at risk (Carson and Kerr, 2001). Many will retire after lives of social disorganization, with no spouse or children, and no assets apart from public pension wealth.

1.6   Ageing, Health, and Long-Term Care Systems

Today, health care accounts for around 10 percent of GDP in more developed countries and runs as high as 15 percent in the case of the United States. While rising costs are a source of concern to policy makers, it must also be remembered that health is inevitably a priority area at both the individual and social levels, one whose solid moral and ethical claims are epitomized in the World Health Organization's slogan of "Health for All" (WHO, 2000).

Population growth and population ageing are the two main demographic drivers of health care expenditure. As populations in the developed world level out, ageing is replacing population growth as the more important of the two. Population ageing, as well as advances in medical knowledge, has led to a dramatic change in the basket of medical conditions and diseases, with infectious diseases being replaced by the chronic diseases of old age, especially heart disease, stroke, and cancer (Mayhew, 2001a). The cost and treatment trajectories of these medical conditions often entail several periods of hospitalization in old age, external assistance with daily living activities, and a concentrated period of long-term institutionalized care at the end of life. International studies consistently show that the costs per capita of health care for the elderly are between six and eight times those for young and middle-aged people (Cichon *et al.*, 1999), and thus there is a built-in ageing cost escalator.

However, all studies agree that the main contributor to rising health expenditure is not demography, but technological change. Key contributors to this upward drive are the costs of medical research and new treatments, which are passed onto consumers via the prices of the ever-increasing range of pharmaceuticals, the very high costs of medical equipment such as CAT scanners, and so on (Mayhew, 2000). While medical technology is often cited as the villain of the piece, it must be kept in mind that the social benefit-cost ratio for most major new technologies and treatments is not merely in excess of unity, but far in excess of unity. The current fad is for "evidence-based" medicine, but such calls for discipline may abate when it emerges that many expensive treatments are based on very strong evidence indeed.

How have health care systems reacted to these challenges? Health care and health care products are part of a huge industry that is renowned for its technological innovation. For countries with a large research base in pharmaceuticals and a medical equipment industry, this has undoubtedly been a large economic benefit contributing substantially to GDP. Health care is also a large employer with a range of job opportunities, from low- to high-skill jobs. Nonetheless, all governments take a keen interest in keeping the lid on health care spending. One reason is that a considerable proportion of health expenditure is from the public purse and therefore has immediate fiscal implications. Second, market peculiarities and imperfections in health care, especially asymmetric information between patient and provider as well as third-party reimbursement systems, conspire to bias costs upward (Barr, 1993), providing a classic rationale for state intervention. Third, access to health care and perceived quality of care are contentious political issues. Since it is often the poor who are in greatest need of health care, the political dimension contains a substantial equity component.

These issues have tended to dominate thinking about how health services should be delivered and financed although no single organizational model has come to dominate (van der Gaag and Preker, 1998). Current delivery systems range from fully nationalized health services that are free to the patient at point of delivery, through to social insurance models with compulsory insurance and co-payments intended to limit overconsumption, all the way to private health care models. The trade-off is that private models are expensive and there are distributional inequalities,[44] whereas fully nationalized systems suffer from poor service or chronic inefficiency because they are starved of resources and not subject to the competitive discipline of the marketplace. Policy makers must navigate between the Scylla of moral hazard in public systems and the Charybdis of adverse selection in private ones.

Ageing also brings into focus the question of where to draw the line between health and adjacent services such as domiciliary care, which in turn raises other issues to do with the allocation of financial responsibilities between the individual, his or her family, and health and social care providers. Traditional support mechanisms within family settings are becoming weaker, yet governments are exceedingly reluctant to step into the breach lest they accelerate the phenomenon. Long-term care, either at home or in an institution, is a case in point, and most countries are backing off any open-ended commitment to provide continuing care for people for whom a hospital environment is no longer appropriate. Indeed, pressure for change is occurring in several countries, such as Germany (Schneider, 1999), but also in Japan, where a new compulsory system of long-term care insurance has been instituted (Ogawa, 2001; Mayhew, 2001b). Because long-term care is concentrated in the months prior to death, demand for long-term care is essentially related to the annual numbers of deaths, which in turn are driven by earlier birth generations, and because of the baby boom these are set to increase significantly.

What Can Policy Makers Do?

There are essentially four courses of action:

- The first is to limit the range of services that are covered by public schemes and place more burden on the consumer to pay at least some of the costs. Cutting back on existing services and forcing consumers to pay is politically unattractive in countries where users are accustomed to what many perceive (incorrectly) to be free services.
- A second course of action is to increase medical insurance contributions, that is, health payroll taxes. The danger here is that voters may regard such increases as a tax increase, not as an actuarially necessary insurance premium adjustment.
- A third course of action is to reduce or limit in some way the growth in health costs. Measures include controlling the cost or limiting the purchase of drugs, regulating types of treatment, setting maximum limits for reimbursement, or introducing management measures aimed at increasing the competition between providers, for example, internal markets. The track record of such measures is mixed.
- The last possibility is to promote the health of the population in ways that over time reduce the cost burden of health and social services. Anti-smoking campaigns and efforts to encourage better diets and exercise, etc., may all make significant contributions, not only to reducing treatment costs, but to lengthening working life. However, the demand for treatments that improve the quality of life (cosmetic drugs, drugs to improve sexual function, operations such as knee replacements to improve mobility, etc.) is so strong that it is unlikely that simply reducing premature mortality will greatly reduce overall health spending.

Conclusion

Health care is a vital sector, and its political importance frequently ranks higher than pensions or other areas of social protection. Health care is covered by a multiplicity of services supplied by the public and private sectors and is supported by large sectors of industry and extremely powerful lobby groups including the medical profession. It enjoys a very high profile and is constantly in the public eye so that scope for political intervention or significant changes of direction or alterations to the status quo is limited.

1.7 Open Economy Aspects of Population Ageing

In a neoclassical world, the differing demographic dynamics described in the early pages of this chapter might set trade and capital flows in motion. Most analyses suggest that capital would flow from the rapidly ageing countries to less rapidly ageing countries, where the capital-labor ratio is lower and the rate of return to capital is higher (Cutler *et al.*, 1990; Masson and Tryon, 1990; Blanchet and Kessler, 1992; Börsch-Supan, 1996; Higgins, 1997; Brooks, 2000b). In this case, the main flows would be from Western Europe and Japan to North America, and from the industrial countries as a group to the less developed countries. By draining capital out of the industrial countries, the impact of these flows would be to raise the domestic rate of return to capital (this might be called a "purging" argument) while lowering it in receiving countries (Kenc and Sayan, 2001). Households would also earn a higher rate of return on capital invested abroad, although some of this would represent a risk premium. Consumption in the regions receiving capital inflows would be higher because more capital would be available per worker.

What Can Policy Makers Do?

The open-economy adjustment mechanism just described has the makings of a virtuous cycle—providing a more efficient way of accumulating assets for the ageing North and promoting more rapid development for the younger South. "Once freed, money may well flow disproportionately to developing countries. For this is the surest way to beat demography," wrote *The Economist* over 10 years ago (20 June 1992). But there are two problems.

The first problem is that model simulations (Turner *et al.*, 1998; MacKellar and Reisen, 1998) conclude that the quantitative significance of the gain in developed countries is likely to be modest, especially relative to the sums of money in play. To some extent this is true because the faster industrial-country capital is poured into developing countries, the faster the productivity of and hence rate of return to capital in the latter region declines. The second problem, closely related to the globalization debate more generally, has to do with distributional issues in the North. The beneficiaries of improved asset allocation are lifetime savers, who are the well-to-do. The lifetime poor, who depend on labor income while young and public transfers when old, suffer twice: when they are young as wage rates are reduced (vis-à-vis an autarchy scenario) by capital outflows, and again when they are old and the lower wage bill places downward pressure on PAYG-financed public pensions (MacKellar *et al.*, 1999).[45] These results are admittedly neoclassical; they do not take into account the benefits of financial deepening in less developed countries and increased openness in both developed and developing regions (Holzmann, 2000).

Finally, the prevailing view may be wrong. If ageing reduced Northern saving and investment equally, there would be no resulting impact on capital flows. Or, if ageing reduced savings while having no impact on investment demand in the North (or if capital market barriers prevented capital from seeking a higher rate of return in the South), the impact would be reduced North–South capital flows. All in all, relying on international capital flows to "beat demography" is a risky proposition, attractive to the business press but less so to those who reflect carefully.

Labor mobility is another open-economy aspect. As Northern societies age, policy makers will almost inevitably be forced to come to terms with significantly higher levels of immigration. Such immigration can significantly improve social security system finances, as found by Lee and Miller (2000) for the United States and Withers (2002) for Australia. Limiting immigration to highly skilled workers in their peak earning years would accentuate the improvement (Storseletten, 2000). However, there is no question of "solving" problems of PAYG pension systems by importing young foreign system participants; the required numbers would be massive.

In business circles, it is taken for granted that high social insurance benefits erode a country's ability to compete internationally, while in labor circles, global-ization is equated with erosion of social benefits and "social dumping." Both views are fallacious. First, countries do not compete in the way that firms do; in fact, the entire concept of "international competitiveness" is ambiguous or even bogus. Even if the flawed notion of international competitiveness is accepted, however, it is not clear that high social insurance contributions raise the net wage (gross wage minus employers' and employees' contributions to social insurance). The economic (as opposed to legal) incidence of the payroll taxes used to finance social insurance depends on the demand and supply elasticities of labor (i.e., their respon-siveness to changes in the real wage rate). All econometric evidence suggests that the economy-wide supply elasticity of labor is near zero.[46] In a world of immobile labor and mobile capital, it is fair to assume that the long-run incidence of social security payroll taxes is entirely on labor. Therefore, in a flexible labor market, high payroll taxes will lead to lower net wages but firms' unit labor costs will be unaffected. In rigid labor markets, however, those workers who are in a strong bargaining position (typically the skilled) benefit in the form of higher net wages, while those who are in a weak bargaining position (typically the unskilled) are made unemployed (Demmel and Keuschnigg, 2000). This is the intuition behind the general feeling that generous European social programs have led to substantial unemployment among low-skilled workers (Siebert, 1997). Add accommodating benefits for the unemployed to the picture and the result is a witch's brew of high labor costs, low price competitiveness, and structural unemployment.[47] However, the root of the problem is the labor market, not the structure of social insurance or population ageing.

Conclusion

Globalization is giving rise to welcome efficiency gains, but its potential to ease the problems of population ageing is limited. Better portfolio allocation will help, at least directly, only those lucky enough to have portfolios to allocate, and the improvement in the rate of return appears to be modest. Reducing barriers to migration will help to balance out the global labor market but has no potential to solve, although it may alleviate somewhat, the financing problems of pension systems in industrial countries. Reducing social insurance benefits might result in lower unit labor costs in some countries, but in many countries it will not; either the labor market is highly flexible (the United States) or social benefits are explicitly taken into account in the tripartite consultative process (Germany, Sweden).

1.8 Conclusion

The economic impacts of population ageing will reflect shifts in availability of factors (capital and labor) and impacts on total factor productivity. Productivity impacts of labor-force ageing are essentially speculative, and we have had little to say about them. Changes in factor availabilities based on partial equilibrium assumptions, such as fixed LFPRs and saving rates, may overstate the actual impacts of ageing, which will occur in a dynamic general equilibrium framework. Moreover, we have stressed that it would be a mistake to analyze ageing as though no policy responses were possible. However, static partial equilibrium results are always of some relevance despite their disadvantages, and a number of the points raised above suggest that policy options are limited. To summarize:

- Policy makers can reduce the distortionary features of public pension systems that encourage workers to retire early. They fail to do so because they are reluctant to forgo redistribution, meaning that they cannot muster the necessary political support. Some have also fallen prey to the fallacy that excluding older workers from the labor force will increase the employment of younger workers. However, firm retirement provisions are much more important than public pension retirement provisions in determining age of exit from the labor force. The key to adapting to the ageing of the labor force lies with the private sector, including unions, not government. Government can, of course, serve as a great example setter (think of the U.S. military when, in the 1950s, it eliminated official race discrimination).
- There is relatively little that the state can do to mobilize savings except to engage in the requisite saving itself. Raising taxes worsens distortions and multiplies deadweight costs, so the only road to greater public savings, short of sustained rapid economic growth, is cutting public expenditure. Voters appear to have no stomach for this. Perhaps it does not really matter: in an ageing world, savings and investment may be overrated because labor force growth

will be slow. Others, however, would reply that the "new economy" places a greater premium than ever on investment in new technology.

- While demographic conditions clearly indicate that there should be a transition from PAYG to capital-reserve financing, the political chances of this occurring are slim. The best we can hope for is probably the allocation of some small fraction of social security contributions to a capital reserve and a modestly increased role for private savings.

- Superior global allocation of retirement saving portfolios can only add a few basis points to the risk-adjusted rate of return. Moreover, the beneficiaries are those who are relatively well-off; the poor who depend on labor income when young and public pensions when old are unambiguous losers from globalization.

- None of the proposed avenues for reducing health care expenditure appears particularly promising. Governments can moderate expenditure growth, but they need to keep in mind that, in an ageing society, health care is deservedly a priority sector and that most technical progress in medicine appears to be well worth the cost.

Thirty years ago, the view was widely held that rapid population growth and the resulting young age structure would prevent developing countries from ever rising above poverty. As that view gave way to a more nuanced interpretation of the effects of population growth, paradoxically, the view took hold that the reverse demographic situation—population decline and an elderly population—implied catastrophe for the developed countries. Each of these extreme views overestimates the importance of demography, especially given that productivity is essentially a wild card. However, the evidence above suggests that young people in the United States, Europe, and Japan (and eventually in China and the more rapidly ageing developing countries) will probably have to pay higher taxes (out of higher incomes), old people are going to have to work longer (at better jobs), and retirees are going to have to get by on pensions that are lower and assets that are worth less than they expected.

The sooner policy makers act to mitigate these adverse effects with the means at their disposal, the better. However, population ageing will have pervasive economic impacts regardless of the extent of government support for the elderly. Policy reforms can mitigate the problems associated with population ageing, but they are unable to eliminate them entirely. Whatever steps policy makers take, and whatever the degree of government involvement in areas such as pensions and health, population ageing will make its presence felt throughout the economy.

Notes

[1] Disney (1996, pp. 59–106) surveyed five pension systems (United States, United Kingdom, Japan, Italy, and Australia) and concluded that only the Australian system will be able to meet its promises to any but the start-up generation.

[2] Anderson *et al.* (1999) found that changes in pension plans and social security arrangements accounted for about a quarter of the reduction in full-time work by American men in their early sixties. Johnson (2000) found that the growth of old-age insurance explains about 11 percent of the reduction in participation of men aged 60–64. On the other hand, Baker and Benjamin (1999) found that the introduction of early retirement provisions in Canada's public pension schemes had little effect on retirement behavior. O'Brien (2000–2001) claims that it is inadequate demand rather than supply incentives that has caused the decline in labor force participation of older workers in Australia. On the other hand, Börsch-Supan (2000a, 2000b) found that pension systems in Europe, and Germany in particular, provide strong incentives to retire early.

[3] In the United States, employer-provided retiree health insurance offers another inducement to leave the workplace (Rust and Phelan, 1997). Blau and Gilleskie (2001) found that such insurance adds 7.5 percentage points to the annual rate of labor force exit for workers aged 61 and over.

[4] Whether wage-based payments into social security schemes represent a tax or a contribution is a philosophical issue over which oceans of ink have flowed. Partly to emphasize that we take no position in this contentious debate, albeit at some risk of confusing the reader, we use the terms "payroll tax" and "social contribution" interchangeably.

[5] An alternative would be to hire more young workers, paying them less than their marginal product and financing early retirement out of the surplus. But it may be difficult to find good younger workers, or the firm may face constraints in the product market.

[6] One of the most elegant pieces in the area of social security (Sala-i-Martin, 1996) is based on the hypothesis that older persons are not only less productive than younger ones, but that their mere presence in the workplace reduces the productivity of the young. In this case, there will be gains to removing the elderly from the labor force. If the externality is intra-firm, then the market will eliminate it as firms find it in their interest to institute pension arrangements. If the externality is inter-firm, then market forces will not eliminate it, and state action, in the form of a public pension scheme, is called for. Trends in OECD countries between 1950 and 1990 provide some support for Sala-i-Martin. While the 50–64 age group contributed positively to labor productivity, workers aged 65 and older had a negative effect (Lindh and Malmberg, 1999).

[7] A simple regression predicted that, holding the investment rate constant, a 1 percentage point decline in the rate of labor force growth would lead to a 0.6 percentage point acceleration in the rate of productivity growth.

[8]   According to this study, in a number of countries, the gains from rationalizing unem-
      ployment benefits for older workers (i.e., recognizing that many older unemployed
      persons are in fact never going to work again and dealing with them through the
      pension system) are greater than the gains from reforming public pensions.

[9]   In this chapter, unless stated otherwise we assume that a capital-reserve funded sys-
      tem is fully funded, in the sense that the present value of assets equals the present
      value of liabilities at all points in time. Most of the points made can be applied to
      a partially funded system. We also make no distinction (unless necessary) between
      public capital-reserve financed pension systems and private retirement savings; both
      amount to the one generation's financing its own retirement by the accumulation of
      capital.

[10] Williamson (2001) argues that the benefits of privatization in Chile go primarily to
      high-wage workers and contribute to income inequality, White (2000) argues that the
      Chilean experience is not relevant for nations with well-developed capital markets,
      and Mesa-Lago (2002) argues that many of the virtuous claims made for the Chilean
      pension reforms are myths.

[11] Workers also may feel that they have been compensated in the form of longer life.

[12] Corsetti and Schmidt-Hebbel (1997) present a model illustrating that a payroll tax of
      20 percent could lead to half of all output's being produced in the informal sector.

[13] From a general equilibrium perspective, the reduction in savings might be exacerbated
      because population ageing should reduce the rate of return on capital (by making labor
      relatively scarce), thus further discouraging saving (Rios-Rull, 2001).

[14] The life-cycle literature is enormous, but a few citations give an idea of its range.
      Thornton (2001) found that the ratios of minors and of retired persons to the working-
      age population are inversely related to the personal saving rate, a finding that supports
      the LCH. By contrast, Banks *et al.* (1998) found that, contrary to the implications
      of the LCH, household heads experience significant falls in consumption when they
      retire. Attanasio *et al.* (1999), in one of the relatively few cross-sectional studies
      to support the LCH, showed that a life-cycle model can generate hump-shaped age-
      consumption profiles that are very similar to those observed in household-level data.
      Deaton and Paxson (1997), while unhappy with the LCH, fail to reject it. Much of
      the evidence casting doubt on the LCH consists of studies showing that the elderly
      continue to save. U.S. panel data show that, while the elderly decumulate non-housing
      wealth (Hurd, 1990, pp. 613–614), they do not decumulate housing wealth (Venti and
      Wise, 1989). Households headed by the elderly fail to dissave in Japan (Yamauchi,
      1997, p. 137) and Germany (Börsch-Supan, 1991), but due to sampling bias, these
      consist disproportionately of households in which the head continues to work (see
      further discussion of this issue in Chapter 2).

[15] Assuming that the LCH is relevant, what proportion of wealth at any point in time can
      be traced to life-cycle saving, as opposed to intergenerational transmission (trans-
      fers and bequests)? Estimates vary from 20 to 80 percent (Reil-Held, 1999, Table
      1 for references). Among the differences between studies are whether bequests are

capitalized, the assumed difference in age between parents and children, and whether the purchase of consumer durables is treated as saving or consumption. In a micro-simulation study, Wolff (1999) finds that U.S. household wealth (excluding social security and private DB pension plan wealth) is attributable in equal part to saving, inheritance, and inter vivos transfers (i.e., two-thirds should be assigned to intergenerational transmission). Most striking, only about one-fourth of the first component is due to saving in the typical national income accounting sense, with the other two-thirds attributable to capital gains, that is, increases in the price of existing assets. These results refer to the birth cohort 1942–1946. The point is that, even if the LCH is true, its significance may be limited.

[16] Another problem with pessimistic fiscal projections is that they do not always take into account expectations and Ricardian equivalence. In a forward-looking, rational expectations framework, the impact of population ageing might be to increase private saving rates as young households anticipate that their pension benefits will be eroded by adverse demographic conditions. Mostly because of the prevalence of liquidity constraints, the hypothesis of full Ricardian equivalence has almost invariably been rejected. However, Roseveare *et al.* (1996; these authors do, to their credit, consider Ricardian equivalence) cite studies indicating that roughly one-quarter to one-half of an increment to the public sector deficit in OECD countries is offset by an increase in private-sector savings.

[17] Specifically, Cutler *et al.* (1990) produced a baseline scenario in which the rates of labor force growth and age structure were kept constant at their 1990 levels and compared this to an alternative scenario in which "news" arrived in the form of the actual demographic projections of the U.S. Social Security Administration. How, the authors asked, would an all-knowing economic planner revise the planned rate of saving? For all plausible parameter values, the result was that the planner would reduce savings. They also examined the efficiency case for "tax smoothing"—instituting moderate tax increases now in order to reduce the magnitude of the tax increases necessary when the members of the baby-boom generation retire—and found it to be weak. This result casts doubt on the wisdom of accumulating the U.S. Social Security "trust fund."

[18] Outside the United States, see Börsch-Supan and Brugiavini (2001), who consider the question of whether there is too much or too little saving in Europe. Guest and McDonald (2001a, 2001b) found that the socially optimal rate of saving for Australia declines after 2010.

[19] A more sophisticated interpretation is that, when a population ages, the consumption of the current elderly rises by more than the consumption of the current young falls. The reason for this is that the current young offload some of the consumption cuts necessary to free resources for transfer to the elderly onto future generations via the Ponzi-scheme nature of PAYG finance (Kotlikoff, 1996, p. 4).

[20] Schieber and Shoven (1997) project that private pension system benefits will start to exceed contributions in 2006. Investment income will mean that real assets continue to rise until 2024, at which point they begin to decline. The date of the switchover is, of course, sensitive to assumed pension contributions and the rate of return.

[21] Increased savings will lead to increased investment if they reduce the price of physical capital, which is the same thing as raising its rate of return. The latter will happen through increased equity prices, if savers purchase equities, or decreased interest rates, if savers purchase government bonds. In both cases, wealth effects on asset holders will tend to increase consumption, giving rise to an offset. Lower government bond yields might also encourage government to borrow more in order to finance expanded consumption. All of these effects would operate in reverse when aged pensioners wished to convert their savings into consumption.

[22] On the other hand, Marini and Scaramozzino (1999) show that a balanced-budget *unfunded* system can be optimal in terms of intergenerational equity and time consistency even in a dynamically efficient economy without uncertainty and externalities. Yoon and Talmain (2001) argue that a PAYG pension system is associated with lower fertility than is a fully funded system; therefore, instituting a PAYG pension system in a developing country can accelerate growth by promoting fertility decline.

[23] It is possible that transition cohorts may pay less than the cost of two retirements, either because of partial refunding or returns to the funded pillar. These are simply devices to shift the costs to other generations who then become effectively "transition generations" as well. In the case of the United Kingdom and Germany, more than one generation would be direct losers if there were a transition to a fully funded pension scheme (Miles and Iben, 2000).

[24] Lewis and Seidman (2002) found that a gradual, three-generation (90-year) conversion from PAYG to full funding would impose only small losses on current workers but yield large gains to future generations.

[25] A precautionary motive would have the same effect as a liquidity constraint—if households felt that they would be unable to gain access to retirement savings in the event of a pre-retirement emergency, they would not fully offset increments to pension wealth by drawing down non-pension wealth.

[26] The silver lining to this cloud is that families lacking other forms of wealth do not, for obvious reasons, engage in offsetting behavior, so imposition of mandatory pensions might tend to even out the distribution of wealth.

[27] The addition of bequests might lead to further offsets if households who expect to receive bequests have a lower propensity to save (Weil, 1996). A change in social security arrangements increasing the assets of the elderly might then affect the saving behavior of younger households.

[28] The same offset applies to government measures to encourage the funding of private pension schemes. As Schieber and Shoven (1994) characterize it, one of the great ironies of recent economic history is that since the early 1980s, U.S. tax policy has explicitly discouraged firms from pre-funding the retirement of the baby-boom generation, the reason being that government is reluctant to forgo tax revenues.

[29] One might expect some of the clearest evidence of demographic impacts on asset prices to come from the housing market. Mankiw and Weil (1989) predicted a nearly 50 percent fall in U.S. housing prices by 2007 owing to demographic effects; no such

decline has been in evidence. Ermisch (1996) also found that changes in the age distribution of the population have important effects on aggregate housing demand in Britain. A contrary prediction is made by Börsch-Supan (1991) for most European countries, where the flow of inherited housing may diminish because of longer life spans.

[30] Future cohorts will receive larger inheritances as the number of heirs declines. However, the increase in these inheritances will not be large enough to offset the increased fiscal burden due to population ageing (Lueth, 2001).

[31] This discussion assumes perfect capital markets, however. The case for investing social security funds in equities is much stronger if individual investors are liquidity constrained or just ill informed. If a majority of households are unable to participate in the equity market because of liquidity constraints, investing part of their social security contributions in the equity market can be Pareto improving (Pestieau and Possen, 2000; Geanakoplos *et al.*, 1999). Bohn (1999) also finds positive welfare effects from equity purchases because stock returns are positively correlated with social security's wage-indexed benefit obligations, and thus such investments would help to stabilize the payroll tax rate.

[32] In the United States, social security and the insurance value of Medicare (public health insurance for the elderly) account for about half the income of persons over age 65 (U.S. Council of Economic Advisors, 1996) and virtually all the income of the poor elderly. For one-quarter of all U.S. elderly households in 1986, social security comprised over 90 percent of income (Hurd, 1990, p. 570; Cubeddu, 2000).

[33] The following example is based on Jackson (1998, pp. 27–33); Disney (1996, pp. 1–34) offers a slightly more complicated model from which the same point can be drawn. Let A represent the aged population, Y the young population, P the output per member of the young population (productivity), B the consumption per capita of the aged, and c the share of output consumed by the young population. Since all output is consumed, by assumption $PY = cPY + BA$, which can be solved to give $c = 1 - (B/P)(A/Y)$. If the dependency ratio A/Y rises while B remains the same, there need be no increase in c as long as P rises proportionally. Now let $B = bcP$, that is, let the consumption of the elderly be proportional to the consumption of the young. In this case $c = 1/[1 + b(A/Y)]$. Productivity has dropped out of the picture, and if the dependency ratio A/Y or the replacement rate b rises, the share of output transferred to the elderly must rise as well.

[34] Disney (2000b) provides a more recent review of the fiscal liabilities of public pension programs in OECD countries.

[35] Tabellini (2000) found that the size of social security programs varies directly with the proportion of elderly in the population and the degree of income inequality; Razin *et al.* (2002) confirm the latter result. The Germans and Italians are aware that their public pension schemes are not sustainable; but most reform proposals lack a majority, and reformers rarely support more than one option (Boeri *et al.*, 2002). Casamatta *et al.* (2000) show that a redistributive PAYG system can be politically sustainable, even when the rate of interest is higher than the rate of population growth. Moreover,

though majority voting typically results in overspending on social security and reform inertia, Cremer and Pestieau (2000) show how it may also result in rapid phasing out of social security in the case of unexpected adverse shocks.

[36] McGarry (1999) argues, furthermore, that observed differences in inter vivos transfers arise from differences in current income, while bequests differ only when indicators of children's permanent income differ.

[37] Barr (2002) argues that, from an economic perspective, the difference between PAYG and funding is secondary, and Bolle (2000) also argues that the debate over PAYG versus fully funded schemes misses the point. Belan and Pestieau (1999) observe that funded and PAYG schemes are equivalent as long as the payroll taxes paid during the inception of the latter are productively invested. Kune (2001) points out that funding generally does not transfer the pension burden over time. Thorgersen (2001), on the other hand, argues that the transition to funded social security schemes would permanently increase the welfare of young and unborn generations.

[38] All of this should lend itself well to the formulation of an optimization program to maximize social welfare by fine-tuning the mix of PAYG and capital-reserve financing. However, it turns out to be difficult to translate Samuelson–Aaron logic into real-world policy advice. Blanchet and Kessler (1991) examined the optimal mixture of PAYG and capital-reserve financing in an ageing population where factor returns are endogenous. The answer turned out to be dominated by the assumed substitutability between consumption of successive cohorts in the social welfare function: if policy makers are concerned about the consumption of future cohorts, capital-reserve financing is the answer; if not, PAYG finance is superior. The optimal policies emerging from the analysis require a degree of flexibility not likely to be feasible in the real world. Simple rules examined did not come anywhere close to optimal policies. Miles (2000) used stochastic simulations to determine the optimal split between funded and unfunded systems when there are sources of uninsurable risk. The solution was dependent on rates of return, risks, and the actuarial fairness of annuity contracts.

[39] Note that we make the simplifying assumptions that mortality decline is concentrated at older ages and that the elderly do not participate in the labor force. To illustrate the magnitude of the longevity effect, Lee and Tuljapurkar (1997, p. 78) calculate for the United States that each one-year increase in life expectancy requires an increase in the payroll tax of 3.6 percent. Based on a current payroll tax rate of 12.6 percent, this translates into an increase of 0.43 percentage points. Roughly speaking, then, if life expectancy increases from its current level of 75 to 85 in 2030, the required payroll tax rate will be about 17 percent. This is roughly equal to the current contribution rate in Japan and the countries of Continental Europe.

[40] A key role of an unfunded social security system is to facilitate the allocation of aggregate risk among generations when financial markets are incomplete (Krueger and Kubler, 2002). Feldstein and Ranguelova (2001) suggest that if an individual saves 6 percent of his earnings during his working years, there is only a 17 percent chance that his annuity will be less than the benchmark social security benefit.

[41] "Privatization," like "rate of return" is a term used loosely in the debate. Gale (1999) pointed out that the gains claimed for privatized systems depend on prefunding not privatization, which is neither necessary nor sufficient for raising national saving.

[42] Note that options other than traditional payroll taxes are available. One option is a PAYG system funded by an *income tax* (Niggle, 2000), another is a PAYG system funded by a payroll tax indexed to longevity (Palley, 2000).

[43] Casamatta *et al.* (2001) argue that from a welfare perspective, fixing a basic pension is superior to a system of pension entitlements. However, substantial efficiency losses might arise if the linkage between contributions and benefits is weakened (Fehr, 2000).

[44] Most systems of health care financing in the European Union currently include elements of income redistribution. Breyer and Haufler (2000) suggest that this redistribution would be more efficient if it were done through the tax system.

[45] The specific question asked by the authors was how a globalization scenario, under which the geographical allocation of savings flows across investment projects changed in line with modern portfolio theory, would compare with an autarchy scenario in which the current geographical allocation of savings was maintained. Two regions, North and South, were employed in the simulation. Taking 2030 as a reference year, GDP in the North was projected to be 2.6 percent lower in the globalization scenario than in the autarchy scenario, while gross national product (GNP) (reflecting increased earnings on foreign assets) was 0.26 percent higher. The rate of return to capital in the North was increased by 40 basis points, not a terribly significant change. Public pension income of the elderly was reduced by US$400 (about 2.5 percent) because of the lower wage bill, but this loss was made up for by more rapid capital accumulation. This is an average; in fact, the well-to-do elderly would gain while the poor elderly would lose. Impacts in less developed countries were more dramatic, with GDP being as much as 7.7 percent higher and GNP being 1.9 percent higher in the globalization scenario. Global GDP was increased by 0.25 percent, an efficiency gain reflecting the improved allocation of capital.

[46] An obvious exception is the case of countries where escape to the informal sector is an option.

[47] Alesina and Perotti (1997) find evidence that when labor unions are either extremely weak (so that they have no effective bargaining power) or extremely strong (so that they are engaged in constant dialogue with government and employers, as in Sweden), payroll taxes result in lower wages. It is when the situation is somewhere in the middle that payroll taxes result in rising unit labor costs. More generally, there is no case to be made in theory that the welfare state impairs macroeconomic performance, nor is there a consensus in the empirical literature on the relationship between the size of transfer programs and the rate of economic growth (see Buti *et al.*, 1997, for references).

Chapter 2

Population Ageing in Japan

2.1 Introduction

In no country is the research surveyed in Chapter 1 of greater importance than in Japan. Japan's population is ageing more rapidly than any population in history. Over the next 50 years, the absolute number of non-elderly will decline while the number of elderly will increase. Here, population ageing in Japan is considered in light of some of the general insights described in the previous chapter.

2.2 Demographic Trends and Outlook

At the time of Japan's last decennial census, 1 October 2000, the nation had a population of 127 million.[1] The only segment of the population that had grown since the previous census was the elderly (aged 65 and older). That group had increased by 20 percent. As a result, for the first time in the history of Japan, the population aged 65 and older outnumbered the population under age 15.

The medium variant of the 2000 projections from National Institute of Population and Social Security Research indicates that the Japanese population will gradually decline from more than 127 million in 2000 to about 100 million by 2050. At the end of this century, the Japanese population is projected to be 64 million, about half its present size (see *Figure 2.1*). The medium variant projection assumes that the total fertility rate (TFR) will rebound to the replacement level (2.07).[2] A more plausible scenario (for reasons we explain later) is that of the low-fertility variant, which projects a population of 46 million at the end of the century. That is about one-third of the current population of Japan.

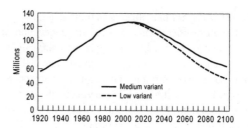

Figure 2.1. Actual and projected total population, two variants, Japan, 1920–2100. *Source*: National Institute of Population and Social Security Research (2002a, Table 1; 2002b, Table 1).

Figure 2.2 provides an international comparison of the old-age shares of the populations of Japan and several other Organisation for Economic Co-operation and Development (OECD) countries. It shows that in 1975 Japan had the lowest old-age share (8 percent), but 25 years later, in 2000, Japan had the second highest share (17 percent). By 2025 Japan is projected to have the highest share (29 percent), and this figure may exceed 36 percent by mid-century. Parenthetically, note that among the countries for which data are presented here (and compared with Germany as well), the country *least* affected by ageing is the United States.

The time required for the proportion of the aged population to double from 7 to 14 percent was less than 25 years in Japan (see *Figure 2.3*). Most European countries took more than 40–50 years to travel the same distance in the ageing of their populations. Japan is, therefore, on the frontier of our knowledge of how to adapt to a rapidly ageing population. It must break the path that other nations will follow.

2.2.1   Fertility, mortality, and migration trends

In Western countries, population ageing is often discussed in terms of the ageing of the baby-boom generation. This is quite misleading for Japan, where the baby boom lasted only three years (as opposed to about 20 years in the West). Rather, the most significant cause of the ageing of the Japanese population is the steep decline in fertility from a TFR of about 4 in 1945 to roughly 1.4 today. Over the 70-year period after 1980, the TFR of Japan has been, and is projected to remain, significantly below the replacement level of 2.07 (see *Figure 2.4*). This leads not only to fewer young persons today, but also to fewer young persons in future decades, as current and future low birthrates translate into a small number of childbearing women in two to three decades.

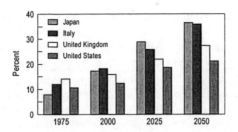

Figure 2.2. Share of the population aged 65 and older, selected OECD countries, 1975–2050. *Source*: UN Population Division (2001a).

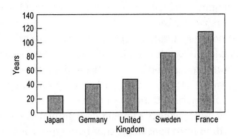

Figure 2.3. Number of years for the percentage of the population aged 65 and older to double from 7 to 14 percent, selected OECD countries. *Source*: Kono (2002, Table 1).

Underlying these changes in the TFR are trends in age-specific fertility rates (ASFRs). As shown in *Figures 2.5* and *2.6*, the most pronounced trend in ASFRs in Japan has been the steady decline in fertility at ages 20–24 and 25–29 since the 1950s. In 2000, the ASFR of Japanese women aged 20–24 stood at just one-fourth of its 1950 level. Since 1950, the highest ASFR has been in the 25–29 age group. However, the ASFR for that group has now fallen to less than half what it was in 1950 and is barely above that of the 30–34 age group.

Figure 2.6 shows that the fertility of older women (aged 30–34 and 35–39) declined rapidly through 1960 as contraception and abortion became available. This stands to reason, since traditionally older women were likely to have completed desired childbearing. Since 1960, however, the fertility of these women has risen somewhat, reflecting the fact that (as we describe below) the mean age at marriage has risen sharply, as a result of which there are more women in their thirties who still wish to have children.

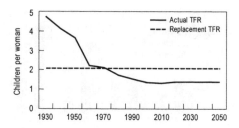

Figure 2.4. Actual and replacement total fertility rates (TFRs), Japan, 1930–2050. *Source*: National Institute of Population and Social Security Research (2002a, Table 9).

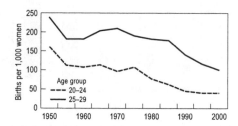

Figure 2.5. Age-specific fertility rates (ages 20–24 and 25–29), Japan, 1950–2000. *Source*: National Institute of Population and Social Security Research (2002a, Table 7).

Decompositions (Ogawa and Retherford, 1993a; Yashiro, 1998) show conclusively that it is not declining marital fertility but rather the growing tendency to delay or forgo marriage that has been the main source of post-1973 fertility decline in Japan.[3] *Figure 2.7* shows that the fertility of *married* women in Japan has remained relatively constant since 1965. It has even risen slightly for all age groups except for women aged 25–29, whose ASFR is almost the same as it was 35 years ago.

Thus, the rapid decline in Japan's TFR is due mostly to the steady decline in the proportion of Japanese women who are married. This has occurred for three reasons: increasingly higher ages at marriage, an increased proportion of women who will never marry at all, and a rising divorce rate. This suggests that the trajectory of Japan's TFR will closely follow the socioeconomic trends affecting the propensity to marry (and stay married).

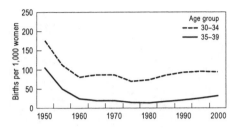

Figure 2.6. Age-specific fertility rates (ages 30–34 and 35–39), Japan, 1950–2000. *Source*: National Institute of Population and Social Security Research (2002a, Table 7).

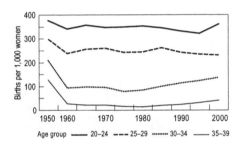

Figure 2.7. Age-specific fertility rates for married women by age group, Japan, 1950–2000. *Source*: National Institute of Population and Social Security Research (2002a, Table 7).

The age at first marriage for women, which was about 22 in 1910, has been rising almost continually and reached 27 in 2000. As a result of the delay in marriage and, of lesser significance, the rising probability of divorce, the proportion of young women who are not married is steadily increasing. The proportion of women in the prime childbearing age group (25–29) that have never married has increased from less than 10 percent in 1930 to 54 percent in 2000 (*Figure 2.8*).[4]

The future of the Japanese population will depend very much on whether the current increase in the proportion of Japanese women who have never married represents merely the postponement of marriage or an increase in the proportion of Japanese women who will never marry. An indicator that current trends represent a delay rather than a rejection of marriage is survey evidence that over 90 percent of 18- to 29-year-old women plan to marry someday (Raymo, 1998). However, not all those women will actually marry. The lifetime celibacy rate for Japanese men

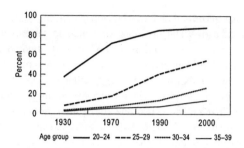

Figure 2.8. Proportion of females never married by age group, Japan, 1930–2000. *Source*: National Institute of Population and Social Security Research (2002a, Table 16).

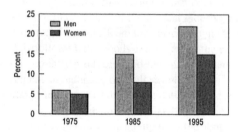

Figure 2.9. Estimated proportion of men and women who will never marry, Japan, 1975–1995. *Source*: Retherford *et al.* (2001, Table 1).

quadrupled from only 6 percent in 1975 to 22 percent in 1995; that of women increased from 5 to 15 percent over the same time period (*Figure 2.9*). Thus Retherford *et al.* (2001) project that in 2010 about 20 percent of men and 8 percent of women aged 45–49 will be unmarried.

Also contributing to the rising proportion of women that are not married is the rising divorce rate. The crude divorce rate in Japan has been rising rapidly since 1960. *Figure 2.10* shows that the level for the year 2000 was 2.10 per thousand of population. That figure is higher than France's divorce rate in 1996 (1.90) and is close to that of Germany (2.14; see Retherford *et al.*, 2001). The total divorce rate in Japan has increased from about 80 per thousand marriages in the 1960s to about twice that number in 1990 (Ogawa and Ermisch, 1994).[5]

While the main factor in population age-structure change has been fertility decline, developments on the mortality side should not be ignored (see discussion in

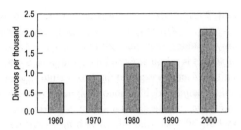

Figure 2.10. Crude divorce rate (divorces per thousand of population), Japan, 1960–2000. *Source*: National Institute of Population and Social Security Research (2002a, Table 5).

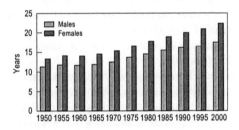

Figure 2.11. Life expectancy at age 65, males and females, Japan, 1950–2000. *Source*: National Institute of Population and Social Security Research (2002a, Table 12).

Chapter 1 on the importance of mortality change for social security systems). Until 1970, increasing life expectancy reflected mostly reduced mortality among infants, children, and youths (Kojima, 1995), which (holding fertility constant) tends to make the population younger. By 1960, however, mortality decline among the middle-aged and elderly had begun to make a major contribution to increasing life expectancy (Feeney, 1999). In 1950, a 65-year-old Japanese woman could expect to live 13 more years. Today she can look forward to living more than 22 additional years. A 65-year-old Japanese male can expect to live more than 17 additional years (see *Figure 2.11*). In 1987, the life expectancy at age 80 for Japanese women was 8.5 years, and the life expectancy at 80 for Japanese men was 6.9 years (Manton and Vaupel, 1995). Not only has the life expectancy of older people been increasing, but it has also been increasing at an accelerating rate, as can be faintly discerned for females in *Figure 2.11* (Nanjo and Kobayashi, 1985).[6] Mayhew (2000) has calculated that, if mortality trends from the late nineteenth century to the present were to continue, by 2020 female life expectancy at age 50 would be 40 years.

Fertility decline combined with increased longevity at older ages must lead to an ageing of the Japanese population unless those trends are offset by international migration. Though it would be possible to prevent the ageing or decline of the Japanese population by allowing increased international migration, Japanese policy makers appear committed to maintaining one of the most restrictive immigration regimes in the OECD.

In the year 2000, foreigners made up only 1 percent of Japan's labor force, and most of these were young men working temporarily in Japan without their families (Martin, 2001). The Japanese government prohibits business firms from importing labor except for ethnic Japanese born abroad and persons with highly specialized skills (Mason and Ogawa, 2001, p. 56). For this reason, the United Nations (UN) population projections for Japan (UN Population Division, 1998) assume no net migration into that country. The UN Population Division (2001b) has, however, calculated the amount of migration necessary to achieve certain population-size and age-structure objectives. In order to prevent population decline by keeping it at the level attained in 2005, Japan would have to admit slightly fewer than 400,000 immigrants per year over the next 50 years. This would mean that by 2050, almost 18 percent of the Japanese population would be composed of immigrants or their descendants. Neither the Japanese public nor policy makers seem likely to accept so fundamental a social change. Moreover, such a policy would maintain population size, but it would not prevent an ageing of the Japanese population. The number of immigrants required to maintain population age structure is astronomical.[7]

2.2.2   Impact on population by age group

What has been the historical impact of these fertility and mortality trends on the Japanese population, and what do projections of future fertility and mortality imply? Demographers often express change in age structure by means of trends in indices such as the old-age dependency ratio (the share of the population over age 60 relative to the share of the population aged 15–59), or they illustrate the age structure with population pyramids. *Figure 2.12* shows the population pyramids for Japan at three points in time, 1950, 2000, and 2050. Clearly, the young cohorts that make up the base are shrinking while the elderly cohorts that make up the top are increasing. However, the most vivid picture of age-structure changes is obtained simply by looking at absolute change of population by age group between two points in time. In the latter half of the twentieth century, the population under age 20 declined while the population over age 20 increased (see *Figure 2.13*). The sum of the bars to the right-hand side of the diagram exceeds that of the bars to

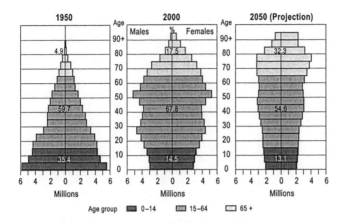

Figure 2.12. Changes in the population pyramid, Japan, 1950–2050. *Source*: Ministry of Public Management, Home Affairs and Posts and Telecommunications (2001, Figure 2.3).

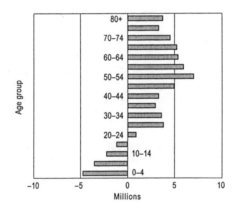

Figure 2.13. Change in total population by age group, Japan, 1950–2000. *Source*: UN Population Division (2002, p. 524).

the left, corresponding to the fact that the total Japanese population increased from approximately 70 to 127 million between 1950 and 2000.

Projections for the first half of the present century indicate that the "twist" observed in *Figure 2.13* will move up the age ladder with a vengeance (see *Figure 2.14*). Not only will the population in young age groups (the groups that would

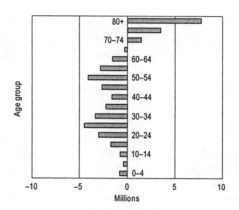

Figure 2.14. Change in total population by age group, Japan, 2000–2050. *Source*: UN Population Division (2002, p. 525).

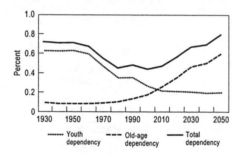

Figure 2.15. Dependency rates (percentage of working-age population), Japan, 1930–2050. *Source*: National Institute of Population and Social Security Research (2002a, Table 1; 2002b, Table 1).

give birth to children) decline, but so too will the population in the working ages. Only the population above age 70 will increase, with most of this increase concentrated among the "oldest old." The sum of the bars on the left-hand side of the diagram outweighs the sum of the bars on the right-hand side, indicating that the total Japanese population is expected to decline over the period.

Between 1950 and 1970, Japan enjoyed a demographic "golden age" where the rapid decline in young dependents caused the total dependency ratio to fall. The total dependency ratio is the sum of the old-age dependency ratio, defined above, and the youth dependency ratio (the population under age 15 relative to the population aged 15–59). But by 2010, the growing old-age dependency ratio will start to push up the total dependency ratio, and by 2050 Japan will have more than 85 dependents for every 100 people of working age (see *Figure 2.15*).

2.3 Uncertainty

How certain is the outlook illustrated in *Figures 2.14* and *2.15*? Demographic projections are only as accurate as the underlying assumptions on mortality, fertility, and migration rates. When long-run demographic projections go wrong, they can go *very* wrong, as small errors in the near term are compounded by the exponential nature of population growth. The most spectacular examples of this are the gross underestimates of future population produced in the 1930s by American and European demographers who extrapolated low Depression-era fertility rates into the future. Only slightly less misleading were the projections of a global "population explosion" produced by demographers in the 1970s who initially thought that fertility in developed countries would quickly return to replacement level and failed to predict the speed with which fertility in most developing countries would decline.

However, the same dynamic characteristics that make long-term demographic forecasts highly uncertain make near- and medium-term forecasts relatively robust. The population that will be above age 50 in 2050 has already been born. Official mortality projections have, if anything, underestimated the observed decline in death rates of the elderly, so the number of persons aged 50 and older in 2050 is more likely to be greater rather than less than projected. The population aged 20–50 in 2050 will have been born between 2000 and 2030. With the exception of girls born between now and about 2010, the mothers of these babies have already been born; that is, their number is known with precision. Therefore, the only real chance that the projections illustrated above underestimate the number of persons aged 20–50 in 2050 is if they are based on a substantial underestimate of the fertility of the girls and young women who are now alive. By the same logic, if the projections greatly underestimate the number of persons under age 20 in 2050, it must be because girls born in coming decades will experience higher fertility than assumed. How likely is this?

If history is a guide, the likelihood that the projection *over*estimates fertility is far greater than the chance that it *under*estimates it. Official fertility projections all over the world are greatly influenced by the homeostatic argument that fertility tends ineluctably toward replacement level (whether from above or below). The appeal of this approach is basically political: population projections that show dwindling national populations can give rise to hysteria, and those that show explosive population growth are hardly less controversial. However, there is a near total lack of empirical evidence for the homeostatic argument (Lutz, 1996), and in

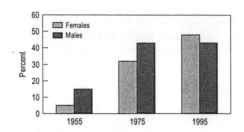

Figure 2.16. Enrollment rates in higher education, Japan, 1955–1995. *Sources*: Ogawa and Clark (1996, p. 312) and Mason and Ogawa (2001, p. 54).

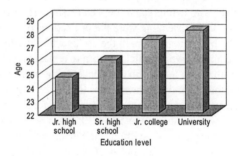

Figure 2.17. Mean age at marriage for women by education level, Japan, 1990. *Source*: Retherford *et al.* (2001, Table 2).

the Japanese (as well as the European) case it has led to consistent overestimates of fertility rates. Since 1975, the Japanese Ministry of Health, Labour and Welfare has been responsible for producing national population projections every five years; since 1975, the Ministry has revised its fertility assumptions downward *every five years*.

As we described above, the main sources of fertility decline in Japan are delayed and, increasingly, forgone marriage. Women are eschewing marriage to take advantage of increased opportunities for higher education and improved employment opportunities (see *Figure 2.16*). In Japan, there is a strong positive relationship between years of education and age at first marriage (Yashiro, 1998; see also *Figure 2.17*). The average age at marriage for women who are university graduates was about 28 years in 1990, compared with about 26 years for high school graduates.

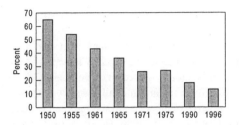

Figure 2.18. Percentage of women expecting old-age support from their children, Japan, 1950–1996. *Sources*: Ogawa and Retherford (1993b, Table 2) and Mason and Ogawa (2001, p. 52).

We know from the example of countries such as Sweden that these trends need not imply low fertility. In Japan, however, the institutional changes to make these opportunity costs manageable, such as moderate-cost day care for children, increased participation in home production by husbands, institutions for care of the infirm elderly, and flexibility in firms' employment and compensation policies, have not been adequate thus far.[8] There have been some governmental initiatives to reduce the opportunity costs of childbearing. The "Angel Plan" has resulted in the provision of day care facilities for children, and the "Golden Plan," along with a newly instituted long-term care insurance program, has resulted in the creation of institutions for care of the infirm elderly. As yet, however, the supply of day care centers for children and institutions for the infirm elderly falls far short of the demand. As we will see shortly, the result has been that many women who would like to work feel unable to do so.

In 1992, Japan implemented a program that gave employed mothers a one-year parental leave. Although this was initially unpaid leave, it allowed a woman to return to the same job and status that she left because of childbirth. Thus she retained her job tenure. In 1995, the scheme was improved so that a mother on parental leave would receive 25 percent of her salary. However, few women availed themselves of this opportunity because of pressure from peers and supervisors (Ogawa, 2000).

At the same time that opportunity costs of taking the traditional life path of marriage and motherhood are rising, the perceived benefits seem to be falling. A declining share of women report that they expect to rely on their children for old-age support. By 1996, that figure had fallen to 13 percent (Atoh, 2001; see also *Figure 2.18*). Perhaps most tellingly, the share of all women with children aged 0–14 who report that they derive pleasure from child rearing has dropped to only

9 percent, as opposed to 40–70 percent in other industrial countries (Ogawa and Ermisch, 1994, p. 211).

Based mostly on considerations of socioeconomic factors impinging on women's status, most experts argue that fertility in Japan is likely to be lower, not higher, than official projections. Moreover, a number of admittedly casual arguments suggest that fertility in Japan could fall even lower. Contraceptive prevalence in Japan is still low relative to other countries, and the methods used are relatively unreliable (as a result of which, some 20 percent of births are unplanned). Recent approval of oral contraceptives (after a delay of 40 years and largely in response to women's outrage over near-instantaneous approval of the male sexual dysfunction drug Viagra) may change this situation.

Turning to mortality, Mayhew (2001b) has shown that increases in Japanese longevity have consistently exceeded expectations. Particularly among women, the number of "oldest old" is increasing rapidly. There is no sign that the pace of mortality improvements at older ages is slackening.

It seems very likely, therefore, that the extreme demographic outlook illustrated in *Figures 2.12* and *2.14* will come to pass, in general if not in precise quantitative terms. Japan will be the first country in history to experience an absolute decline in its working-age population combined with an absolute increase in its elderly population. If any alternative demographic scenarios deserve attention, it is those in which fertility is lower than officially expected and longevity is greater than officially expected. Such alternative scenarios are presented in Chapter 4 of this book.

2.4   Economic Impacts of Ageing in Japan

In this section, we look at impacts of population ageing on availability of economic resources and their productivity, reaching the conclusion that economic stagnation will be difficult to avoid.

2.4.1   Labor

While the impact of population ageing on savings and capital formation has received more attention from economists, its impacts on the labor market will be more direct. Much of Japan's economic growth occurred in the latter half of the 1950s and 1960s, when the labor force was growing rapidly and therefore was relatively young. At that time, employers could draw on a large stock of well-educated young workers who were willing to work for relatively low wages. The lower wages paid to young workers, combined with their high levels of education, powered Japan's economic growth. In the twenty-first century, however, population ageing will slow labor force growth as numbers in the peak labor supply age

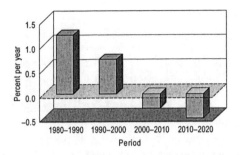

Figure 2.19. Labor force growth rates, Japan, 1980–1990 to 2010–2020. *Source*: Yashiro (1997, Table 1).

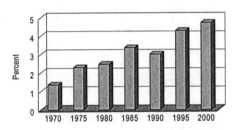

Figure 2.20. Unemployment rate, Japan, 1970–2000. *Source*: National Institute of Population and Social Security Research (2002a, Table 17).

groups decline. The male labor force peaked in 1998 at 40.3 million and the female labor force peaked one year later at 27.7 million (Ministry of Public Management, Home Affairs and Posts and Telecommunications, 2001). Yashiro (1997) projects that labor force growth will be negative in the 2000–2010 period and will fall even further in the 2010–2020 period (see *Figure 2.19*).

The decline in the size of the labor force understates the reduction in the labor component of Japan's productive capacity. The unemployment rate has been climbing since 1970 (see *Figure 2.20*), reaching a level comparable with those of the United States and the United Kingdom, though considerably below the levels of Germany and France (see *Figure 2.21*). Unemployment is especially high for elderly males. *Figure 2.22* shows that in 2000, the unemployment rate for males aged 60–64 was almost 11 percent. The situation for elderly women is not so serious, though female unemployment for the 60–64 age group is significant.

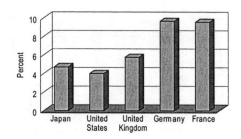

Figure 2.21. Unemployment rate, selected OECD countries, 2000. *Source*: Japan Institute of Labour (2002).

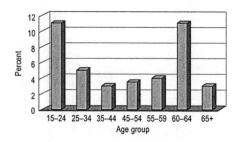

Figure 2.22. Male unemployment rates by age group, Japan, 2000. *Source*: Ministry of Public Management, Home Affairs and Posts and Telecommunications (2001, Figure 4.5).

A further reduction in the effective labor input is occurring through the steady decline in the average number of hours worked per month. In 1990, the average Japanese employee worked 172 hours per month. In 2000 that figure had fallen to 154 hours, a reduction of more than 10 percent in a decade (see *Figure 2.23*).

To deal with the declining labor supply, Japanese policy makers often speak of lengthening working life and have implemented a number of measures to remove disincentives to elderly employment (Katsumata, 2000). However, elderly labor force participation in Japan is already extraordinarily high by OECD standards (see *Figure 2.24* for men). Therefore, it is not surprising that these rates have been falling (see *Figure 2.25*). It is possible that this downward trend might be reversed. Yashiro *et al.* (1997) suggest that the labor force participation of older workers may increase as a result the 2000 pension reforms, which increased the age of eligibility for public pensions to 65 and reduced benefits. Furthermore, since labor force participation among the elderly is positively correlated with wages and education,

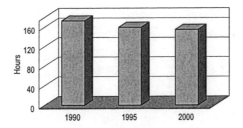

Figure 2.23. Average hours worked per month, Japan, 1990–2000. *Source*: Ministry of Public Management, Home Affairs and Posts and Telecommunications (2001, Figure 4.6).

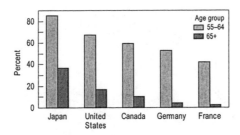

Figure 2.24. Labor force participation rates of older men, selected OECD countries, 1996. *Source*: Organisation for Economic Co-operation and Development (1997).

it is possible that the labor force participation of elderly males will increase as their average educational level increases. In Western countries, however, policy makers have found that raising the statutory retirement age does not necessarily translate into a higher effective retirement age. Well-educated, well-to-do workers may simply accept lower pension income.

Historically, the distinguishing features of the Japanese labor market were a seniority-based wage system and lifetime employment (Ogawa and Clark, 1996). Those institutions provided workers with job stability and employers with high levels of effort and low turnover (Itoh, 1996). According to the system that evolved during the period of rapid labor force growth, a large pool of younger workers who were receiving less than their productivity warranted were supporting deferred payments to a smaller group of older workers who were receiving more than their productivity justified (see *Figure 2.26*). Since older workers were being paid more

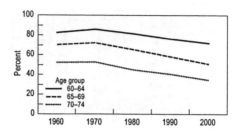

Figure 2.25. Labor force participation of men aged 60–74, Japan, 1960–2000. *Source*: National Institute of Population and Social Security Research (2002a, Table 18).

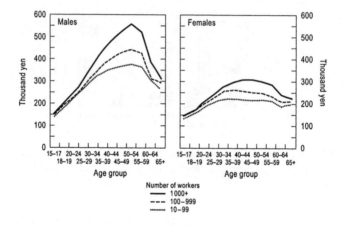

Figure 2.26. Monthly contractual earnings by size of enterprise, Japan, 1999. *Source*: Ministry of Public Management, Home Affairs and Posts and Telecommunications (2003, Figure 12.10).

than their productivity, however, employers needed a system of mandatory retirement.

By the year 2000, virtually all firms had set their mandatory retirement age at 60 or older (Ohtake and Yamaga, 2002). However, more than 70 percent of the firms allowed some workers to continue past the mandatory retirement age or re-employed them in lower-status jobs at lower pay. On average, men work about five years after mandatory retirement, receiving wages 20–40 percent below their

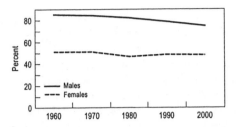

Figure 2.27. Labor force participation rates for males and females aged 15 and older, Japan, 1960–2000. *Source*: National Institute of Population and Social Security Research (2002a, Table 18).

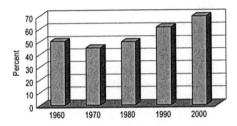

Figure 2.28. Labor force participation rates for women aged 25–29, Japan, 1960–2000. *Source*: National Institute of Population and Social Security Research (2002a, Table 18).

pre-retirement wages. It is this reduction in wages that has made it economical for employers to continue employing elderly workers.

Chiefly as a result of economic development, but also as a result of changes in household composition, education, and social welfare systems, there has been a decline in the labor force participation rates (LFPRs) of Japanese men and a much smaller decline in the LFPRs of women (see *Figure 2.27*). The slight decline in the average female LFPR occurred despite a very substantial increase in the LFPR of women aged 25–29 (see *Figure 2.28*). Among the reasons for the rise was the increasing proportion of young women that were unmarried. However, the LFPR of married women aged 25–29 increased as well.

A number of disincentives reduce female LFPRs, especially for women in their thirties and forties, and encourage those women who do work to take relatively low-productivity jobs. The poor supply of child and elder care is a factor that has already been mentioned. High marginal tax rates and social security taxation strongly discourage wives from working. Some authors have suggested that measures to address such disincentives could substantially counteract the expected negative impact of demographic trends on the Japanese economy (Kosai and Yashiro, 1998).

There is evidence that the observed increases in the labor force participation of women understate significantly the potential labor supply of women. In 1997, the Japanese Ministry of Public Management, Home Affairs and Posts and Telecommunications conducted a labor force survey in which they attempted to identify the number of "invisible workers"; that is, persons who would like to be in the labor force but are unable to do so for reasons such as lack of child care, need to care for elderly parents, lack of suitable labor market opportunities, etc. As *Figure 2.29* shows, male "invisible workers" tend to be in their sixties, where over 10 percent of men say that they would like to work but cannot. Among women, by contrast, the number of "invisible workers" is above 20 percent for respondents aged 25–40 and remains above 10 percent through age 65 before tapering off. The characteristic "M-shaped" Japanese female labor force participation curve (high labor force participation in the early twenties, then low labor force participation while caring for young children until the forties, then high labor force participation after children are more independent) is exactly mirrored, in reverse, by the curve of female "invisible workers."

We argued above that demographic trends are fairly robust to changes in assumptions. What about the outlook for labor supply? In *Figure 2.30*, we illustrate several alternative labor force scenarios. In the baseline scenario, labeled Scenario 1, which assumes constant LFPRs, labor force declines steadily from its 2000 level of 67 million workers to 45 million workers in 2050. In Scenario 2, we assume that, between 2000 and 2050, the LFPRs of workers aged 60 and older gradually rise 20 percentage points above their 2000 levels. As the figure makes clear, this does not substantially forestall the declining trend. By contrast, when "invisible workers," mostly women in their thirties, forties, and fifties, are brought into the labor force (gradually between 2000 and 2050), the decline in the Japanese labor force is delayed until 2025 (Scenario 3). However, from 2025 through 2050, even bringing all "invisible workers" into the labor force cannot prevent a substantial decline.

We reach two conclusions: First, a long-run decline in labor force is almost inevitable. Not only is the working-age population shrinking, but hours worked per month and LFPRs are also declining. Furthermore, Japan can no longer assume that its labor force will be fully employed. Second, in delaying this decline, policies to make it easier for women to work are likely to be more effective than policies to discourage the elderly from retiring. Moreover, while policies to encourage elderly labor force participation make the labor force older, those to employ discouraged female workers may have the opposite effect.

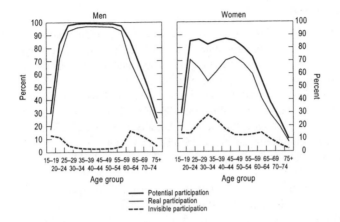

Figure 2.29. Potential labor force participation rates by sex and age group, Japan, 1997. *Source*: Ministry of Public Management, Home Affairs and Posts and Telecommunications (1997).

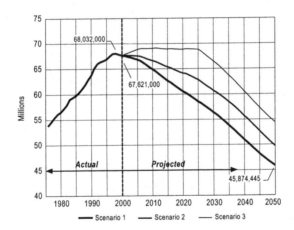

Figure 2.30. Actual and projected future labor force, 1976–2050. *Sources*: Ministry of Public Management, Home Affairs and Posts and Telecommunications (1976–2000); Institute of Population and Social Security Research (1997); authors' projections.

2.4.2 Capital

Japan at the end of World War II was a poor country. Production was concentrated in a poorly performing agriculture sector, capital was scarce, few young people attended secondary school (let alone university), and income was low. Fertility and mortality, as we saw above, were high, albeit somewhat lower than in the Japan of the pre-war era. In the course of a few decades, Japan transformed itself into an economic superpower. While the causes of the Japanese economic miracle, and the East Asian economic miracle more broadly, remain the subject of discussion, there is a growing feeling among economists that favorable demographic conditions played a significant role (Radalet *et al.*, 1997; Bloom and Williamson, 1997; Kelley and Schmidt, 2001).

When a rapidly growing population (as Japan's was) experiences sharp fertility decline, a relatively large generation of young working people finds itself with few dependents to support—a relatively small generation of parents because their parents' fertility was high and a relatively small generation of children because their own fertility is low. There is evidence that during the opening of this window of demographic opportunity, a large share of income is saved and devoted to capital formation, including human capital formation. Eventually, however, the window closes. Fertility, being bounded from below, cannot decline at the same proportional rate indefinitely. It is only a matter of time before a generation of workers finds itself supporting an approximately equal-sized generation of children (assuming roughly replacement-level fertility) and a relatively large generation of aged parents.

When the window of opportunity is open, the relative generation sizes, from youngest to oldest, are small–large–small. The total dependency ratio is low. At the second point in time, corresponding to the closing of the window of opportunity, the relative generation sizes are small–small–large.

In the United States and Western Europe, where demographic change has been, and will be, less pronounced than in Asia, few economists would be willing to identify the simple demographic model of savings just described as the driving force underlying trends in capital formation. As we saw in Chapter 1, the relationship between population age structure and savings is extraordinarily complicated. In the case of Japan, however, and the East Asia region as a whole, it is fair to say that most economists believe that favorable demographic conditions were a major determinant of high post-war saving rates (Williamson and Higgins, 2001). Therefore, there is a large literature asking whether the demographic trends described above will bring the era of high Japanese saving rates to an end.

National savings consist of public (government) and private savings. Regarding the first, there seems little doubt that the overall trend over time in Japan will be toward a public sector deficit, as population ageing will put pressure on the public

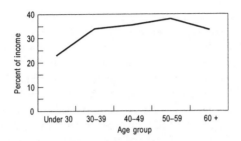

Figure 2.31. Saving rates by age group, Japan, 1999. *Source*: Yoshikawa *et al.* (2002, Figure 4).

pension and health systems. Even studies (Meredith, 1995; Yashiro *et al.*, 1997) that incorporate a thorough reform of the public pension system (lower replacement rates, higher contribution rates, longer working lives, etc.) into their projections conclude that the government balance will decline over the 2000–2050 period. We discuss the public pension and health systems in detail in Sections 2.5 and 2.6, respectively.

Private savings consist mostly of household (personal) savings. The remainder is the savings of firms (corporate savings), which have been relatively little studied in Japan but are often assumed to track household savings closely (firms are, after all, owned by households).

As discussed in Chapter 1, household saving behavior is usually described in terms of the life-cycle model of consumption, in which households build up assets during middle age and then dissave (consume in excess of current income) after retirement. In an economy characterized by such behavior, the household saving rate will decline as a result of population ageing. Some researchers have questioned whether the elderly in Japan really dissave as predicted by the life-cycle hypothesis (LCH; see Hayashi *et al.*, 1988; Dekle, 1990; Ando *et al.*, 1995). Household surveys often yield an age profile of saving rates indicating positive saving at older ages. *Figure 2.31* presents a typical age profile of saving rates in Japan. It shows that even the oldest age group has a positive saving rate.[9]

However, most evidence shows that the *retired* elderly actually do dissave (Meredith, 1995; Horioka *et al.*, 1996). One reason for the apparently high saving rate of the elderly is that many studies have concentrated on households as the unit of analysis. This imparts a serious bias to results, since elderly heads of household consist disproportionately of persons who are still working or are well-to-do, while elderly non-heads of household are likely to have been absorbed into their children's households (Yashiro, 1997).

Assuming that the LCH is valid, then evidence should reveal an inverse relationship between the old-age dependency ratio and the household saving rate. Studies by Horioka (1989, 1991) based on both cross-sectional and time-series evidence have confirmed that there is such an inverse relationship.

In the simple life-cycle model, all bequests are accidental. Yet approximately one-third of wealth in Japan is received via inheritance, especially housing wealth (because of the advantageous tax treatment of housing bequests).[10] Based on a variety of evidence, Horioka (2002) concluded that in Japan (and the United States), most bequests are motivated by selfish strategic or exchange motives. (Such selfish bequests, if considered as deferred payment to children for support during old age, are consistent with the LCH.) Even if the bequest motive were a significant factor, it is not clear that aggregate household savings would be high as a result, as younger households might save less in anticipation of a bequest (Tachibanaki, 1996).

Liquidity constraints play no role in the simple life-cycle model. However, consumer credit has traditionally been scarce in Japan, so households have been forced to accumulate in order to make major purchases. Mortgage credit is also scarce, and saving for residential investment is an important motive for saving (Horioka, 1988). However, when saving for housing purchases (or, equivalently, the paying down of mortgage debt) is balanced against rapid depreciation of the housing stock, it is not clear that the residential sector is a net source of capital to the economy.[11] Moreover, in equilibrium, low levels of consumer and mortgage borrowing correspond to low levels of repayment (a form of saving). It is thus not clear that Japanese saving has been high because credit has been scarce.

Other explanations for Japan's high saving rate have included cultural factors, risk aversion, habit persistence, rebuilding of wealth ratios after the war, and so on. None of these add up to a consistent, parsimonious explanation for Japan's apparently high saving rate.

Given the paucity of strong alternatives and the conceptual and computational simplicity of the model, most projections of Japanese savings have been based in one way or another on the LCH. Virtually all such studies project that the Japanese household saving rate will decline, although there is not unanimity on the size of the decline (Horioka, 1989,1991; Ando *et al.*, 1995; Meredith, 1995; Yashiro *et al.*, 1997; Williamson and Higgins, 2001).

Capital formation is, of course, most directly a function of domestic investment, not savings. One of the features of the Japanese economy, however, has been that large amounts of domestic savings have financed investment, not in Japan, but abroad. This capital outflow, or acquisition of foreign assets, corresponds to the huge current account surplus (about 3 percent of gross domestic product) that has characterized the Japanese economy for nearly three decades.[12] If the volume of Japanese savings declines but demand for domestic investment continues to be

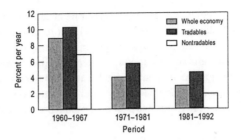

Figure 2.32. Growth rate of productivity, Japan, 1960–1992. *Source*: Itoh (1996, Table 3).

strong, the net outflow of capital from Japan will decline and eventually turn into a net inflow (corresponding to a current account deficit). Most authors agree, or implicitly accept, that ageing is likely to have a greater negative impact on savings than on investment.[13] Therefore, a feature common to almost all macroeconomic projections for Japan is a decline in Japan's current account surplus, often to the extent of turning into a deficit (Noguchi, 1989; Auerbach *et al.*, 1989; Masson and Tryon, 1990; Hamada and Iwata, 1989). This implies that the ageing of Japan's population will have not just domestic, but international economic consequences, including potentially significant impacts on financial markets and asset prices worldwide.

2.4.3 Productivity growth

Kosai and Yashiro (1998) used a macroeconomic model to demonstrate that increasing the efficiency of the economic system might largely offset the effects of population ageing and allow sustained economic growth in spite of a declining population. In the face of an increasing scarcity of labor, firms would seek to employ their workers more efficiently. Thus a decline in the labor supply should be accompanied by an increase in productivity.

Curiously, this does not seem to have happened in Japan, where the slowing of labor force growth has been accompanied by a steady decline in the growth of various measures of productivity. From 1983 to 1990, Japanese total factor productivity grew at about 2.4 percent per year. However, that rate fell precipitously to 0.2 percent per year in the 1991–2000 period (Hayashi and Prescott, 2002). Itoh (1996) earlier showed that the rate of productivity growth had slowed, especially in the non-tradable sector, where Japan does not face international competition (see *Figure 2.32*). Wolff (2001) found that the growth rate of labor productivity in manufacturing has been falling since the 1970–1979 period and was below 1 percent per year in the early part of the 1990s.

Since population ageing will surely slow the rate of capital formation and bring about an absolute decline in the effective labor input to production, Japan's only real hope for avoiding economic stagnation is an offsetting increase in productivity. Unless Japan can turn around its long-term productivity growth deceleration, economic stagnation appears inevitable. Such a reversal would be no small order: Japan is already on the technological frontier and there are no signs of rapid social or institutional change of the sort that would stimulate productivity.

2.5   Pensions

Not only are the pension and health insurance schemes vitally important to the elderly population of Japan, but they are also major determinants of whether the government's accounts are in surplus or deficit. Thus they are major determinants of the national saving rate. In the future, the national saving rate may fall precipitously because of deficits in these schemes (which would have to be covered by resources taken from elsewhere in the government fiscal accounts). This was not always the case. It was less than 10 years ago that Meredith (1995) observed that the seeming fiscal health of the Japanese government was due to large surpluses in the social security accounts.

The Japanese social security system has three major components: pensions, medical care, and welfare. Measured by expenditures, public pension schemes are the most significant component of the system. However, if regular medical care insurance is added to public health expenditures and health care for the elderly, the total medical component of social security is larger than public pensions (see *Figure 2.33*).

The economic impact of the social security system is enormous. In fiscal year 2002, social security contributions equaled 15.5 percent of national income (Japan Institute of Labor, 2002). Together, social security contributions and income taxes accounted for about 38 percent of national income. *Figure 2.34* shows that the combined burden of social security contributions and the income tax has remained relatively constant since 1985 because the growth in the social security share in national income has been largely offset by a decline in the income tax share.

Compared with those of other OECD countries, the combined burden of tax and social security contributions is still low in Japan (see *Figure 2.35*). It is slightly higher than the combined burden in the United States, but it is considerably lower than those in the United Kingdom, Germany, and France.

One fairly recent study (Ogawa and Retherford, 1997) projected that contributions to social security would rise from 13 percent of national income in 1993 to 21 percent in 2025 (see *Figure 2.36*). If the other tax payments are added to that

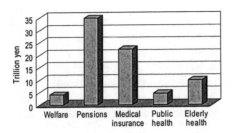

Figure 2.33. Social security expenditures, Japan, 1997. *Source*: Ministry of Public Management, Home Affairs and Posts and Telecommunications (2001, Table 13.1).

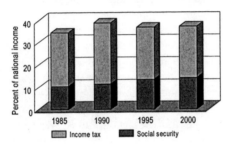

Figure 2.34. Ratio of income tax and social security contributions to national income, Japan, 1985–2000. *Source*: Japan Institute of Labor (2002).

figure, the total would rise from 40 percent of national income in 1993 to 56 percent in 2025. Three-quarters of this increase would be due to increases in social security contributions (Ogawa and Retherford, 1997, p. 68). However, significant steps have been taken to slow the growth of social security spending.

2.5.1 The pension system

Yashiro *et al.* (1997, p. 7) point out that Japan's public pension system began as something close to a fully funded scheme in which contributors accumulated savings to be withdrawn after retirement. Over time, however, revenues fell short of expenditures and inflation lowered the value of previously accumulated reserves. As a result, the public pension system evolved into what is now, essentially, despite the existence of substantial trust funds to cover temporary deficits, a pay-as-you-go (PAYG) system in which current benefits are financed by current contributions.

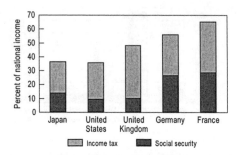

Figure 2.35. Income tax and social security contributions as a percentage of national income, selected OECD countries, 1997–2000. *Source*: Ministry of Public Management, Home Affairs and Posts and Telecommunications (2001, Table 13.2).

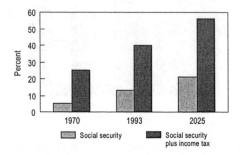

Figure 2.36. Social security contributions and taxes as a percentage of national income, Japan, 1970–2025. *Source*: Ogawa and Retherford (1997, Figure 2).

The Japanese pension system is a two-tier system. The first tier, or National Pension Scheme (NPS), is a public program that covers all residents older than 65 and provides them with a flat pension.[14] It covers about 80 percent of the working-age population and has almost 70 million participants. This is the only plan for farmers, the self-employed, the unemployed, students, and non-working married women. The second tier, or Employees' Pension Insurance (EPI), is for salaried workers and covers about 32 million private sector employees. Though the plan covers private sector employees, it is publicly managed.

In addition to the public pension system, retirement income is provided by Employees' Pension Funds (EPS), which are private corporate pension funds. These funds cover about 12 million employees. There are five Mutual Aid Pensions schemes, which cover about 6 million public employees, such as teachers.

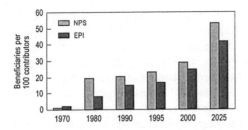

Figure 2.37. Program dependency rate, public pension programs, Japan, 1970–2025; NPS = National Pension Scheme, EPI = Employees' Pension Insurance. *Source*: Endo and Katayama (1998, Table 5-6).

Defined-contribution plans have been allowed since 1 October 2001. Employer contributions on behalf of each employee are deductible up to about US$3,600 per year if the employer has no other pension plan. They are deductible up to US$1,800 for companies that also sponsor a defined-benefit plan. These plans do not permit employees to make contributions. A hybrid similar to U.S. "cash balance plans" has been authorized since April 2002.

Ninety percent of Japanese firms offer private retirement packages of some sort. Of these firms, 90 percent provide a lump-sum retirement bonus. In the case of a worker who has worked a full career with the firm, that lump-sum payment usually amounts to a little less than four years' salary.[15] About half the workplaces in Japan offer only this type of private retirement benefit.

The demographic tendencies described above are crucial to the pension system. The program dependency ratio (PDR) for a public pension program is defined as the ratio of beneficiaries to covered workers (i.e., contributors). Looked at from a historical perspective, the great attraction of PAYG financing is that PDRs in a new pension scheme are low. However, as the plans mature, the PDRs increase. The evolution of PDRs for the two largest public pension plans, the NPS and the EPI, is shown in *Figure 2.37*. In 1993, there were 23 beneficiaries from the NPS for every 100 contributors. By 2025, that figure should more than double to 53 beneficiaries per 100 contributors. Unlike the NPS, where the age for receiving a pension is already 65, the age of eligibility of the EPI is rising toward age 65. Thus the PDR of the EPI, which was 17 in 1995, will "only" rise to 42 in 2025.

2.5.2 Contributions

The NPS requires a fixed contribution of 13,300 yen (about US$112) per month, scheduled to rise to 21,700 yen (about US$184) in 2015 according to the 1994 reassessment. Everyone except salaried workers must contribute to the NPS between the ages of 20 and 59.[16] The spouses of salaried workers are exempt from contributing if their annual income is below a specified level. In 1999, that level was 1.3 million yen (about US$11,017). As discussed above, this is a strong disincentive to labor force participation of married women.

In October 1996, the EPI contribution rate was 17.35 percent of monthly wages.[17] As of the fiscal year 2003, however, the contribution base was shifted to *annual* earnings, including semi-annual bonuses (Takayama, 2001). When the 2002 reassessment was made, this rate was scheduled to rise to about 32 percent in 2025. However, the 2000 pension reforms cut benefits and, as a result, this rate is projected to go only to about 25 percent.

The contribution rate for EPS corporate pension plans depends on the particular plan. Many of these plans are seriously underfunded, as a result of which, contribution rates must rise or promised benefits must be cut (Dawson, 2000). This situation reflects not only demographic conditions, but also the collapse of the "bubble economy" in the 1990s. As the Japanese stock market has declined, so have the assets of corporate pension plans, giving rise to the underfunding problem. However, the situation also reflects extremely low interest rates, which have the effect of ballooning the present value of future liabilities through the discounting calculation. To the extent that these low (near-zero) interest rates reflect current macroeconomic imbalances, the underfunding may shrink of its own accord in coming years.

2.5.3 Benefits

For those who belong only to the NPS, the pensionable age is 65. However, salaried workers belong both to the NPS and to one of the second-tier pension systems. Up until 2001 they received the basic pension plus an earnings-related component starting at age 60. The age at which salaried workers can begin receiving the basic pension will be gradually raised from 60 to 65 over the 2001–2013 period (Horioka, 2001).[18]

Under the system as it was designed, a retiree who belonged only to the NPS would receive only a basic pension. The pension of a retiree who contributed for the maximum number of years would be 67,000 yen (about US$567) per month. However, the average monthly benefit under the NPS is only 49,000 yen (about US$415). A retiree belonging to any other pension scheme would receive both a basic pension from the NPS and an earnings-related pension from the scheme to which he or she belonged. In the case of an employee who contributed for the maximum period to the EPI scheme, the earnings-related component would amount to 30 percent of average monthly earnings. The average monthly benefit for participants in the EPI is 177,000 yen (about US$1,500). This would be equal to about 56 percent of the average salary in 1999. As a result of the 2000 reforms, however, there will be a gradual reduction of 20 percent in overall lifetime benefits.

Total NPS plus EPI benefits for a typical retired male salaried worker amount to about 70 percent of average pre-tax monthly earnings and about 80 percent of average after-tax earnings. However, if bonuses are included, public pensions will replace about 50 percent of pre-tax salary and about 60 percent of after-tax salary.

At present, one-third of NPS basic pension benefits are financed by subsidies from the general accounts of central government. However, this subsidy is scheduled to rise to one-half by 2004. Though the government does not directly subsidize the EPI system, employer and employee contributions to those plans are tax deductible. In principle, benefits are taxed. However, there is a large deduction for pension benefits, so they remain largely untaxed.

2.5.4   Pension reform

There was a major expansion of benefits in 1973. At that time, there was a belief that Japan, having made great material progress, should give more attention to improving the quality of life for its citizens. Benefit levels were increased so as to make the replacement rate about 60 percent, a level comparable with those in the major developed countries. The newly expanded pension system quickly ran into trouble, however, and a set of adjustments was made in 1986. Measures taken included an increase in contribution rates, mandatory coverage of employees' spouses in the NPS, imposition of a 40-year participation minimum in order to qualify for the full NPS pension, and partial unification of the various public pension systems into the current two-tier system.

By 1994, there had been further deterioration of system finances and a new round of reform measures was introduced. They called for gradually raising to 65 the age at which salaried workers are eligible to start receiving the NPS basic pension.[19] Pension benefits were to be indexed to after-tax wages and public health insurance premiums were deducted from benefits.[20] A special levy on bonuses was instituted and pensioners were prevented from drawing pension and unemployment benefits at the same time. The benefit formula was adjusted to discourage early retirement. However, even after instituting these cost-containment measures, the 1994 reforms called for public pension premiums to rise from 14.5 percent of regular wages in 1994 to 29 percent of wages in 2025.

The goal of the 1994 reform was to ensure that there would be adequate reserves even at the peak period of population ageing. In the event, however, the reforms were not nearly sufficient to meet the demands placed on the pension system by Japan's rapidly ageing population. Yashiro *et al.* (1997) warned that the large current net assets of the pension system would be exhausted well before the peak

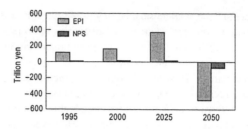

Figure 2.38. Projection of pension fund balances, Japan, 1995–2050; EPI = Employees' Pension Insurance, NPS = National Pension Scheme. *Source*: Yashiro *et al.* (1997, Table 1).

in PDRs.[21] In the absence of further reforms, they projected huge deficits in the pension fund balances by 2050 (see *Figure 2.38*).

It soon became clear to everyone that the 1994 pension reforms were not enough to restore the Japanese social security program to an actuarially sound basis. In March 2000, the Japanese Diet enacted an additional set of reforms that would cut lifetime pensions by about 20 percent (Mulheisen and Faruquee, 2001). Benefit levels were cut by 5 percent and there was a gradual increase in the age of eligibility for the earnings-related pensions from 60 to 65. Furthermore, the then-current accrual rate for earnings-related benefits of 0.75 percent per year was reduced to 0.7125 percent beginning in fiscal year 2000. Before this change, an average worker who had contributed for 40 years would receive 30 percent of his or her final salary. Now the retiree would receive only 28.5 percent (Takayama, 2001).

The 2000 reforms to the Japanese public pension scheme called for indexing both the basic and the earnings-related pension schemes to prices instead of net wages. This was the most important element of the pension reform scenario investigated by Yashiro *et al.* (1997). The impact of this change can be gauged by comparing their projected replacement ratios with and without pension reform. If pensions had continued to be indexed to wages, the replacement ratio in 2050 would have exceeded 50 percent of after-tax income.[22] By indexing pensions to prices, the replacement ratio will be cut to less than 20 percent.[23] However, Mulheisen and Faruquee (2001) argue that further benefit cuts or contribution rate increases will be needed to prevent the depletion of pension fund assets.[24]

Since even the 2000 reforms may not be adequate to meet the pension obligations to a rapidly growing population of retirees, various options for reducing outflow and increasing the revenues of the pension system have been proposed. One way to cut benefits is to link them to average life expectancy. The actuarial value of benefits would be maintained, but the monthly benefits would be reduced to take into account increasing life expectancy. Another option is to raise the age at which individuals become eligible for payments from the current level of 65 years to 67 years.

The main drawback of these strategies is their adverse impact on the standard of living of the elderly. In 1999, public pension payments accounted for roughly 60 percent of the income of elderly households (i.e., households headed by an elderly person) and about half of such households rely solely on public pensions for support (Masuda and Kojima, 2001).[25] An additional problem is that an extension of the eligibility age for receiving a full pension may raise the already high unemployment rate of the elderly.

Reducing pension benefits raises serious distributional issues. However, the unreformed pension system is also replete with distributional issues. Many Japanese are concerned that the present system unfairly redistributes income from younger to older generations (Horioka, 2001). According to Hatta and Oguchi (1997), cohorts born before 1950 will receive benefits that are much greater than their lifetime contributions. The excess of benefits over contributions is greater among older cohorts.[26] *Figure 2.39*, based on Takayama (1992), shows that older cohorts will receive pension benefits worth many times more than their contributions. Conversely, cohorts born after 1965 will receive less in benefits than their lifetime contributions. Current public pension beneficiaries on average have only contributed 30 percent of the benefits they have received.[27]

Masuda and Kojima (2001) found that in 1996, the effect of Japan's pension programs was to redistribute income to those aged 60 and older, and especially those aged 65 and older, who would have had quite low incomes otherwise (see *Figure 2.40*). Though these benefits to the elderly come at the expense of all younger Japanese, that cost is quite evenly allocated among the earlier generations.

The public pension system also redistributes incomes within generations in three ways: benefit formulae favor the wealthy; spouses of salaried workers are exempt from contributions, yet receive significant benefits; and contributions are based on salary and semi-annual bonuses, even though a significant part of an employed person's income may come from the retirement bonus. In any given older cohort, the amount by which benefits exceed contributions is positively related to the size of the benefit. Prior to 2000, contributions were based on salary rather than total compensation. That favored those, such as full-time workers and workers in larger firms, who are likely to receive a greater part of their incomes in the form of bonuses. The lump-sum retirement payment is still exempted, and thus the system continues to favor those who receive large retirement payments.

Another concern about the pension system is its adverse effect on the labor supply. When they reach age 60, the better employees often have the option of

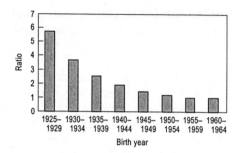

Figure 2.39. Ratio of social security wealth to contributions by birth year, Japan. *Source*: Takayama (1992, Table 4.3).

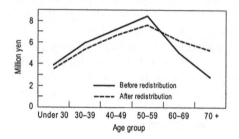

Figure 2.40. Effect of social security on per capita family income by age group, Japan, 1996. *Source*: Masuda and Kojima (2001, Table 2).

continuing to work for the same company or a subsidiary, but at a considerably lower wage. If they do so, they may lose a part of their pension, because public pensions are subject to an earnings test until the worker reaches age 65 (Yashiro, 1997). If there are any earnings at all, benefits are reduced by 20 percent. These earnings tests are likely to reduce the labor force participation of older workers, because an older worker can often earn more by retiring and collecting pension benefits or unemployment benefits than he or she could by continuing to work at a reduced wage.

Because dependent spouses of employees are exempt from making social security contributions as long as their incomes are below a certain amount, wives often limit their participation in the labor force to part-time employment. Horioka (2001) reports that about 12 percent of wives reduce their working hours to stay below this amount. Overall, there is little doubt that the Japanese pension system is contributing to the decline in the labor force participation of women and the elderly.

2.6   Health and Long-Term Care

Total medical care expenditures (both public and private) were at about 6 percent of national income in 1982 and at 7.1 percent in 1995 (Yashiro, 1997, p. 256). By 2000, health care expenditures had reached US$300 billion, or about 8 percent of gross domestic product (Pearson, 2002). Per capita medical expenditures grew at 5.5 percent per annum between 1980 and 1997, and they have been projected to grow by an additional 40 percent over the next three decades (Iwamoto, 2002).

Health care in Japan is organized basically along social insurance lines, in which finance is public (i.e., citizens pay health insurance premiums to public insurance funds) and provision is private. There is, however, a great deal of cross-subsidization among the various health insurance funds (i.e., some persons pay more than an actuarially fair premium in order to subsidize others), in addition to which, the funds receive a substantial government subsidy from general revenue. Over 80 percent of health care providers are in the private sector, although there is heavy government control over the pricing of services.

There are five main medical plans in Japan, and together they cover almost the entire population. The three largest plans are the Association-managed Health Insurance Plan (AHIP), which covers the employees of large enterprises; the Government-managed Health Insurance Plan (GHIP), which covers employees of small and medium-sized firms; and the National Health Insurance Plan (NHIP), which covers the self-employed, proprietors of small businesses, and farmers. Members of the AHIP tend to be young; members of the NHIP tend to be old.

The premiums for the AHIP and the GHIP are 8 percent of workers' earnings, divided equally between employers and employees. Premiums for the NHIP are collected directly from households and are varied according to the enrollees' assets and income. In general, these premiums have not been sufficient to cover the costs associated with the NHIP's older age structure. Hence, government and the other health plans have subsidized the NHIP.

Medical care costs are paid directly to doctors and hospitals by the government. Patient co-payments vary from 10 to 30 percent of costs.

The government has submitted a health finance reform bill, broadly aiming to cut costs and increase revenues. It would gradually raise the minimum age to qualify for reduced co-payments from 70 to 75. It would also raise the co-payment rate to 20 percent for those elderly with high incomes. The share of medical expenses for persons aged 70 and older paid for by the government would increase from 30 to 50 percent. The co-payment rate for active employees would be raised from 20 to 30 percent. Ceilings on co-payments by employees and the elderly would go up. The contribution base for civil servants and employees of large firms would be expanded to include semi-annual bonuses, and the contribution rate for employees of small firms would be increased (Takayama, 2002).

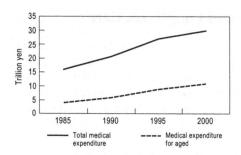

Figure 2.41. Medical care expenditure, Japan, 1985–1998. *Source*: Ministry of Public Management, Home Affairs and Posts and Telecommunications (2003, Figure 15.4).

Health care for the elderly has been heavily subsidized in Japan since 1972. Medical care costs of the elderly, growing at the rate of 9 percent annually, are the main driver of the increase in medical expenditure. *Figure 2.41* shows the rapid growth of total medical care expenditure in Japan and medical care expenditure for the "aged" (persons aged 70 and older) since 1985. The share of the elderly in total health care costs has risen from about 14 percent in 1975 (not shown in figure) to 35 percent in 2000 (see *Figure 2.42*); by 2025, the aged are projected to account for half of total costs. Yashiro (1997) and Yashiro *et al.* (1997) report that patients who are over age 65 use more than three times as much medical care as other individuals. The lifetime medical expenditure of the average Japanese is about US$17,000. About half this amount is spent after age 70 (Aging, 2001). Takayama (2002, p. 19) reported that in 1999, the annual medical costs of persons over 65 were 8.3 times the costs of those between 15 and 44 years old (see *Figure 2.43*). While most of this reflects the greater need for medical care among the aged, some of it also reflects the fact that this group can receive care for a very low fee.

Not all researchers agree, however, that population ageing is the key cause of rising medical expenditures in Japan. An analysis of the relative contribution of population growth, population ageing, and other factors (such as cost increases) to rising medical expenditure led Endo and Katayama (1998) to conclude that the role of demographic factors is small relative to other factors. Iwamoto (2002) assessed the contribution of population ageing by varying the age structure while keeping the per capita medical costs of each age group constant. He found that only about one-fourth of the annual growth rate was due to population ageing.

The primary source of higher costs is not the elderly as a group, but rather the bedridden elderly, which consists disproportionately of the very aged. The number of bedridden elderly, 1 million in 1993, is projected to increase to 2.6 million in

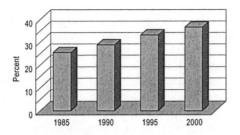

Figure 2.42. Medical expenditure for the aged as a percentage of total medical expenditure, Japan, 1985–1998. *Source*: Ministry of Public Management, Home Affairs and Posts and Telecommunications (2003, Figure 15.4).

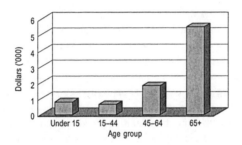

Figure 2.43. Annual medical cost per person (in US$) by age group, Japan, 1999. *Source*: Takayama (2002, p. 19).

2025 (Ministry of Health, Labour and Welfare, 2002). A large portion of the frail elderly are found among those aged 80 and older. As discussed previously, the "oldest old" are the most rapidly growing segment of the Japanese population.

In April 2000, Japan implemented a system of long-term care insurance. It will cover the long-term care of the elderly, which was previously provided partly through the health insurance system and partly by welfare measures. The cost of the long-term care insurance program will be paid by insurance premiums (45 percent), a government subsidy (45 percent), and the co-payments of users (10 percent). Only after the municipal government has determined that the applicant is disabled will he or she be eligible for benefits. The system will provide nursing-home care, but emphasis is placed on home-domiciliary care. The Ministry of Health, Labour and Welfare estimates that the cost of the insurance will be about US$20 a month, rising to about US$35 a month in 2010. The current cost of the long-term care program is only 1 percent of national income but it is projected to absorb 3.5 percent of national income by 2025.

In some aspects the Japanese health system is puzzlingly inefficient. The average length of hospital stay, at 35 days, is many times the average in the United Kingdom and the United States (about 6 days). The average length of hospitalization for persons aged 65 and older was 79 days in 1990 (though it had decreased to 71 days in 1993). This was quite long compared with 20 days for Sweden in 1997 (Ogawa and Retherford, 1997, p. 71). The monthly co-payments for hospital stays are only two-thirds of the co-payments for intermediate-care nursing homes, thus favoring long hospital stays. Hospital stays are also related, perversely, to reliance on middle-age housewives to provide elder care. Physicians will commonly admit the bedridden elderly to hospital simply to give the care-giver a much-needed break.

In recognition of the shortage of appropriate health care for the elderly, in 1990 the government instituted the "Golden Plan" to provide long-term care services and improve social services for the elderly and their families (Japan Aging Research Center, 1996). The Golden Plan is primarily directed toward increasing the number of beds in nursing homes. It also aims to improve home-based services for the elderly by providing home-helpers, short-term stay facilities, and elder day care centers. In the early 1990s Japan had only 360 home-helpers per 100,000 elderly persons, compared with more than 5,000 in Sweden (Ogawa and Retherford, 1997, p. 70). Japan was, on the other hand, well supplied with short-term-stay services. "Golden Plan" services are provided at low cost or no cost to the elderly and their families.

In addition to pensions and medical care, the elderly are provided with a variety of welfare programs. In 1995, those programs absorbed about 2 percent of national income. However, the implementation of the new public long-term care insurance program will significantly decrease welfare spending. The program to provide long-term care should reduce the demand for hospitalization and thereby slow the growth of medical spending as well.

2.7   Conclusion

Japanese population ageing is breaking new ground—no population in history has ever aged this much, this fast. The review in Chapter 1 suggests that age-structure changes on this scale, combined with absolute population decline, cannot but have profound impacts on the Japanese economy. Among the conclusions that emerge from this chapter, three in particular stand out:

- Although inefficiencies in the labor market can be eliminated by bringing discouraged workers, mostly women, into the workplace, labor force decline appears to be inevitable after 2025. Moreover, this is a best-case scenario; in the absence of policies to encourage additional labor supply, shrinkage in the Japanese workforce is beginning right now, at the turn of the century.
- While great uncertainty must be attached to impacts of demographic change on saving rates, there is near unanimity among researchers that the availability of savings will decline, with implications not only for Japan, but for the world economy as well.
- Financing problems in the Japanese public pension system are already beginning to surface, in the form of increasing contribution rates, and are likely to be exacerbated by projected demographic developments in the future. The same, it appears, holds for the health system.

Two things might change this rather pessimistic assessment: the demographic projections might be wrong, and an acceleration in productivity might occur. Regarding the first, we have stressed throughout the discussion that demographic trends over the next 50 years are fairly robust to changes in assumptions. All evidence, including the track record of previous official forecasts, is that fertility in Japan is likely to be lower than predicted and longevity, to be higher. In Chapter 4, we will apply an economic–demographic simulation model to assess the sensitivity of the economic outlook to these alternative demographic scenarios. Regarding the second, Japan is already one of the most technologically advanced countries in the world; at the same time, it appears to the outside observer to be one of the slowest to embrace changes in economic, social, and political institutions. It would be a brave forecaster indeed who relied on productivity to solve some of the deep-seated structural problems we have described above.

Notes

[1] Unless otherwise indicated, demographic data are taken from National Institute of Population and Social Security Research (2002a, 2002b).

[2] The total fertility rate (TFR), a synthetic index, is the number of births that a hypothetical woman would experience if she were to live from age 15 to 49 according to the age-specific fertility rates observed in a given year. Replacement level fertility, which corresponds in long-run equilibrium to a stable population, results from a TFR of approximately 2.1. Japan's TFR in 2000 was 1.36 (National Institute of Population and Social Security Research, 2002a, p. 6).

[3] One factor supporting European fertility levels is the high number of births outside marriage. Extramarital fertility has traditionally been very low in Japan. It is difficult to imagine this situation changing in the absence of the effective institutions that support working single mothers in Europe.

[4] Similarly, Kojima (1995, p. 201) notes that the percentage of women in the 20–34 age group who were married in 1990 was only three-fourths what it was in 1975.

[5] The total divorce rate is the sum of the current age-specific divorce rates of married women aged 16–49.

[6] In 1960, female life expectancy at age 65 exceeded male life expectancy by 2.5 years. By the year 2000, that difference had almost doubled.

[7] The UN calculated that, in order to keep the ratio of the working-age population to the retired-age population at its 1995 level, Japan would have to admit an average of 10 million immigrants per year over the next 50 years. Though such an immigration policy would maintain the age structure, it would result in the growth of the total population to 818 million in 2050. Furthermore, 87 percent of that population would be made up of immigrants or their descendants.

[8] Traditionally, aged parents in Japan are cared for by the eldest son's wife. Due to fertility decline, a rising share of all prospective spouses consists of eldest sons, thus further reducing the attractiveness of marriage from a woman's point of view. On the other hand, the proportion of elderly residing with their children is declining, in addition to which, the burden of elder care must be balanced against childcare provided by co-resident grandparents.

[9] In Japan, the bulk of saving is done by a very small number of households (Campbell and Watanabe, 2001). Most households, young or old, save very little. Household data may do little to explain private saving in Japan because such surveys are not likely to include these high savers.

[10] Yoshikawa *et al.* (2002, p. 2) report that a recent Bank of Japan survey showed that bequest motives were weak and most saving by the old is for precautionary reasons.

[11] Hayashi (1991, p. 86) suggested that "the Japanese housing depreciation rate of about 9 percent is reasonable given that a large fraction of Japanese housing is made of paper and wood."

[12] Most Japanese foreign assets consist of financial assets in the United States; however, Southeast Asia and Europe also account for significant shares of Japanese foreign assets.

[13] There are exceptions, however. Williamson and Higgins (2001) predict that between 1990–1992 and 2025, the Japanese saving rate will fall by 18 percentage points while the investment rate will fall by 20 percent. Hence, the share of the current account balance in Japan's GDP will increase from 2.5 percent in 1990–1992 to 4.5 percent in 2025.

[14] The NPS achieved almost universal coverage in 1986 when it was extended to self-employed workers.

[15] A full term with a firm would be 38 years for a college graduate and 42 years for a high school graduate.

[16] Salaried workers contribute indirectly through EPI and EPF pension plans. All plans share in the cost of the NPS in proportion to the number of persons they cover.

[17] The employer pays half this amount.

[18] Employees who retire between the ages of 60 and 64 will be eligible for reduced benefits.

[19] Employed workers would still be able to start drawing the earnings-related component of their pension at age 60.

[20] Since taxes are expected to rise over time, the impact is expected to be to reduce the rate of growth of benefits.

[21] For example, the Ministry of Health, Labour and Welfare, using the 1992 demographic projections and assuming a 2 percent growth rate of gross domestic product, a 2 percent inflation rate, and a 5.5 percent long-term interest rate, projected that there would be a surplus in the EPI pension fund through 2050. However, the effect of using the 1997 population projections is that a deficit begins to accumulate after 2030 in both the earnings-related and basic pension funds. The same exercise carried out using the most recent population projections would be even more pessimistic (Yashiro *et al.*, 1997).

[22] The gross replacement ratio refers to pre-tax income.

[23] The authors point out that although pensioners have a lower replacement rate under the pension reform case, they will have paid less in taxes when they were young and could thus save more.

[24] A report by the Finance Ministry found that the total value of Japan's pension liabilities now equals about one year's gross domestic product (Takinawa, 2000).

[25] Only 4 percent of their income comes from transfers from other family members.

[26] These comparisons refer to the undiscounted sums of costs and benefits.

[27] Takayama (1992), as reported by Yashiro (1997, p. 254).

Chapter 3

An Economic–Demographic Simulation Model for Japan

3.1   Introduction

Having reviewed the economics of population ageing and the demographic situation in Japan, in this chapter we present an economic–demographic growth model to study linkages between population dynamics, the macro-economy, the pension and health care systems, and intergenerational distribution. We describe the model structure in general terms, leaving a full algebraic presentation for Annex 3.1. We describe baseline assumptions and show that these reasonable exogenous assumptions give rise to a reasonable economic scenario. The baseline scenario described in this chapter is the basis for the alternative demographic scenarios presented in Chapter 4.

3.2   Model Structure

The IIASA model, which extends work originally presented by Blanchet and Kessler (1992), is theoretically heterodox. At its core is a two-factor (labor and capital) Cobb-Douglas production function with constant returns to scale:

$$GDP(t) = A(1 + g)^t K(t)^\beta L(t)^{1-\beta} , \qquad (3.1)$$

where g, the rate of total factor productivity growth, is exogenous. Rates of return to factors are neoclassical:

$$R(t) = \beta \left[\frac{GDP(t)}{K(t)} \right] ,$$ (3.2)

$$\overline{WageRate}(t) = (1 - \beta) \left[\frac{GDP(t)}{L(t)} \right] ,$$ (3.3)

where R is the gross profit rate, including depreciation and indirect taxes net of subsidies, and $\overline{WageRate}$ is average (over all age groups) employee compensation, including payroll taxes (contributions to public and private pension schemes as well as to health and long-term care schemes). Age-specific wages are calculated on the basis of the average wage rate, an age-wage profile based on empirical data, and the labor force age structure.

Thanks to the Cobb-Douglas function, the basic features of the neoclassical analysis of population ageing are maintained: a decline in the ratio of active labor force members to inactive persons results in a higher capital-output ratio (i.e., abundant capital is substituted for scarce labor) and a lower rate of profit relative to the wage rate (i.e., capital is less productive because it has less labor to work with). We speak here of static model response properties. Over the long run, impacts on the capital-output ratio reflect the nature of the saving function.

While factor prices are neoclassical, saving in the model is classical, with age-specific consumption rates (i.e., average propensities to consume) out of disposable wage income and profit income representing exogenous assumptions. Sometimes, although not here, this ultimately Marxian approach is taken to the limit of assuming that all wages are consumed and all profits are saved. Consumer utility maximization, based in most models on the life-cycle hypothesis and some form of forward-looking behavior, plays no role in the model save to the extent that current income can be considered a proxy for lifetime wealth. Clearly, incorporating different behavioral consumption functions would lead to differing model simulation properties; however, our review (in Chapter 2) of the Japanese saving literature has shown that there are widely diverging views on the nature and determinants of household consumption in Japan (as well as elsewhere).

Utilizing an accounting system based on the Organisation for Economic Co-operation and Development (OECD) System of National Accounts (SNA), the model tracks income, expenditure, and assets of each single-year cohort as it ages. Members of a cohort accumulate assets while young, then consume these assets during retirement, bequeathing to the living population whatever is left over when they die.[1] In this way, consumers' inter-temporal budget constraint is respected. Underscoring the classical roots of the approach implemented, this is a "corn model": wages are paid in corn, profits are paid in corn, taxes are paid and transfers are received in the form of corn, etc., and corn comprises the sole consumption and capital good. There are no asset prices to equilibrate the amount of capital that the elderly (and firms, and the government) wish to sell with the amount that the young (and firms, and the government) wish to buy. However, it may be possible to infer asset price movements from movements in the rate of return to capital, that is, corn.

In a non-welfare-state setting, since the elderly derive their livelihood from rents and the sale of assets while the young earn wages, population ageing would be expected to lead to a decline in the income of the elderly relative to the income of the young. In practice, however, this picture is complicated by the fact that most of the elderly's income in OECD countries comes from public pay-as-you-go (PAYG) pension systems. In our model, a PAYG public pension system collects contributions (at a rate calculated to maintain system balance) out of wages (as well as profits of the self-employed, i.e., entrepreneurial income) and pays benefits calculated on the basis of wage at retirement and indexed to growth in real wages after retirement.[2] In addition, some workers participate in a private sector PAYG-financed defined-benefit (DB) pension system where, again, the contribution rate is calculated endogenously to maintain system balance. A private fully funded defined-contribution (DC) pension system, which might be assumed to represent individual retirement saving accounts as well as firm-sponsored DC pension plans, also collects contributions and, after retirement, pays out benefits. In addition, households engage in saving outside the pension system. Finally, most persons over the pensionable age are assumed to receive a small "flat" pension indexed to the prevailing average wage rate.

A public health system is financed on a PAYG basis, with patient co-payments (i.e., deductibles) calculated as an exogenous share of age-specific health care expenditure and payroll tax contributions collected out of wages and entrepreneurial income at a rate calculated to balance total expenditure minus total co-payments. Change in the share of health care spending in gross domestic product (GDP) is expressed as a function of an "underlying" rate of health care expenditure growth and change in the age structure of the population. The situation is particularly simple when (i) the underlying rate of growth is assumed to be equal to the rate of GDP growth and (ii) relative age-specific health care costs (e.g., the health care costs of persons aged 70–74 relative to those of persons aged 0–4) are assumed to be constant over time at their base-year value. Under these admittedly restrictive assumptions, the share of health care spending in GDP can be expressed as a function of its initial-year value and changes since the initial year in the age structure of the population. While we are unable to analyze the most important sources of health care spending growth, such as changes in technology, we are at least able to translate changes in population age structure into consistent impacts on health care spending. The model also contains a public long-term care system module that is structurally identical to the health care system; only the parameters differ.

When the population ages, the pension, health, and long-term care payroll tax rates increase to balance the respective systems unless the model user makes explicit assumptions about government subsidies paid for out of general revenue or changes exogenous assumptions such as the retirement age, the rate of DB pension indexation to real wages, etc. Put differently, while the qualitative population ageing story told by some models (e.g., Roseveare *et al.*, 1996) is a flood of red ink as public pension and health systems go into deficit, the qualitative story told by our model is that payroll taxes rise. Another way of characterizing this approach is that, absent adjustments imposed by the model user, demographic risk is borne by the working-age population, whose social contribution rates change to accommodate population ageing. A final interpretation is that, while in some models ageing primarily affects public savings, in ours, it primarily affects private savings.

Savings consist of personal household savings (which can, in turn, be split into savings captured by the private DB and DC pension systems and other savings), government savings, and corporate savings. Age-specific pension savings (contributions plus investment income minus payouts) are assumed to be invested entirely in capital operated by firms. Age-specific non-pension savings are allocated over investment in three asset classes—residential capital, capital operated by unincorporated enterprises, and capital operated by firms and held on households' behalf by non-pension financial institutions—using shares that sum to unity. For accounting consistency (total wealth must be age indexed), age-specific non-pension personal savings are augmented by the age group's imputed share of the savings of firms and government before being allocated over the three asset classes.

In the case of residential capital and capital operated by unincorporated enterprises, profits are directly credited to households. In the case of capital operated by firms, profits are credited to firms, who then distribute dividends to the financial intermediary, namely, either the private DB or DC pension system or the non-pension financial institution sector. Non-pension financial institutions are assumed to pay out these dividends immediately in full to households; pension institutions, by contrast, retain dividends on participants' behalf.

Since government savings have no offsetting impact on personal savings (although such a link would be simple to implement), there is no Ricardian equivalence in the model; a dollar of government savings translates into a dollar of capital formation. In order to impose inter-temporal consistency on the government budget, an automatic adjustment mechanism is built in which limits government debt as a proportion of GDP by adjusting public consumption expenditure. Interest on government debt is credited to households as income. Note also that the government does not own or operate capital in this model.

Underscoring the partial equilibrium nature of the model, there is no behavioral investment demand function; total capital formation simply equals domestic savings minus acquisition of net foreign assets. The model is multiregional (at the global scale) and tracks bilateral capital flows between regions, but as with the domestic portfolio allocation process, the treatment of international allocation is ad hoc. All residential capital formation and formation of capital operated by private unincorporated enterprises is, for obvious reasons, allocated to the home region. Private pension funds and non-pension financial institutions are assumed to allocate capital to investment projects located in the domestic region and in foreign regions in accordance with exogenous coefficients summing to unity. This approach adds little from a behavioral point of view, but from a scenario-building point of view, it forces the model user to make explicit assumptions regarding the foreign sector and enforces global consistency on capital stocks and flows.

The comparative advantage of the model lies in its fine-grained accounting treatment of age-specific stocks and flows, and the inclusion of explicit pension, health, and long-term care modules; its comparative *dis*advantage lies in the limited amount of endogenous economic behavior built into the model and the large number of exogenous assumptions that must be made as a result. General equilibrium overlapping generations (OLG) models combine demographic detail with inter-temporal market-clearing behavior. This offers advantages, but carries with it its own set of restrictive assumptions, such as model-consistent expectations reaching many decades into the future (because of the long-term nature of demographic trends). A number of global macroeconomic model-based analyses (e.g., Masson and Tryon, 1990; Turner *et al.*, 1998) incorporate indices of age structure such as the dependency ratio into the major macroeconomic functions; however, these have limited age detail on economic stocks and flows. There are trade-offs in economic–demographic modeling, and we have chosen to emphasize the demographic rather than the economic side. One benefit of the emphasis on demographic detail, combined with the fact that different income streams are treated separately, is that the model is arguably better suited to addressing distributional issues than conventional neoclassical models.[3]

3.3 Baseline Scenario Assumptions

Model Initialization

The initial year of the model solution is 1995, and we present results in 10-year intervals from 2000 on. The model has been solved for 55 time periods, that is, out to 2050. Since this is a "test run" of the model and most attention will be focused on differences between the baseline and alternative demographic scenarios, only limited attention was given to fine-tuning assumptions. Therefore, the following scenario should not be interpreted as a forecast (or even as a particularly accurate depiction of the situation in the early years of the model solution). Rather, it illustrates trends and contributes to model validation by demonstrating that reasonable assumptions give rise to a reasonable scenario.

While we present results only for Japan, the model has been solved simultaneously for four countries/regions: Japan, the United States, Other Industrial Countries (according to the United Nations definition; this is effectively the OECD countries minus the United States and Japan plus Eastern Europe and the former Soviet Union), and Less Developed Countries (LDCs). The full set of exogenous assumptions made for Japan can be found in Annex 3.2; assumptions for other regions are given in MacKellar *et al.* (2002). In the following, we give only the highlights. In view of the multiregional nature of the model and the international audience for our results, all calculations have been performed in U.S. dollar terms.

In the following paragraphs, we describe exogenous assumptions for Japan and then discuss baseline solution results.

Demography

Baseline scenario age-specific (single-year) population data for Japan are from the United Nations (UN) Population Division's 1998 *Revision* (UN Population Division, 1998). The decision to use UN population data, as opposed to data from the Japanese Ministry of Population and Social Security, reflects the desire for consistency with the data used for other regions. The construction of the baseline demographic scenario is described at the beginning of Annex 4.1, which also presents our approach to constructing alternative low-fertility and low-mortality scenarios.

Economic Parameters, Rates, and so on

Among the driving economic assumptions for Japan are that the capital coefficient in the two-factor Cobb-Douglas production function is 0.333 (meaning that the labor coefficient is 0.667) and that the total factor productivity growth and depreciation rates are 1 and 5 percent per year, respectively. Age-specific labor force participation rates (LFPRs) for Japan were taken from the National Institute of Population and Social Security Research's *Selected Demographic Indicators for Japan*, Table 18 (see www.ipss.go.jp) and assumed to remain constant throughout the solution period. This is an important assumption and could be thought of as representing "business as usual" in labor market institutions and behavior.[4] An aggregate unemployment rate of 4 percent, invariant over time and uniform over the age spectrum, was assumed. As unemployment is higher among the elderly than among those in the prime working years, this simplification results in an overstatement of the number of elderly workers and, given population ageing, an overestimate of the rate of labor force growth. The age-wage profile, assumed to be time invariant over the simulation period, was taken from data from the Statistic Bureau of the Ministry of Public Management, Home Affairs and Posts and Telecommunications (2002, Figure 4.9).[5]

The model is initialized on an initial-year per capita GDP of approximately US$36,000 and a capital-output ratio of 2.6. The direct tax rate is set equal to 12 percent of wages and profits, and the indirect tax rate is set equal to 5 percent of GDP. Government consumption is assumed to be 15 percent of GDP and is automatically adjusted to ensure a government debt–GDP level not in excess of 30 percent. All of these notional estimates were derived from recent issues of the OECD *National Accounts Yearbook*.

The consumption rate out of wages is set equal to 90 percent, and that out of entrepreneurial income is set equal to 60 percent.[6] It is assumed that 60 percent of the elderly population's "annuity income" (really just the drawdown of accumulated assets), 100 percent of pension benefits (public DB, private DB, and private DC), and 100 percent of rents imputed to residential capital are allocated to consumption. Ten percent of inherited wealth is assumed to be converted into consumption; the remaining 90 percent represents an intergenerational wealth transfer. Note that all of these exogenous consumption rates are assumed to remain constant over the solution period. Given the assumed consumption rates and the fact that the elderly consume out of annuity income in addition to current income, persons aged 15–59 are net savers whereas persons aged 60 and older are net dissavers.

These consumption rates represent ad hoc assumptions based on assorted stylized facts—that workers consume while capitalists save, that bequests in Japan are substantial, that there is no saving out of pensions income, and so on. All of these simplifying assumptions could be refined.

Pension Systems

Our model tracks cohorts, not individuals, as they age. While we focus on the average worker and the average elderly person, some attention to institutional detail is nonetheless necessary to justify assumptions. However, the pension system in Japan is complicated, and our assumptions are for the most part rough.

Ninety percent of all workers are assumed to participate in a public earnings-related DB PAYG pension system (see National Institute of Population and Social Security Research, 2002c, especially the schematic outline of the Japanese pension system at the end of Chapter 2; all pension system detail in the following paragraphs is based on information from this source). Our public DB PAYG pension system corresponds more or less to the combined Employees' Pension Insurance (EPI) scheme and the civil servants' Mutual Aid Pensions scheme. Participation of eligible persons is reported to be 100 percent. Eligibility is limited to workers in firms employing more than five persons, so we adjust the 100 percent figure down somewhat. The accrual rate, in line with the new rate set for the EPI scheme by the 1999 Pension Reform Bill, is assumed to be 0.7125 percent. This means that upon retirement, a beneficiary annually receives 0.7125 percent of his or her final salary for each year of system participation.

Sixty percent of the population over the pensionable age is assumed to receive a flat-rate benefit equal to 10 percent of the current average wage; like the earnings-related public pension, this pension is financed out of payroll taxes. This corresponds roughly to the Basic Pension. For simplicity, we combine the public flat-rate and earnings-related pensions into one hypothetical scheme.[7] Assuming that 80 percent of the wage bill is subject to taxation, we estimate a total payroll tax of 22.6 percent in 2000, not far from reality.[8]

After retirement, pensions in the earnings-related scheme are indexed to rise each year by one-fifth of the growth rate of the real wage. The 1999 Pension Reform Bill abolished wage indexing in Japan, but we assume that political forces will give rise, over the long run, to some form of disguised indexing. We have implicitly indexed the flat Basic Pension to the average wage; this is probably not too far from what will actually happen.

Forty-five percent of workers are assumed to participate in an optional private DB pension scheme loosely corresponding to the Employees' Pension Funds scheme. No replacement ratio that would allow calculation of an accrual rate is available. However, since workers eligible for the Employees' Pension Funds scheme earn, on average, close to twice as much as those eligible for the mandatory public EPI scheme, the accrual rate has been set equal to 0.333 percent.

Pensions from the private sector DB PAYG pension system are assumed to rise each year by 10 percent of the growth rate of the wage rate; that is, by half as much as public pensions. Assets of the private DB pension system are assumed to belong to the firm, not the individual; in other words, they are not heritable. However, for accounting purposes, private DB pension system assets are imputed to cohorts, as are other forms of capital.

Private DC pension funds were instituted in Japan only in 2001, but firms have expressed keen interest in converting their seriously underfunded DB pension schemes into DC ones. On the assumption that DC pension schemes will successfully take root, we assume that 30 percent of workers (and entrepreneurs) contribute 5 percent of their gross income to a private DC pension fund. In contrast to DB pension wealth, assets of the DC pension system are assumed to be heritable. Pre-retirement withdrawals from the DC pension system are set equal to 3 percent of assets every year; this would be consistent with, say, about 10 percent of system participants changing jobs every year and one-third of these deciding to withdraw their accumulation.

Beginning at the pensionable age, cohorts are assumed to engage in a program of asset sales, including sales of DC pension system assets, designed to deplete their wealth at age 105; that is, if the pensionable age is 60, persons aged 60 sell one-forty-fifth of their assets, persons aged 61 sell one-forty-fourth of their remaining assets, and so forth. Note that these "sales" are in reality just the consumption of accumulated corn-savings. Any assets remaining upon death are bequeathed to the surviving population using shares based on the age structure of the population.

Pensionable age is assumed to rise from 60 in 1995 to 65 in 2015. As we will discuss below, this assumption and the assumption of unchanging age-specific labor force participation rates have important implications for intergenerational distribution (see endnote 3).

Health and Long-Term Care

For modeling purposes, the main health insurance schemes (Government-managed Health Insurance, Association-managed Health Insurance, and National Health Insurance, each covering about 30 percent of the population) are consolidated into a single hypothetical health system financed on a PAYG basis. According to the National Institute of Population and Social Security Research (2002c, Chapter 3), in 1998 the sources of finance for the consolidated Japanese health system were insurance premiums (52.9 percent), government subsidies from general revenue (32.2 percent), and patient co-payments (14.9 percent). Initial-year health spending is assumed to be 6 percent of GDP (National Institute of Population and Social Security Research, 1997, Table 5). The age profile of health care costs (assumed to remain constant over time) is taken from Cichon *et al.* (1999, Table 9, p. 325; these data are taken, in turn, from the Japanese Ministry of Health, Labour and Welfare).

The statutory co-payment rate is 20 percent for persons insured under the Government-managed and Association-managed Health Insurance schemes and 30 percent under the National Health Insurance scheme. Effective co-payment rates are difficult to calculate, however, owing to the operation of caps for low-income households, special rules governing drugs, favorable rules for the elderly, and so on. We simply make the assumption that 20 percent of all health expenditure is covered by patient co-payments.

Under these assumptions, the insurance premium calculated for 2000 is 7.3 percent of wages and profits of unincorporated enterprises. For comparison, in 2001 the combined employer–employee premium in the Government-managed and Association-managed Health Insurance schemes was 8.5 percent. No premium is reported for the National Health Insurance scheme, but this scheme is heavily subsidized.

Long-term care insurance in Japan came into force only in 2000 and is complicated in terms of financing and eligibility for benefits (Ogawa, 2001). We do not try to model these structural details; rather, we adopt the same approach as for health. We initialize long-term care costs at 2 percent of GDP based on the estimate that total turnover in the long-term care market for the elderly is 1.5 percent of GDP (Karlsson, 2002, p. 20). We did not succeed in finding age-specific disability rates for Japan, so we use rates for the United Kingdom instead (UK Office of Population Censuses and Statistics, 1988).

Initializing the Capital Stock

Capital stock estimates, never very reliable, are especially problematic in Japan because of wide historical movements of asset prices. For initialization purposes, we calculated a total capital stock based on our initial-year GDP and the assumed capital-output ratio of 2.6. Investment shares were used to split this into residential (14 percent) and nonresidential (86 percent) capital; this allocation corresponds to recent national expenditure account estimates of the share of housing in gross capital formation. Nonresidential capital was further split into capital operated by private unincorporated enterprises (33 percent) and capital operated by firms (67 percent). Capital operated by firms was further split into capital held on households' behalf by the private DB pension system (15 percent), the private DC pension system (15 percent), and non-pension financial institutions (70 percent). We used an age profile of household wealth from the United States (Hoynes and McFadden, 1997, Table 7.7, p. 174) to allocate all these forms of wealth over initial-year cohorts. Data sources described in MacKellar et al. (1999) were used to estimate initial-year cross-border holdings for the pension system and other financial institutions. For obvious reasons, all residential capital and capital operated by private unincorporated enterprises is assumed to be installed in Japan.

Allocating Savings across Asset Classes

In each year and for each age group, 14 percent of savings not captured by the pension system was allocated to residential investment. Of the remaining 86 percent, 33 percent was allocated to investment in capital operated by unincorporated enterprises and the remaining 67 percent, to investment in capital operated by firms. Based on estimates discussed in MacKellar et al. (1999), 85 percent of change in assets held on households' behalf by the non-pension financial system was assumed to finance domestic capital formation and 15 percent was assumed to finance capital formation abroad. The corresponding figures for capital held on households' behalf by the private pension system are 90 percent and 10 percent. The share of foreign-region savings invested in Japan varies from 1 to 3 percent, depending on the sending region and whether the hypothetical portfolio manager is the foreign pension system or the foreign non-pension financial sector.

3.4   Baseline Scenario Results

The demographic outlook in Japan has given rise to worry and even alarm among Japanese policy makers and the public. Most economic analyses have concluded that this concern is justified (see summaries of these analyses in Annex 3.3). Despite both theoretical and empirical controversies regarding the determinants of household savings, virtually all studies agree that the Japanese household saving rate will decline (Horioka, 1989, 1991; Ando *et al.*, 1995; Meredith, 1995; Yashiro *et al.*, 1997). Most projections call for a decline in the aggregate saving rate (net national savings over GDP, expressed as a percentage) as well, even into negative territory (Horioka, 1989; Kato, 1998). Most authors agree that ageing is likely to depress the supply of savings more than the demand for investment; therefore, a common feature of macroeconomic projections is a decline in Japan's historical current account surplus, often to the extent of turning into a deficit (Auerbach *et al.*, 1989; Hamada and Iwata, 1989; Noguchi, 1989; Masson and Tryon, 1990). The rate of return on capital is likely to decline, which is another way of saying that the productivity of capital will be reduced by labor scarcity, and the move toward deficit in the current account will be held in check by foreign investors' reluctance to invest in a country characterized by a low rate of return on capital. Higher payroll contribution rates—or subsidies from general revenue—will be required to maintain promised benefits in the public pension and health systems (Meredith, 1995a; Yashiro *et al.*, 1997).

   Some of the major demographic, macroeconomic, and distributional variables from the baseline scenario are shown in *Table 3.1* and illustrated in *Figure 3.1*. The demographic assumptions call for the aggregate population growth rate, which is currently decelerating, to reach zero between 2000 and 2010 and to be negative thereafter. Labor force growth, currently about zero, is significantly negative throughout the period. The dependency ratio (ratio of population aged 60 and older to population aged 15–59, expressed as a percentage) more than doubles from its recent level (34.7 percent in 2000) by mid-century.

   The macroeconomic consequences of these trends are well described by the Keynesian phrase "demographic stagnation." The aggregate saving rate declines from an estimated 7.2 percent in 2000 to 2.6 percent at the end of the solution period. Per capita growth of GDP decelerates from 1.8 percent per year in 1995 (not shown in *Table 3.1* and *Figure 3.1*) to 1.7 percent in 2000 to 1.3 percent per year in 2040, turning up slightly at the very end of the simulation period. Note that, since the 1990s were a decade of economic crisis in Japan, further deceleration of growth in the following decades would signal a very dramatic break with historical experience. The apparent cycle in *Figure 3.1* is entirely due to labor force dynamics. The capital-output ratio rises from 2.6 in 2000 to 3.5 in 2050, steadily decelerating as cumulative effects of the decrease in the aggregate saving rate become pronounced.

Table 3.1. Baseline scenario: Summary presentation.

	2000	2010	2020	2030	2040	2050
Demography						
Population (annual % change)	0.2	−0.1	−0.4	−0.5	−0.6	−0.6
Labor force (annual % change)	0.1	−1.2	−0.6	−0.8	−1.0	−0.8
Population 60+ : population 15–59 (%)	34.7	49.0	57.1	61.9	73.1	74.9
Macro-economy						
GDP per capita (US$)	39,943	46,253	53,435	62,399	71,317	80,249
GDP per capita (annual % change)	1.7	1.4	1.6	1.5	1.3	1.4
Capital-output ratio	2.6	2.9	3.1	3.3	3.4	3.5
Rate of return to capital (%)	5.6	4.8	4.0	3.4	2.9	2.6
Net savings (% of GDP)	7.2	6.6	5.6	4.6	3.5	2.6
Change in net foreign assets (% of GDP)	0.4	0.3	0.1	0.1	0.0	−0.1
Gross foreign investment in Japan (% of GDP)	5.9	5.3	4.5	3.7	2.7	2.0
Gross Japanese investment abroad (% of GDP)	5.5	5.1	4.3	3.6	2.8	2.1
Social insurance						
Public pension system						
Contribution rate (%)	22.6	24.6	25.4	25.7	29.3	32.3
Contributions (% of GDP)	8.4	9.1	9.3	9.4	10.7	11.7
Health system						
Contribution rate (%)	7.3	8.4	9.2	9.7	10.1	10.4
Contributions (% of GDP)	5.2	5.9	6.5	6.8	7.1	7.2
Long-term care system						
Contribution rate (%)	2.4	2.8	3.1	3.2	3.4	3.5
Contributions (% of GDP)	1.7	2.0	2.2	2.3	2.4	2.4
Intergenerational distribution						
Disposable income per capita,						
pop. 60+ : pop. 15–59 (%)	127.6	97.3	83.6	78.8	79.4	86.6
Non-health-related consumption per capita,						
pop. 60+ : pop. 15–59 (%)	134.5	103.4	88.9	84.5	86.8	95.2
Assets per capita,						
pop. 60+ : pop. 15–59 (%)	203.4	160.3	140.1	137.2	137.3	148.5

The rate of return to capital declines from 5.6 percent in 2000 to 2.6 percent in 2050. Change in net foreign assets, a proxy (albeit not a close one) for the current account balance, is projected to shift from +0.4 percent of GDP in 2000 to −0.1 percent of GDP in 2050; this would correspond to a move toward deficit in the current account. All in all, these results are in line with results presented by other researchers.

We also show some indices of intergenerational distribution in *Table 3.1* and *Figure 3.1*.[9] Trends in these indices depend on how policy makers allocate the impact of population ageing among higher social security payroll taxes, lower benefits, and greater government budget deficits; thus, these trends represent assumptions as much as results. Our model structure places the burden of adjustment

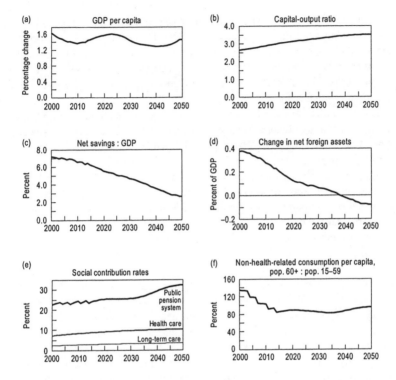

Figure 3.1. Baseline scenario: Summary results.

on system contributors by allowing payroll tax rates to rise while not modifying benefit calculation rules. However, we also assume that the pensionable age rises from 60 in 1995 to 65 in 2015 with no accompanying change in LFPRs. This explains the decline in the relative disposable income of the elderly (aged 60 and older) during the initial years of the simulation. Per capita disposable income of the elderly population declines from nearly 130 percent that of the non-elderly population (aged 15–59) in 2000 to less than 90 percent in 2015 (not shown in the table).[10] If labor force participation in the 60–64 age group were to increase in response to reduced availability of pension income, the distributional shift would be moderated (however, see the discussion of this issue in endnote 3). In level terms, disposable income of the elderly declines by about 15 percent between 2000 and 2014, then rises to approximately regain its initial level in 2025 and continues to rise for the rest of the simulation (see *Table A4.2.4* in Annex 4.2). Disposable income of the working-age population (see *Table A4.2.3* in Annex 4.2) increases throughout.

After 2015 (when the pensionable age ceases to rise), the trend in intergenerational distribution of disposable income reflects the combination of two opposing forces. The wage rate rises over the entire solution period while the rate of return to capital declines, both tending to favor younger persons. However, increases in payroll tax rates after 2015 reduce the disposable income of the young much more than the disposable income of the elderly. These opposing influences roughly cancel each other; as a result, there is little change in the intergenerational distribution of disposable income between 2015 and 2050. Given the offset between rising wages and rising payroll tax rates, policies that govern the generosity of pensions (such as pensionable age) and possible associated shifts in elderly labor force participation are clearly important determinants of intergenerational distribution.

The relative non-health-related consumption of the working-age population (i.e., total consumption minus consumption of health care minus consumption of long-term care), which includes consumption financed by decumulation of assets as well as consumption out of disposable income, broadly tracks the trend in relative disposable income (see *Table 3.1* and *Figure 3.1f*). So, too, does the ratio of assets of the elderly to assets of the non-elderly (bottom of *Table 3.1*). Among the developments affecting the latter are the ageing of the elderly population, which raises the share of the elderly who have mostly depleted their assets, as well as the ageing of the population aged 15–59 into the age groups whose wealth is highest.

Despite the assumed increase in pensionable age, the contribution rate necessary to balance the public pension system rises from 22.6 percent in 2000 to approximately 25 percent in 2015, after which it continues to increase to 32.3 percent in 2050 (see *Table 3.1* and *Figure 3.1e*). Note that this scenario is less extreme than some others (see Annex 3.3) that did not feature an increase in pensionable age. The health system contribution rate is estimated to rise from 7.3 percent in 2000 to 10.4 percent in 2050 and the long-term care contribution rate, from 2.4 percent to 3.5 percent. These rising payroll tax rates are, in effect, the price paid for the smooth intergenerational distribution of income after 2015.

Table 3.2 gives details on the evolution of the income, expenditure, and balances of the three components of the pension system. Public pension system contributions and benefits increase from 8.4 percent of GDP in 2000 to 11.8 percent in 2050; this corresponds to the rising payroll tax rates described above. Private DB pension system contributions are stable at 1.6 percent of GDP through 2030, at which point they begin to rise, reaching 2 percent at the end of the simulation. Taking the private DB and private DC pension systems together, the contribution of the private pension system as a whole to capital formation (i.e., the balance of the system) falls from 0.7 percent of GDP in 2000 to 0.1 percent of GDP in 2050.[11] This duplicates the trend projected for the United States by Schieber and Shoven (1997), albeit less dramatically because those authors kept private DB pension

Table 3.2. Baseline scenario: Pension systems, billion US dollars.

	2000	2010	2020	2030	2040	2050
Public						
Benefits	421	530	602	685	841	983
% of GDP	8.4	9.1	9.3	9.4	10.7	11.8
Contributions	421	530	602	685	841	983
% of GDP	8.4	9.1	9.3	9.4	10.7	11.7
Investment income	0	0	0	0	0	0
Bequests	0	0	0	0	0	·0
Withdrawals	0	0	0	0	0	0
Balance	0	0	0	0	0	0
% of GDP	0.0	0.0	0.0	0.0	−0.1	−0.1
% of net savings	0.0	0.0	0.0	0.0	0.0	0.0
Assets	0	0	0	0	0	0
Change in assets	0	0	0	0	0	0
Private DC						
Benefits	6	9	12	18	24	28
% of GDP	0.1	0.2	0.2	0.2	0.3	0.3
Contributions	48	56	63	70	74	79
% of GDP	1.0	1.0	1.0	1.0	0.9	0.9
Investment income	5	7	7	8	8	8
Bequests	6	9	12	17	20	22
Withdrawals	12	16	19	22	22	24
Balance	29	28	26	22	17	13
% of GDP	0.6	0.5	0.4	0.3	0.2	0.2
% of net savings	8.0	7.3	7.0	6.5	5.9	5.9
Assets	606	891	1,145	1,411	1,610	1,740
Change in assets	27	28	27	22	17	13
Private DB						
Benefits	78	94	104	117	143	168
% of GDP	1.6	1.6	1.6	1.6	1.8	2.0
Contributions	78	94	104	117	143	168
% of GDP	1.6	1.6	1.6	1.6	1.8	2.0
Investment income	4	4	4	3	3	3
Bequests	0	0	0	0	0	0
Withdrawals	0	0	0	0	0	0
Balance	4	4	4	3	3	3
% of GDP	0.1	0.1	0.1	0.0	0.0	0.0
% of net savings	1.2	1.0	1.0	1.0	1.2	1.5
Assets	489	530	565	604	637	666
Change in assets	4	4	4	3	3	3
Total						
Benefits	505	633	718	820	1,008	1,180
% of GDP	10.1	10.9	11.1	11.2	12.8	14.1
Contributions	546	680	768	872	1,059	1,230
% of GDP	10.9	11.7	11.8	11.9	13.4	14.6
Investment income	10	11	11	11	11	12
Bequests	6	9	12	17	20	22
Withdrawals	12	16	19	22	22	24
Balance	33	32	30	25	20	16
% of GDP	0.7	0.5	0.5	0.3	0.2	0.1
% of net savings	9.1	8.3	8.0	7.5	7.1	7.4
Assets	1,095	1,421	1,710	2,015	2,247	2,406
Change in assets	31	32	30	26	21	16

system contribution rates fixed instead of letting them rise in response to increasing benefit outflows. Another way of looking at the role of the private pension system in savings is to express net savings of the pension system as a share of total net savings. In our baseline scenario, this variable declines from 9.1 percent in 2000 to 7.4 percent in 2050.

The Global Picture

Because this study concentrates on Japan, only cursory attention has been given to the exogenous assumptions made for the rest of the world. Nonetheless, it is worth reviewing briefly what these rough assumptions imply for the global economy. As illustrated in *Figure 3.2*, many of the macroeconomic trends evident in Japan are repeated in other regions. Among these are decelerating rates of growth in GDP per capita, declining aggregate net saving rates, and rising public pension contribution rates. These trends serve as a reminder that slowing total population growth and population ageing are trends that are in place in every major world region. However, it is discernible in *Figure 3.2* that the United States, projected to experience the least-pronounced population ageing of any industrial country, is less subject to demographic stagnation than Japan or the other industrial countries. Given the caveat above about the rudimentary nature of the international linkage system, we do not attach too much significance to the capital flow trends in *Figure 3.2d*; however, the "mirror image" nature of the figure illustrates the global consistency characteristic of the approach used.

Comparison with Other Studies

In Annex 3.3, we compare our results with those of some other studies. Given the range of demographic assumptions, initial years, and model structures, it is not surprising that there is a broad range of model results.

3.5   Deterministic Simulation Properties

As the main application of this model is simulation of alternative economic and demographic scenarios, it is important to establish systematically how the model behaves when perturbed.

The basic deterministic simulation properties of the model are reported in *Table 3.3* (macroeconomic variables) and *Table 3.4* (variables related to intergenerational distribution and the social security system). Shocks are administered (to the baseline solution described above) in the initial year of the simulation and maintained throughout the solution period. Results for three years are given: year 0, representing the near term; year 10, representing the medium term; and year 50,

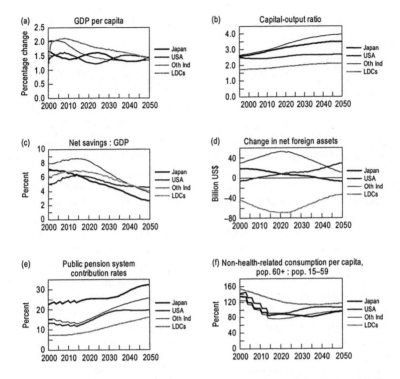

Figure 3.2. Baseline scenario: Global summary. Oth Ind = Other Industrial Countries; LDCs = Less Developed Countries.

representing the long term. All differences, whether measured in terms of percentage change or absolute percentage point change, are calculated by comparing the shocked alternative solution to the baseline solution. The first two shocks relate to population and establish the basic neoclassical properties of the model with respect to the role of demography. The remaining shocks relate to the main behavioral assumptions in the model, namely, labor force participation rates and age-specific consumption rates, as well as overall shocks to the level of economic output, which can be interpreted as shocks to total factor productivity.

Note that these shocks are designed to check the marginal response properties of the model, not to simulate the effects of foreseeable exogenous changes. An instantaneous 10 percent change in population is, for example, absurd, but can give insight into how the model would respond to a scenario with high population growth.

Increase in Aggregate Population

In the first shock, population in all age groups is increased by 10 percent (see first set of rows of *Tables 3.3* and *3.4*). As ensured by the neoclassical production function, the result is an immediate decline in GDP per capita (vis-à-vis the baseline scenario; see first column of *Table 3.3*). Since the shock is equiproportional across the age spectrum, the percentage change in labor force is the same as the percentage change in population, as a result of which the wage rate experiences the same percentage decline as GDP per capita. The capital-output ratio is reduced, reflecting substitution toward more abundant labor, and the rate of return to capital rises pari passu as a consequence of the higher productivity of capital. Note that this substitution response, to which we will allude a number of times, is the sole determinant of change in the capital-output ratio (and rate of return to capital) in the near term; however, in the long term, shifts in the capital-output ratio will also reflect the nature of the saving function and impacts of the shock on income streams (effectively, on GDP). In this case, the aggregate saving rate increases vis-à-vis the baseline in the near and medium terms and returns to its baseline level in the long term. A number of underlying factors are at work, but the easiest way to interpret this model property is to recall that when population is increased, the wage and profit shares in GDP remain fixed, as do all assumed saving rates out of the various income streams. As total GDP is increased, so are factor incomes and consumption therefrom. However, consumption corresponding to decumulation of assets by the elderly remains fixed. Thus, total consumption rises by less than total GDP and the aggregate saving rate is increased. Over the long term, this effect is dissipated as assets of the elderly "catch up" with GDP.

Disposable income of the non-elderly consists essentially of wages; that of the elderly consists mostly of pension benefits, the bulk of which come from the public pension system. In the initial year, the impact of the population shock is to increase the relative disposable income of the elderly by 2.2 percentage points because wages are lower (see first column of *Table 3.4*). This effect is dampened over time as the wage rate gradually returns to close to its baseline level (see fourth column of *Table 3.3*) and the ranks of retirees are filled with persons whose pensions reflect lower wage rates.

The initial impact of the population shock is to dilute assets per capita equiproportionally across the age spectrum, with zero impact on relative wealth (see second column of *Table 3.4*). By year 10, the assets of the elderly have not recovered from the initial dilution; by contrast, the assets of the population aged 15–59 include the wealth of persons in their twenties and thirties, which was not affected by the initial dilution effect because it was, at the time, zero or very low. This explains why the wealth of the elderly, expressed as a percentage of the wealth of the non-elderly, is significantly (2.2 percentage points in year 10) lower in the

Table 3.3. Sensitivity of macroeconomic variables to changes in baseline exogenous assumptions.

	GDP per capita (% change)	Capital-output ratio (% change)	Rate of return to capital (%-point change)	Wage rate (% change)	Net savings : GDP (%-point change)
Population increased 10% (age structure unchanged)					
Year 0	-3.1	-6.2	0.8	-3.1	0.6
Year 10	-2.3	-4.5	0.6	-2.3	0.5
Year 50	-0.4	-0.8	0.1	-0.4	0.2
Older age structure (total population unchanged)					
Year 0	0.0	0.0	0.0	0.0	0.0
Year 10	0.7	-0.6	0.1	-0.3	0.0
Year 50	-2.9	-1.3	0.1	0.6	-1.4
Labor force participation rates increased 10%					
Year 0	6.6	-6.2	0.8	-3.1	0.7
Year 10	7.6	-4.3	0.5	-2.2	0.6
Year 50	9.7	-0.6	0.1	-0.3	0.1
Age-specific propensities to consume increased 10%					
Year 0	0.0	0.0	0.0	0.0	-4.6
Year 10	-5.0	-9.8	1.3	-5.0	-4.0
Year 50	-12.3	-23.5	2.9	-12.3	-0.9
Total factor productivity increased 10%					
Year 0	10.0	-9.1	1.3	10.0	0.9
Year 10	11.5	-6.6	0.9	11.5	0.7
Year 50	14.3	-1.7	0.2	14.3	0.3

Table 3.4. Sensitivity of intergenerational distribution and variables related to pension, health, and long-term care to changes in baseline exogenous assumptions, percentage-point change.

	Disposable income per capita, pop. aged 60+ : pop. aged 15–59	Assets per capita, pop. aged 60+ : pop. aged 15–59	Public pension system contribution rate	Health and long-term care systems combined contribution rate	Assets of private DB and DC pension systems combined : GDP
Population increased 10% (age structure unchanged)					
Year 0	2.2	0.0	0.5	0.0	-1.3
Year 10	0.8	-2.2	0.2	0.0	-0.9
Year 50	-0.1	0.1	-0.1	0.0	-0.6
Older age structure (total population unchanged)					
Year 0	0.0	0.0	0.0	0.0	0.0
Year 10	0.6	0.5	0.2	0.1	0.0
Year 50	5.5	-5.8	8.7	2.4	2.5
Labor force participation rates increased 10%					
Year 0	-5.0	0.0	-1.5	0.0	-1.3
Year 10	-3.2	-2.7	-1.2	0.0	-1.0
Year 50	-1.4	0.0	-0.8	0.0	-0.6
Age-specific propensities to consume increased 10%					
Year 0	0.0	0.0	0.0	0.0	0.0
Year 10	5.6	34.0	0.5	-0.1	1.2
Year 50	3.9	36.1	-0.2	-0.2	4.1
Total factor productivity increased 10%					
Year 0	-5.6	0.0	-1.7	0.0	-1.9
Year 10	-3.0	-3.9	-1.2	0.0	-1.4
Year 50	0.0	0.4	-0.1	0.0	-0.8

high-population alternative scenario than it is in the baseline. By the end of the solution period, the asset dilution effect has disappeared as young persons unaffected
by the initial shock move up the age ladder.

Public pension contribution rates are not very significantly affected, and health
and long-term care contribution rates are unaffected, by change in total population.
This makes sense, since the ratio of contributors to beneficiaries is unchanged by an
across-the-board change in population. The ratio of assets of the combined private
DC and DB pension systems is reduced by 1.3 percentage points in year 0 because
GDP increases whereas assets do not. The effect is dissipated over the simulation
period as the higher volume of savings in the private DC system allows assets to
catch up.

Older Age Structure

In the second simulation (see second set of rows in *Tables 3.3* and *3.4*), the level
of population is left unchanged, but its age structure is changed to correspond to
a Maximum Population Ageing demographic scenario (see the beginning of Annex 4.3 for details on demographic scenarios; to summarize, this scenario combines
the fertility, mortality, and migration assumptions that produce the oldest population age structure). Note that the alternative versus baseline observations made
in this exercise can in no way be construed as estimates of the impact of actual
population ageing trends, as the baseline demographic scenario already contains
substantial ageing.

From the beginning of the solution period through 2025, labor force in the Maximum Population Ageing scenario is *higher* than it is in the baseline scenario, not
lower as might be intuitively thought. This is because reduced mortality immediately increases the number of workers, whereas reduced fertility does not make its
impact felt, in the form of fewer labor force entrants, for roughly 20 years. Thus,
results for year 10 in *Tables 3.3* and *3.4*, which might appear counterintuitive in the
context of a rapid ageing scenario, must be interpreted keeping in mind that labor
force is initially higher, not lower, in the alternative scenario.[12]

In year 10, because of the increase in the labor force described above, GDP per
capita is higher than the baseline (albeit by only 0.7 percent). Because labor force
is higher and capital stock is almost unchanged, the year 10 capital-output ratio and
wage rate are slightly lower in the alternative scenario than in the baseline. By the
end of the simulation period, slower capital accumulation (see the next paragraph)
and a smaller labor force result in a 2.9 percent reduction in GDP per capita vis-
à-vis the baseline. The long-term impact for the wage rate is the reverse of the
medium-term impact, because after 2025, labor force is lower in the alternative
than in the baseline scenario. The long-term impact of the older age structure is to
reduce the saving rate, further reducing the capital-output ratio.

This reduction in the saving rate occurs as the age-structure change redistributes population from the saving years (15–59) to the dissaving years (60 and older). While the impact on the aggregate saving rate is slow to develop, by the end of the simulation period it amounts to a 1.4 percentage point reduction. This corresponds to cutting the baseline rate (2.6 percent) approximately in half. The payroll tax rate for the public pension system is increased by 8.7 percentage points in the long term, and the combined health and long-term care payroll tax rate is also significantly increased, by 2.4 percentage points. By the end of the simulation, the ratio of pension system assets to GDP is 2.5 percentage points higher in the Maximum Population Ageing scenario than in the baseline. This makes sense since, generally speaking, an older population will be characterized by a higher pension wealth–income ratio.

As we wrote above, the risk of demographic shocks is, in this model, borne by the working-age population that pays payroll taxes. Proportionally speaking, and not taking indirect effects into account, the long-term 8.7 percentage point increase in the public pension system payroll tax rate and 2.4 percentage point increase in the combined health and long-term care payroll tax rate amount to roughly a 20 percent reduction in the disposable income of contributors. These increases in payroll tax rates explain the fact that, by the end of the simulation period, the per capita disposable income of the elderly increases 5.5 percentage points relative to the disposable income of the working-age population. The ratio of per capita assets of the elderly to per capita assets of the working-age population is reduced by 5.8 percentage points in year 50 (from roughly 150 to 145 percent). This reflects the compounded effects of lower saving rates out of lower disposable wage income in the middle years of the alternative scenario.[13] Moreover, in the Maximum Population Ageing scenario, the average age of the 60 and older population increases, placing a higher proportion of the elderly in the "oldest old" age group, which is characterized by low levels of wealth.

Higher Age-Specific Labor Force Participation Rates

In this simulation, we increase all age-specific LFPRs by 10 percent (i.e., multiply baseline rates by 1.1), leading to an immediate increase in output (see third set of rows in *Tables 3.3* and *3.4*). The wage rate falls to reflect greater abundance of labor, the capital-output ratio is reduced, and the rate of return to capital rises, all of which reflect neoclassical aspects of the model. Note that, because the proportional impact on the labor force is the same as in the population shock (first set of rows in *Tables 3.3* and *3.4*), the impact on the wage rate and the rate of return to capital is essentially the same in these two simulations. The aggregate saving rate initially increases because, while factor incomes and consumption out of them rise pari passu, consumption of the elderly financed by the sale of assets is fixed in the near term. Over the long term, the consumption of the elderly adjusts upward and the impact on the saving rate is gradually reduced. Not surprising in view of the fact that LFPRs were held constant in the first simulation described above (increasing the entire population by 10 percent), the aggregate saving rate impacts in the labor force simulation are almost identical to those in the baseline scenario. Recall that the impacts of higher labor force on social insurance contribution rates, described below, do not result in changes in the aggregate saving rate because these systems are balanced by assumption.

The initial impact of higher labor supply is to reduce the disposable income of the elderly by 5.0 percentage points relative to the disposable income of the non-elderly, as the wage income of the non-elderly increases while the pensions of the elderly do not. However, this impact is attenuated over time as higher LFPRs translate into a greater proportion of the elderly population receiving an earnings-related pension. The increase in labor force does nothing to affect assets in year 0, hence there is no initial-year change in the assets of the elderly relative to the assets of the non-elderly. In the medium term (year 10), the distribution of assets is shifted (by 2.7 percentage points) against the elderly, because many assets of the elderly in year 10 already existed in year 0 and hence were unaffected by the labor force shock. Put differently, in year 10, few elderly will have experienced the higher labor force participation, and hence greater asset accumulation, in the alternative scenario. In the longer term, however, assets of the elderly population gradually reflect higher labor force participation while young, as a result of which the age distribution of assets returns to its baseline pattern.

Higher labor force participation reduces the contribution rate required to balance the public PAYG pension system by 1.5 percentage points in year 0. In the longer run, however, the impact of the higher LFPR on the pension system is less significant because more workers in the near term means more pensioners in the long term. Note that the payroll tax rate necessary to balance the health and long-term care systems is unaffected by higher labor force participation: as discussed above, our simplifying assumptions imply that effectively the only determinant of this rate is the age structure of the population. The impact on assets of the private pension system relative to GDP is virtually the same for an increase in labor force as it was for an increase in population.

Higher Age-Specific Propensities to Consume

In this simulation, all age-specific consumption rates were increased by 10 percent (i.e., were multiplied by 1.1).[14] As there are no demand-side multiplier effects in the model, there is no impact on GDP in the initial year (see fourth set of rows in *Table 3.3*). By the end of the simulation, however, the cumulative effect of lower savings is to reduce GDP by 12.3 percent vis-à-vis the baseline. The capital-output ratio is reduced by nearly a quarter (23.5 percent, to be exact) owing to lower savings, the rate of return to capital is increased by 2.9 percentage points, and the wage rate falls in step with GDP.

The ratio of the disposable income of the elderly to that of the non-elderly is higher in the alternative than in the baseline scenario for three reasons. First, the wage rate is lower (see fourth column of *Table 3.3*). Second, the rate of return to capital is higher (see third column of *Table 3.3*), and while *rentier* income of the elderly is not nearly as important as pension income, it is nonetheless a significant component of their total income. Note that the distributional impact is greater in the medium term, before pensions have had a chance to adjust downward to reflect the lower salaries of new retirees. Third, and related to the second point, the age distribution of wealth is shifted decisively toward the elderly (see second column of *Table 3.4*). The difference in the age distribution of wealth observed in year 10 has to do mostly with the inertia of capital accumulation. The assets of the elderly population in year 10 reflect primarily pre-shock accumulation behavior; that is, relatively high baseline-scenario propensities to save combined with relatively high baseline wage rates. The assets of the non-elderly in year 10, by contrast, reflect to a significant degree post-shock accumulation behavior; that is, relatively low alternative-scenario propensities to save and relatively low alternative-scenario wage rates. Because the wage rate continues to fall and the rate of return to capital continues to rise between years 10 and 50, the shift in the age distribution of wealth persists in the long run.

The increase in consumption rates does not very significantly affect the payroll tax rates necessary to balance the public pension system, because while the contribution base is lower owing to reduced wages, so too, eventually, are the pensions that must be paid. The combined health and long-term care contribution rate, for reasons described above, is largely unaffected. The ratio of assets of the private pension system to GDP is increased by 1.2 percentage points in year 10 and by 4.1 percentage points in year 50. This can be explained by noting that, when propensities to consume are multiplied by 1.1, saving rates associated with the private pension system are unaffected (the DC pension system contribution rate remains 5 percent and the private DB contribution rate is still calculated to balance the system). Therefore, a larger share of household savings consists of an increase in pension wealth, specifically DC pension wealth. This effect is consistent with the significant observed redistribution of wealth, proportionally speaking, from the working-age to the elderly population.

Higher Total Factor Productivity

A particularly simple but interesting shock is the scaling up or down of GDP by a shift in total factor productivity. The results of a sustained 10 percent increase in the constant term of the Cobb-Douglas production function are shown in the fifth set of rows in *Tables 3.3* and *3.4*. Because the pensions and assets of the elderly are unaffected by the shock in the near term, consumption rises by less than income, leading to an immediate 0.9 percentage point increase in the aggregate saving rate. Eventually, consumption catches up with income and the saving rate impact is dampened. In the meantime, however, the higher saving rate translates into more rapid GDP growth: the shock increases GDP per capita by 10 percent in year 0 (there are no Keynesian multiplier effects in the model), but by 11.5 percent in year 10 and 14.3 percent in year 55. The capital-output ratio is decreased in the near term because GDP is a fast-moving variable whereas capital stock is a slow-moving one; in the long term, it returns to roughly its baseline value, thanks in part to the higher aggregate saving rates. The wage rate changes in step with GDP, because in an economy characterized by a Cobb-Douglas production function, the exponent in the production determines the share of wages in GDP, and this parameter is the same in the baseline and alternative solutions.

As the shock increases wages without affecting the pensions of those already receiving them, its initial impact is to reduce the disposable income of the elderly relative to the disposable income of the young (by 5.6 percentage points). Also playing a role in this distributional shift is the reduction in the payroll tax rate necessary to balance the public pension system. Owing to the pension catch-up phenomenon, both these shifts are dissipated over time. Since higher wage income translates into enhanced asset accumulation by the population aged 15–59 while leaving the existing elderly wealth largely unaffected, the ratio of the wealth of the elderly to the wealth of the working-age population is reduced (by 3.9 percentage points) in year 10, then returns to roughly its baseline value in the long term. The ratio of assets of the pension system to GDP is immediately reduced by the upward shock to GDP but gradually approaches its baseline value from above as private DC savings are accumulated from the higher wage bill.

3.6   Robustness Analysis

Particularly in view of the long-term nature of questions involving social security, attention should be given to model robustness. One subjective definition of robustness might be that, when model parameters and/or exogenous assumptions are randomized and the model is solved in Monte Carlo fashion, the mean and median of the stochastic forecasts lie "reasonably close" to the deterministic baseline forecast throughout the simulation period and uncertainty bands are not "too wide." Robustness does not mean that results are little changed when exogenous assumptions or model parameters are subject to massive fluctuations (Hackl and Westlund,

1991). It means, rather, that reasonable stochasticity in model input gives rise to reasonable stochasticity in model results.

Most economic variables have trends and exhibit periods of volatility followed by periods of relative tranquility. It is common practice (see, e.g., Enders, 1995) to represent variables such as GDP, investment, government consumption, and price indices using autoregressive conditional heteroscedastic (ARCH)-type processes. In the rest of this section, we illustrate model behavior when a key model parameter (the constant term in the Cobb-Douglas production function) and the main exogenous assumptions (age-specific average propensities to consume and LFPRs) are assumed to follow an ARCH-M process, in which the mean of the variable depends on its own conditional variance. Taking the Cobb-Douglas production function scale parameter A as an example, the process is modeled as

$$A(t) = \mu(t) + \varepsilon(t) \,, \tag{3.4}$$

where $\mu(t) = A^* + \delta h(t), \delta > 0, h(t) = \alpha_0 + \sum_{i=1}^{q} \alpha_i \varepsilon^2(t - i)$, A^* is the baseline parameter, and we assume $\varepsilon(t) \sim N(0, 0.05A^*)$. We model $A(t)$ as ARCH(q), where the conditional forecast of $A(t)$ is based on the error term in $t - 1$; that is, $q = 1$. In empirical analysis, the parameters δ, α_0, and α_i must be econometrically estimated. For our analysis we assumed $\delta = 1$, $\alpha_0 = 0$, and $\alpha_1 = 0.65$ (see, e.g., Enders, 1995).

In addition to being interested in the "drift" of the mean parameter value due to conditional volatility, we are concerned with the possibility of unforeseen changes in parameters. In order to incorporate such effects, we define a shock function that gradually shifts the selected parameter by 1 percent per year over a 10-year period. During the remainder of the simulation, the parameter remains at its shifted value.

We illustrate these numerical experiments with the scale parameter $A(t)$. At $t = 0$, the baseline parameter A^* is shocked by a random variable $\varepsilon(t) \sim N(0, 0.05A^*)$; that is, $A(0) = A^* + \varepsilon(t)$. For $0 < t < 18$ (i.e., from 1995 through 2013), the parameter is simulated according to the process $A(t) = A^* + \varepsilon(t)$, $\varepsilon(t) \sim N(0, 0.05A^*)$. We then impose a shift in the parameter, as follows: In 2014, the variable is shocked upward by a factor of $(1+0.01)$. In 2015, it is shocked upward by a factor of $(1+0.01)^2$, and so on through 2023, when the shock factor is $(1+0.01)^{10}$. That is, for $19 \leq t \leq 28$ (i.e., 2014 through 2023), we define $A^{*i} = (1 + 0.01)^i A^*$, $i = 1, \ldots, 10$ and set $A(t) = \mu(t) + \varepsilon(t)$, $\mu(t) = A^{*i} + h(t), h(t) = \sqrt{0.65\varepsilon^2(t - 1)}$, with $\varepsilon(t) \sim N(0, 0.05A^{*i})$. For $t \geq 29$ (i.e., 2024–2055), we let $A(t) = \mu(t) + \varepsilon(t)$, where $\mu(t) = A^{*10} + h(t)$ and $\varepsilon(t) \sim N(0, 0.05A^{*10})$.

Results are shown in *Figure 3.3* (uncertainty in the production function scale parameter A), *Figure 3.4* (uncertainty in age-specific LFPRs), and *Figure 3.5* (uncertainty in age-specific average propensities to consume). The uncertainty bands

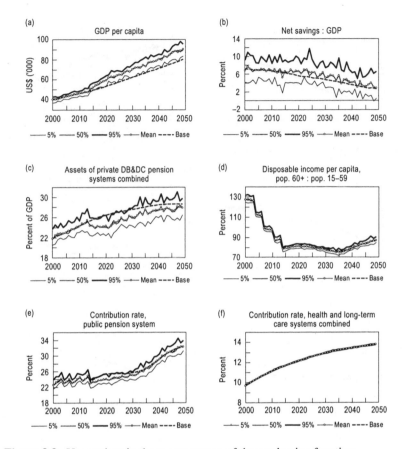

Figure 3.3. Uncertainty in the constant term of the production function.

in *Figures 3.3* to *3.5* were calculated based on Monte Carlo runs and can be strictly interpreted as confidence intervals corresponding to the assumed probability distribution. Note, however, that shocks that are the same in proportional terms (across variables) cannot be compared in the real world. For example, a 10 percent shock (or uncertainty) that increases a consumption rate from 90 to 99 percent is not meaningfully comparable to a 10 percent shock that shifts an LFPR from 75 to 82.5 percent.

Figure 3.3 contains results for the scale parameter *A*. The mean and median of the stochastic solutions correspond to the baseline until 2014, when the upward intervention commences. The 90 percent uncertainty range during the interval

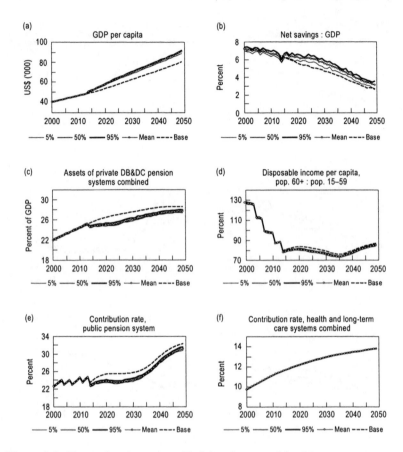

Figure 3.4. Uncertainty in age-specific labor force participation rates.

2000–2013 is roughly US$5,000 for per capita income (*Figure 3.3a*), 5 percent-
age points for the aggregate saving rate (*Figure 3.3b*), 3 percentage points for total
private pension system assets as a share of GDP (*Figure 3.3c*), 5 percentage points
for relative disposable income of the elderly (*Figure 3.3d*), and 2 percentage points
for the public pension system contribution rate (*Figure 3.3e*). The insensitivity of
the combined health and long-term care contribution rate (*Figure 3.3f*) reflects the
fact that this variable is a function only of age distribution.

Of particular interest is the question of whether the mean and median stochastic scenarios return to the deterministic baseline path even after the 10-year intervention commencing in 2014. *Figure 3.3* shows that in the case of all variables

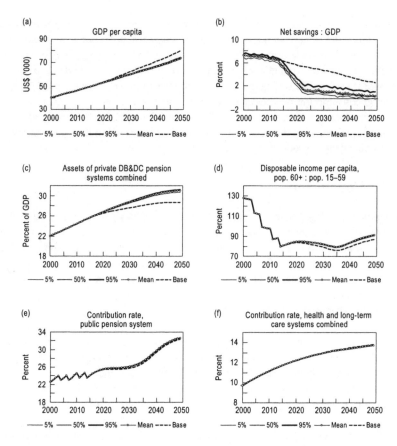

Figure 3.5. Uncertainty in age-specific average propensities to consume.

calculated as a rate or a percentage—that is, all variables except GDP per capita—
the mean and median stochastic variables finish the simulation period quite close
to the deterministic baseline. In the case of GDP per capita, at the end of the simulation period the stochastic mean and median are a little more than 10 percent
above the baseline, a result of the persistent multiplier effect of the 10 percent intervention. As a general proposition, however, the stochastic uncertainty bands in
Figure 3.3 are relatively narrow and symmetric around the baseline, even at the end
of the simulation period.

Figures 3.4 and *3.5* give results for stochasticity in LFPRs and consumption rates, respectively. In all cases, stochastic uncertainty bands around the

deterministic baseline are extremely narrow for the early years of the simulation and, despite the 10 percent intervention, the stochastic bundles finish the simulation fairly close to the deterministic baseline scenario. The great sensitivity of the aggregate saving rate to the intervention in consumption rates (see *Figure 3.5b*) arises because the aggregate saving rate is practically the complement of the average age-specific consumption rate. Because GDP is a flow and assets are a stock, private pension system assets as a share of GDP (*Figure 3.5c*) and GDP (*Figure 3.5a*) move in opposite directions; this is also the case in *Figure 3.3*, illustrating uncertainty in the Cobb-Douglas production function constant term.

3.7   Conclusion

The model described in this chapter and its annexes is designed to study the evolution of GDP, factor incomes, pension and health systems, and the age distribution of income and wealth in a consistent macroeconomic framework. The driving forces are population growth and age structure and exogenous assumptions about productivity growth, consumption rates, LFPRs, and the nature of pension and health arrangements.

In this chapter we have shown that

- sensible exogenous assumptions give rise to a credible long-run model solution;
- when exogenous assumptions or model parameters are changed, the model performs plausibly on a baseline-versus-alternative basis; and
- model projection results are robust, in the sense that reasonable stochasticity in assumptions leads to reasonable stochasticity in model results.

Subject to normal cautions regarding the restrictive simplifying assumptions, and so on, the model is appropriate for long-run simulations related to demography, social security systems, the macro-economy, and the intergenerational distribution of income and wealth.

The baseline scenario presented here corresponds to what we have termed "demographic stagnation"—decelerating growth, declining saving rates, and so on. Because of our assumptions about increasing pensionable age and constant elderly LFPRs, disposable income of the elderly declines in the initial years of the simulation. It is striking, however, that in the longer term, disposable income of *both* the young and old rises and the intergenerational distribution of income is relatively stable. In this sense, the baseline scenario presented here is fundamentally an optimistic one despite lower growth and depressed savings. The key to this outlook is a steady rise in both the wage rate and payroll tax rates.

Notes

[1] We do not calculate life annuities and survivor benefits for several reasons. The first is that in many countries, and particularly in Japan, very few elderly persons purchase annuities. They retain their assets as precautionary balances or may have explicit bequest motives, be they selfish or altruistic. Second, population in this model is single-sex. At best, survivor's benefits could be calculated only through ad hoc adjustments. Needless to say, disaggregating population by sex would be a major step forward in the further development of this model. Bequests are simply distributed over living cohorts using population age shares. Incorporating a model age schedule of inheritance would, likewise, be a significant advance.

[2] It is computationally much simpler to calculate pensions based on wage at retirement than to track contributions over the entire work life of a cohort. Moreover, there is no reason to believe that final salary is not proportional to lifetime earnings. Note that we use the term "entrepreneurial income" rather loosely. In this model, there are no pure economic profits; that is, no return to entrepreneurship as traditionally defined. What we call "entrepreneurs" are the owners of capital operated by unincorporated enterprises. Their income contains no element of wages; it is a pure return on capital owned by the "entrepreneur."

[3] One reviewer regretted that we did not utilize the distributional detail available in the model to pay more attention to intergenerational equity issues. However, this is a descriptive, not a normative, model. It was not intended for developing specific objectives such as maximizing per capita income or achieving intergenerational equity. There is no consensus on the meaning of the general concept of intergenerational equity (indeed, of any sort of equity) in quantitative terms. In the narrow pensions sphere, for example, there are many unresolved (and perhaps unresolvable) technical issues concerning life expectancies and appropriate rates of discount in calculating intergenerational pension equity—to mention just one, should later generations receive lower monthly pensions because they have longer life expectancies? Even if the pension system could be made intergenerationally equitable, there is no assurance that this would make the total economic system more equitable. There are other important wealth flows between generations, most importantly, the flows between working parents and their children. Horioka (2002) and others argue that current PAYG pension systems in Japan and elsewhere are not equitable because they favor older generations. However, that imbalance favoring the elderly in Japan may simply offset the sacrifices made by the older generation to equip younger generations with human capital. If there are other intergenerational inequalities in the economic system, making the pension (and health) system intergenerationally equitable according to some criterion might make the overall system less equitable. In short, we place no equity or fairness interpretation on our descriptive measures of income distribution.

[4] As we note below, assuming that the pensionable age rises from 60 to 65 while keeping elderly LFPRs constant implies a large reduction in the per capita disposable income of the population aged 60 and older relative to the population aged 15–59. It is indeed possible that, as the pensionable age rises, an increasing number of workers aged 60–64 will choose to remain in the labor force. However, it is also possible

that cohorts entering the over-60 category are wealthier than those that went before them and will choose to retire despite the increase in pensionable age—this is what has happened in the United States and Europe, and what has happened so far in the case of Japanese males. Recall that elderly LFPRs in Japan are already extremely high compared with those of other OECD countries. All things considered, it has seemed to us even more speculative to hypothesize a labor supply response to the rising pensionable age than to assume business as usual.

[5] For simplicity, the observed age profile was stylized to one in which wages rise linearly (by a factor of 3.6) from age 15 to 55, then decline linearly (by a factor of 2.9) through age 75, then remain constant until age 86, whereupon they fall to zero.

[6] Propensities to consume can be varied by age; in view of the fact that our assumptions are essentially ad hoc, we have chosen to make them uniform across the age spectrum.

[7] In reality, owners of unincorporated enterprises (whom we refer to as "entrepreneurs") contribute only to the flat-rate pension system and not to the earnings-based scheme. However, we adopt the simplification of combining wages and the profits of unincorporated enterprises into one contribution base for a consolidated public PAYG-financed pension scheme, taking the same 80 percent catchment rate for both.

[8] The combined employer–employee payroll tax rate for the EPI scheme is now 17.35 percent (it is slightly higher for the small civil servants' Mutual Aid Pensions scheme). The flat-rate contribution to the Basic Pension scheme reported in 2001 is about 2.5 percent of the average wage. However, one-third of the benefits paid out under the Basic Pension scheme are subsidized out of general government revenue, so the true contribution rate is closer to 4 percent. Broadly speaking, the 22.6 percent payroll tax rate that we estimate is in the right neighborhood.

[9] An alternative measure of income is "adjusted" disposable income, which controls for change in pension wealth. Since the disposable income of the elderly includes benefits from DC pension schemes, a decrement to wealth, and the disposable income of the young excludes contributions to DC pension schemes, an increment to wealth, the impact of the adjustment is to reduce the income of the elderly relative to the income of the young. It is also worth noting that we do not take account of current income transfers between the generations such as the transfer that takes place when adult children live in their elderly parents' homes. This practice is common in Japan, and because the relative value of residential capital is very high, co-residence implies a significant transfer from old to young. Failure to take this into account biases upward the ratio of disposable income of the elderly relative to that of the working-age population. The relative non-health-related consumption variable in the second-to-last line of *Table 3.1* and *Figure 3.1f* is subject to the same bias.

[10] Since this decline is caused by the lower income of the 60–64 age group, the trend in the index could be moderated by the simple expedient of redefining the elderly as the population over age 65. Such definitional problems are not easily resolved, but the example reminds us how policy decisions are frequently swayed by the definition of the elderly. Note also that the saw-tooth patterns of change in the pension contribution rate and relative income and consumption measures are due to the fact that we raise the retirement age in discrete steps.

[11] Investment income of the private pension system includes only distributed dividends, in this case 15 percent of total profits. The remainder is retained by firms where, presumably, it will be reflected as a capital gain.

[12] In the initial year of the simulation, the population age structure is identical in the baseline and alternative scenarios; this explains the row of zeros in *Tables 3.3* and *3.4*.

[13] *Table 3.3* reports average (over all ages) rates. Under the Maximum Population Ageing scenario, the working-age population is concentrated, proportionally speaking, in the peak wage rate and peak saving rate years (ca. 40–50). If age-structure changes in the population were controlled for, the 60 and older cohort being observed in year 50 would be seen to have experienced age-specific wage and saving rate impacts more negative than those visible in *Table 3.3*.

[14] Among the exogenous variables are the proportion of inherited wealth converted to consumption and the proportion of "annuity income" (i.e., the proceeds of the elderly population's asset sales) consumed, the complement of the latter being the proportion of wealth the elderly wish to bequeath. These "propensities to consume" were also multiplied by 1.1. Propensities to consume out of pension income, already 1.0 in the baseline scenario, were kept at the same level in the alternative scenario. Note that shocks to consumption and saving rates are proportionally asymmetric; that is, a 10 percent consumption rate shock from 90 to 99 percent produces a more than 10 percent saving rate decline from 10 to 1 percent.

Annex 3.1:
The Model

This annex presents the algebraic structure of the model described in Chapter 3. Because we are reporting what is essentially a one-country application of the model, a single-region version of the model is described. For a presentation of the interregional linkage mechanism, see MacKellar and Ermolieva (1999).

1. Population, Labor Force, and Employment

1.1 Population

Population is divided into age groups $age = \overline{0, MaxAge}$, where $MaxAge$ is the beginning year of the terminal age category (for example, $MaxAge = 85$ if the terminal age category is 85 and older). We implement the simplest possible approach to population, namely, importing from another source a deterministic demographic scenario consisting of population by single-year age groups. Incorporating a population projection module would not be conceptually difficult, but would not add much depth to the model unless mortality and/or fertility were endogenized. Arguably, a higher-payoff extension would be disaggregating population by sex, which would allow finer-grained treatment of the labor market, pensions, health, and long-term care.

1.2 Labor force and employment

Total labor force is the sum over age groups:

$$LabForce(t) = \sum_{age=15}^{MaxAge} LabForce(t, age) ,$$

where

$$LabForce(t) = Pop(t, age) LabForcePartRate(t, age) .$$

Age-specific LFPRs are exogenous assumptions, as are unemployment rates:

$$Emp(t) = LabForce(t, age)[1 - UnempRate(t, age)] ,$$

$$Emp(t) = \sum_{age=15}^{MaxAge} Emp(t, age) .$$

114

2. Capital and the Nature of Claims

As stressed in Section 3.1 of this chapter, this is a corn model: output consists of corn, wages are paid in corn, and corn capital earns a corn rate of return. However, we impose an accounting system that distinguishes between different income streams and different types of capital.

The four types of capital are residential capital ($KRsdntial$), capital operated by private unincorporated enterprises ($KPvtUnincorpEnt$), capital operated by incorporated enterprises and held on households' behalf by the private pension system ($KPvtPenSys$), and capital operated by incorporated enterprises and held on households' behalf by other (i.e., non-pension system) financial institutions ($KOthFinIns$).[1] The private pension system is divided into two components: a partially funded defined-benefit (DB) system ($PvtPenSysDB$) and a fully funded defined-contribution (DC) system ($PvtPenSysDC$). Implicitly assigned to $OthFinIns$ are households themselves to the extent that they individually hold claims on capital operated by firms (i.e., disintermediated claims). Firms operate capital, either distributing or reinvesting earnings; they do not own shares in other firms. Claims on the capital operated by firms are held on behalf of households by institutions ($PvtPenSys$ and $OthFinIns$) that collect and distribute dividends. All claims consist of equity.

Total assets of a cohort in a given year are

$$
\begin{aligned}
KTot(t, age) \;=\; & KRsdntial(t, age) + KPvtUnincorpEnt(t, age) \\
+\; & KPvtPenSysDC(t, age) + KPvtPenSysDB(t, age) \\
+\; & KOthFinIns(t, age),
\end{aligned}
$$

or, aggregating the two components of the private pension system,

$$
\begin{aligned}
KTot(t, age) \;=\; & KPvtPenSys(t, age) + KRsdntial(t, age) \\
+\; & KPvtUnincorpEnt(t, age) + KOthFinIns(t, age),
\end{aligned}
$$

which expresses a cohort's wealth as the sum of pension and non-pension wealth.

As described below in Section 9 of this annex, corresponding to each type of capital is an age-specific capital accumulation equation that tracks the building up and drawing down of assets for each cohort as it ages. There is a structural difference between the dynamics of $KPvtPensSys$ and the dynamics of the other three asset classes. Funds flow into $PvtPenSys$ only through payroll deductions, including deductions from entrepreneurial income, on behalf of system participants. Dividends earned on assets held by the $PvtPenSys$ remain within the system. By contrast, savings of all origins, not just captive pension savings, are invested in $KOthFinIns$, $KRsdntial$, and $KPvtUnincorpEnt$. Dividends earned on assets held by $OthFinIns$ accrue to households, instead of being retained by the intermediary, and may be allocated to consumption at any point during the life cycle, as may profits accruing to $KPvtUnincorpEnt$. Implicit rents on $KRsdntial$ are consumed, by assumption, in their entirety; equivalently, all housing is assumed to be occupied by the owner. If saved, dividends earned on assets held by $OthFinIns$ may remain within $OthFinIns$ or be allocated to residential investment or investment in capital operated by $PvtUnincorpEnt$.

3. Output and Rates of Return to Factors

3.1 GDP, wage rate, and rate of return to capital

Gross domestic product (GDP) is given by a Cobb-Douglas production function:

$$GDP(t) = \alpha(1+g)^t KTot(t)^\beta Emp(t)^{1-\beta} ,$$

where g, the rate of total factor productivity growth, is exogenous. Rates of return to factors are neoclassical:

$$R(t) = \beta \left[\frac{GDP(t)}{KTot(t)} \right] ,$$

$$\overline{WageRate}(t) = (1-\beta) \left[\frac{GDP(t)}{Emp(t)} \right] ,$$

where R is the gross profit rate, including depreciation and indirect taxes net of subsidies; and $\overline{WageRate}$ is average (over all age groups) employee compensation, including social insurance contributions (contributions to public and private pension schemes, as well as the health and long-term care systems).

In order to net depreciation and indirect taxes out of the rate of return to capital, we define

$$r(t) = R(t) - \frac{IndTaxRate(t)GDP(t)}{KTot(t)} - DeprRate(t) ,$$

where $IndTaxRate$ is defined with respect to GDP and $DeprRate$ is the depreciation rate. The advantage of netting out depreciation and indirect taxes immediately is that we can henceforth ignore them in calculating income, outlay, and net savings.

3.2 Age-specific wage rates

There is no explicit accounting for human capital formation in our model; nonetheless, we wish to take into account the universal observation that wages vary by age. We have approached this problem by defining a scale factor $\sigma(t, age)$ and then calculating age-specific wage rates as

$$WageRate(t, age) = \sigma(t, age)\overline{WageRate}(t) .$$

The $\sigma(t, age)$ function used for Japan is described in endnote 5 of Chapter 3.

Having calculated age-specific wages, however, we now must ensure that the average wage rate calculated from the economy-wide marginal productivity condition equals the average wage rate calculated across age groups (i.e., the weighted average of age-specific wages, the weights corresponding to the age structure of the workforce). Let $WageAdj(t, age)$ be an adjustment factor to be applied to age-specific wages in order to force consistency. The required consistency condition is

$$\overline{WageRate}(t) = \frac{\displaystyle\sum_{age=15}^{MaxAge} WageAdj(t, age)\sigma(t, age)\overline{WageRate}(t)Emp(t, age)}{\displaystyle\sum_{age=15}^{MaxAge} Emp(t, age)} .$$

The simplest approach to this problem is to let $WageAdj(t, age)$ be the age-invariant

$$WageAdj(t) = \frac{\overline{WageRate}(t) \sum\limits_{age=15}^{MaxAge} Emp(t, age)}{\sum\limits_{age=15}^{MaxAge} \sigma(t, age)\overline{WageRate}(t)Emp(t, age)} = \frac{\sum\limits_{age=15}^{MaxAge} Emp(t, age)}{\sum\limits_{age=15}^{MaxAge} \sigma(t, age)Emp(t, age)},$$

that is, total "nominal" employment relative to total "effective" (human-capital adjusted) employment. Then the identity required for consistency may be rewritten as

$$\overline{WageRate}(t) = \frac{\sum\limits_{age=15}^{MaxAge} \left\{ \dfrac{\sum\limits_{age=15}^{MaxAge} Emp(t, age)}{\sum\limits_{age=15}^{MaxAge} \sigma(t, age)Emp(t, age)} \sigma(t, age)\overline{WageRate}(t)Emp(t, age) \right\}}{\sum\limits_{age=15}^{MaxAge} Emp(t, age)}.$$

Moving age-invariant terms outside the brackets,

$$\overline{WageRate}(t) = \frac{\dfrac{\sum\limits_{age=15}^{MaxAge} Emp(t, age)}{\sum\limits_{age=15}^{MaxAge} \sigma(t, age)Emp(t, age)} \overline{WageRate}(t) \sum\limits_{age=15}^{MaxAge} \sigma(t, age)Emp(t, age)}{\sum\limits_{age=15}^{MaxAge} Emp(t, age)},$$

which clearly will always hold true.

Accordingly, we calculate age-specific wages as

$$WageRate(t, age) = WageAdj(t)\sigma(t, age)\overline{WageRate}(t),$$

where $WageAdj(t)$ is as defined above and $\sigma(t, age)$ will be defined on a case-by-case basis.

4. Income, Capital Transfers, Outlay, and Net Savings of Households

4.1 Income

The sources of household income are wages, imputed rents from residential capital, profits that accrue to capital operated by unincorporated enterprises, dividends distributed from earnings on capital operated by firms, public pension system benefits, private pension benefits, and health and long-term care benefits.

4.1.1 A note on taxation

The taxation of factor incomes in this model follows three simplifying assumptions. First, factor income is taxed once and only once, when it is earned. Thus, dividend income of households is not taxed because profits have already been taxed at the level of the firm. Second, no distinction is made from a taxation point of view between different types of capital: profits on capital operated by firms, profits on capital operated by private unincorporated enterprises, and the imputed services of residential housing are all assumed to be taxed at the same rate. Third, tax rates are not indexed by income or age.

4.1.2 Wage income

Disposable wage income is equal to gross wages minus direct taxes minus social insurance contributions to the public and private pension systems as well as the health and long-term care systems:

$$WageY(t, age) \ = \ WageRate(t, age)Emp(t, age),$$

$$
\begin{aligned}
DispWageY(t, age) \ = \ & WageY(t, age) - DirTaxWageY(t, age) \\
- \ & ContPubPenSysWageY(t, age) \\
- \ & ContPvtPenSysWageY(t, age) \\
- \ & ContHlthCareSysWageY(t, age) \\
- \ & ContLngTrmCareSysWageY(t, age),
\end{aligned}
$$

where $ContPvtPenSysWageY(t, age)$ consists of the sum of contributions to the DB and DC components of the private pension system. Calculation of direct taxes is described in Section 6 of this annex; that of pension system contributions, in Section 7 of this annex. Contributions to the health and long-term care systems are described in Section 8 of this annex. Note that, even though $PvtPenSys$ contributions represent the acquisition of a financial asset, rather than a current expenditure flow, the System of National Accounts (SNA) nonetheless counts such transactions as a debit in the calculation of disposable income. However, an adjustment is made (see Section 4.1.11 below) to ensure that the savings associated with such flows are credited to households.

4.1.3 Rental income

Imputed rental income is taxed like any other form of income; however, payroll taxes are assumed to be zero:

$$RntlY(t, age) = r(t)KRsdntial(t, age),$$

$$DispRntlY(t, age) = RntlY(t, age) - DirTaxRntlY(t, age).$$

Recall that capital returns are already net of depreciation and indirect taxes.

4.1.4 Entrepreneurial income

Profits from capital operated by unincorporated enterprises are treated the same as wages:

$$EntrY(t, age) = r(t)KPvtUnincorpEnt(t, age),$$

$$
\begin{aligned}
DispEntrY(t, age) = \ & EntrY(t, age) - DirTaxEntrY(t, age) \\
& - ContPubPenSysEntrY(t, age) \\
& - ContPvtPenSysEntrY(t, age) \\
& - ContHlthCareSysEntrY(t, age) \\
& - ContLngTrmCareSysEntrY(t, age).
\end{aligned}
$$

See endnote 7 of Chapter 3 for a discussion of the interpretation of entrepreneurial income in the model.

4.1.5 Dividend income

The assets held on households' behalf by $PvtPenSys$ and $OthFinIns$ earn dividends. However, in the first case, dividends are not considered by the SNA to be part of household income; rather, they are considered to represent the acquisition of a financial asset. The adjustment described in Section 4.1.11 will add these dividend earnings captured by the private pension system to household income. Unadjusted household disposable income includes only dividends (i.e., distributed earnings) on assets held by $OthFinIns$:

$$DividY(t, age) = DistErngsFirmsKOthFinIns(t, age).$$

The calculation of distributed earnings is given in Section 5.2.2 of this annex. Having already been taxed when earned, dividends are not taxed when received by households. Disposable dividend income is thus simply

$$DispDividY(t, age) = DividY(t, age).$$

4.1.6 Interest on government debt

Interest income on government debt is

$$IntGovDebt(t, age) = r(t)GovDebt(t, age),$$

and the derived disposable income is

$$DispIntGovDebt(t, age) = IntGovDebt(t, age) - DirTaxIntGovDebt(t, age).$$

4.1.7 Pension income

Pension income comes from three sources: the public pay-as-you-go (PAYG) financed DB pension system, the private fully funded DC pension system, and a private partially funded DB pension system which, for our purposes, is assumed to be essentially PAYG financed. All three systems provide benefits; in the first case they are current transfers, while in the second two cases they represent sales of capital assets, which for accounting purposes are nonetheless considered to represent income. The calculation of pension benefits is described in Section 7 of this annex.

In any year, some persons will change jobs and a given proportion of these will choose to withdraw their assets from the private pension system rather than rolling them over into new schemes. These withdrawals are also treated as income in our framework. We assume that withdrawals occur only from the DC pension system. While this point is debatable, most countries have in place measures that strongly encourage job switchers to transfer their DB pension assets into another scheme.[2] Combining the two components of the private pension system, we get

$$\begin{aligned} PensionY(t, age) \ &= \ BenPubPenSys(t, age) + BenPvtPenSys(t, age) \\ &+ \ WthdrwlKPvtPenSys(t, age) \,. \end{aligned}$$

Public pension income is subject to taxation because it is a current transfer. Private DB pension system income, private DC pension income, and early withdrawals from the private DC pension system are not taxed because these represent the drawing down of capital assets. Disposable pension income is therefore

$$\begin{aligned} DispPensionY(t, age) \ &= \ [1 - DirTaxRate(t)] \, BenPubPenSys(t, age) \\ &+ \ BenPvtPenSys(t, age) \\ &+ \ WthdrwlKPvtPenSys(t, age) \,. \end{aligned}$$

Private pension system benefits are included in the adjustment to disposable income described in Section 4.1.11. Early withdrawals from the private DC pension system are described in Section 4.2.3; these are also included in the adjustment to disposable income described below.

4.1.8 Health and long-term care benefits

The calculation of health and long-term care benefits is described in Section 8 below. These are assumed to be untaxed.

4.1.9 Total income

Total income of households is equal to the sum over all income sources:

$$\begin{aligned} TotYHH(t, age) \ &= \ WageY(t, age) + RntlY(t, age) + EntrY(t, age) \\ &+ \ DividY(t, age) + IntGovDebt(t, age) + PensionY(t, age) \\ &+ \ BenHlthCareSys(t, age) + BenLngTrmCareSys(t, age) \,. \end{aligned}$$

4.1.10 Disposable income

Disposable income is analogous:

$$\begin{aligned} DispYHH(t, age) \ &= \ DispWageY(t, age) + DispRntlY(t, age) \\ &+ \ DispEntrY(t, age) + DispDividY(t, age) \\ &+ \ DispIntGovDebt(t, age) + DispPensionY(t, age) \\ &+ \ BenHlthCareSys(t, age) + BenLngTrmCareSys(t, age) \,. \end{aligned}$$

4.1.11 Adjusted disposable income

Adjusted disposable income is equal to disposable income

- plus contributions to $PvtPenSys$
- plus dividends earned on assets held by $PvtPenSys$
- minus benefits received from $PvtPenSys$
- minus early withdrawals from the private DC private pension system (recall that these were included in pension income),

where the purpose of the adjustment is to ensure that savings that go into the private pension system are credited to households:

$$
\begin{aligned}
AdjDispYHH(t, age) \;=\; & DispYHH(t, age) + ContPvtPenSys(t, age) \\
+ \;& DividPvtPenSys(t, age) - BenPvtPenSys(t, age) \\
- \;& WthdrwlKPvtPenSysDC(t, age) \,.
\end{aligned}
$$

The third term on the right-hand side of the equation represents the sum over DB and DC components of the private pension systems of dividends paid out by firms (given in Sections 7.2.1 and 7.3.1 of this annex, respectively).

Adjusted disposable income is close to, but not exactly the same as, disposable income plus change in pension wealth. The latter would be equal to

$$
\begin{aligned}
\Delta KPvtPenSys(t, age) \;=\; & ContPvtPenSys(t, age) + DividPvtPenSys(t, age) \\
- \;& BenPvtPenSys(t, age) - BeqKPvtPenSys(t, age) \\
- \;& WthdrwlKPvtPenSysDC(t, age) \,,
\end{aligned}
$$

where bequests $BeqKPvtPenSys(t, age)$ reflect the fact that upon the death of the claimant, accumulated pension assets are paid out to heirs.[3] We do not include inheriting (i.e., being on the receiving end of a bequest) pension wealth because all inherited pension assets are assumed to be either converted to consumption or re-allocated to non-pension capital asset classes. Stated differently, there is no explicit modeling of survivors' benefits; that is, reassigning title to existing pension assets. Combining the last two expressions, we could also write

$$
\begin{aligned}
AdjDispYHH(t, age) \;=\; & DispYHH(t, age) + \Delta KPvtPenSys(t, age) \\
+ \;& BeqPvtPenSys(t, age) \,.
\end{aligned}
$$

The last term is necessary because, in its absence, disposable income would be debited by the pension wealth bequests occurring as a consequence of deaths within the cohort.

4.2 Capital

Resources available for household consumption take the form of disposable income and capital assets. In this section, the second of these is described.

4.2.1 "Annuitization" of assets in old age

Starting at the pensionable age, households are assumed to divest themselves of non-pension assets in a way calculated to exhaust assets at age 105. This "annuitization" process—which for simplicity's sake we model as a program according to which corn-assets are consumed—is assumed to begin whether households are still in the labor force or not. For $[\bullet] = Rsdntial, PvtUnincorpEnt, OthFinIns$, "annuity income" is

$$AnnYK[\bullet](age, t) = \frac{K[\bullet](t, age)}{105 - age}, age \geq EligAge .$$

4.2.2 Bequests/inheritance

In all asset classes, age-specific bequests are equal to assets times the proportion of persons in the age group dying. For the capital asset classes $[\bullet] = Rsdntial, PvtUnincorpEnt,$ $OthFinIns, PvtPenSysDC, PvtPenSysDB,$

$$BeqK[\bullet](t, age) = K[\bullet](t, age) \left[\frac{Deaths(t, age)}{Pop(t - 1, age - 1)} \right] .$$

Without question, DC pension system assets, like non-pension wealth, belong to the individual and are heritable. As we discuss in Section 9.2 of this annex, the case of assets of the DB pension system is debatable.

Bequests are received, in the form of inheritance, by the surviving population. For simplicity, we estimate age-specific inheritance by dividing total bequests by population age shares, excluding the population under age 15. Total bequests are

$$BeqK[\bullet](t) = \sum_{age=15}^{MaxAge} BeqK[\bullet](t, age) ,$$

and inheritance (for age groups over 15) is

$$InhK[\bullet](t, t) = \left[\frac{Pop(t, age)}{\sum\limits_{age=15}^{MaxAge-1} Pop(t, age)} \right] \sum_{age=15}^{MaxAge} BeqK[\bullet](t, age) .$$

Summing over age groups leads to

$$InhK[\bullet](t) = \sum_{age=15}^{MaxAge} InhK[\bullet](t, age) .$$

This simplification admittedly exaggerates the number of "backward" bequests (elderly persons inheriting wealth from middle-aged persons, who are in fact more likely to bequeath assets to their children than to their parents).[4]

The assumption is made that, when "corn wealth" is inherited, some is converted to consumption and the remainder is allocated among $\Delta KOthFinIns$, $\Delta KRsdntial$, and

$\Delta PvtUnincorpEnt$ using the same share coefficients applied to household net saving (see Section 9.3 of this annex). Note, however, that the portion not consumed does not comprise new household savings; it represents the acquisition of an asset formed as the result of past saving. We define "sale" of inherited assets as

$$SaleInhK[\bullet](t, age) = InhK[\bullet](t, age) \,.$$

Consumption out of the proceeds of such sales is described in Section 4.3.4.1 of this annex.

4.2.3 Early withdrawals from the private DC pension system

These withdrawals are described in Section 7.2.2 of this annex; the associated consumption is described in Section 4.3.4.3 below.

4.3 Outlay

4.3.1 Direct taxes

These are described in Section 6.1 of this annex.

4.3.2 Social insurance contributions

These are described in Section 7 of this annex.

4.3.3 Consumption out of income

Average propensities to consume ($AvgPropCons$) out of disposable income streams are exogenous assumptions:

$$ConsWageY(t, age) =$$
$$DispWageY(t, age)AvgPropConsWageY(t, age) \,,$$

$$ConsEntrY(t, age) =$$
$$DispEntrY(t, age)AvgPropConsEntrY(t, age) \,,$$

$$ConsDividY(t, age) =$$
$$DispDividY(t, age)AvgPropConsDividY(t, age) \,,$$

$$ConsIntGovDebt(t, age) =$$
$$DispIntGovDebt(t, age)AvgPropConsIntGovDebt(t, age) \,,$$

$$ConsBenPubPenSys(t, age) =$$
$$BenPubPenSys(t, age)AvgPropConsBenPubPenSys(t, age) \,,$$

$$ConsBenPvtPenSysDC(t, age) =$$

$$BenPvtPenSysDC(t, age) AvgPropConsBenPvtPenSysDC(t, age) \,,$$

$$ConsBenPvtPenSysDB(t, age) =$$

$$BenPvtPenSysDB(t, age) AvgPropConsBenPvtPenSysDB(t, age) \,.$$

It is assumed that all imputed housing services received are consumed:

$$ConsRntlY(t, age) = DispRntlY(t, age) \,.$$

4.3.4 Consumption out of the proceeds of asset sales

4.3.4.1 Consumption out of the proceeds of selling inherited assets

For $[\bullet] = Rsdntial, PvtUnincorpEnt, OthFinIns, PvtPenSysDC, PvtPenSysDB$, consumption out of the sales of inherited assets is

$$ConsSaleInhK[\bullet](t, age) = SaleInhK[\bullet](t, age) ConsShareSaleInhK[\bullet](t, age) \,,$$

and the sharing out of what is not consumed between $\Delta K\,OthFinIns$, $\Delta K\,Rsdntial$, and $\Delta K\,PvtUnincorpEnt$ is as described in Section 9.3 of this annex. We use a mnemonic corresponding to "consumption share" instead of $AvgPropCons$ because average propensity to consume is properly considered with reference to income.

4.3.4.2 Consumption out of "annuity income"

Because private pension system benefits are classified for purposes of the SNA as income, rather than capital transfers, this component has already been described above. For the remaining components $[\bullet] = Rsdntial, PvtUnincorpEnt, OthFinIns$,

$$ConsAnnYK[\bullet](t, age) = AnnYK[\bullet](t, age) ConsShareAnnYK[\bullet](t, age) \,.$$

If the propensity to consume out of the annuity income is assumed to be unity, there is no bequest motive; if, for example, the propensity is assumed to be 0.95, elderly households aim to die with 5 percent of their wealth intact, and so on.

4.3.4.3 Consumption out of the proceeds of selling assets withdrawn from the private DC pension system

The final component of consumption is

$$ConsWthdrwlKPvtPenSysDC(t, age) =$$

$$WthdrwlKPvtPenSysDC(t, age) ConsShareWthdrwlKPvtPenSys \,.$$

Early withdrawals from the private DB pension system are assumed to be zero.

4.3.5 Consumption of health and long-term care

Determination of age-specific consumption of health and long-term care services is described in Section 8 of this annex.

4.4 Net savings of households

Recapitulating, disposable and adjusted disposable household incomes are

$$
\begin{aligned}
DispYHH(t, age) = {} & DispWageY(t, age) + DispRntlY(t, age) \\
+ {} & DispEntrY(t, age) + DispDividY(t, age) \\
+ {} & DispIntGovDebt(t, age) + DispPensionY(t, age) \\
+ {} & BenHlthCareSys(t, age) + BenLngTrmCareSys(t, age) ,
\end{aligned}
$$

$$
\begin{aligned}
AdjDispYHH(t, age) = {} & DispYHH(t, age) + ContPvtPenSys(t, age) \\
+ {} & DividPvtPenSys(t, age) - BenPvtPenSys(t, age) \\
- {} & WthdrwlPvtPenSys(t, age) ,
\end{aligned}
$$

and total consumption is

$$
\begin{aligned}
PvtCons(t, age) = {} & ConsWageY(t, age) + ConsRntlY(t, age) \\
+ {} & ConsEntrY(t, age) + ConsDividY(t, age) \\
+ {} & ConsIntGovDebt(t, age)ConsPensionY(t, age) \\
+ {} & ConsSaleInhKRsdntial(t, age) \\
+ {} & ConsSaleInhKPvtUnincorpEnt(t, age) \\
+ {} & ConsSaleInhKOthFinIns(t, age) \\
+ {} & ConsSaleInhKPvtPenSysDC(t, age) \\
+ {} & ConsAnnYKRsdntial(t, age) \\
+ {} & ConsAnnYKPvtUnincorpEnt(t, age) \\
+ {} & ConsAnnYKOthFinIns(t, age) \\
+ {} & ConsWthdrwlKPvtPenSysDC(t, age) \\
+ {} & ConsHlthCare(t, age) \\
+ {} & ConsLngTrmCare(t, age) .
\end{aligned}
$$

The first three lines on the right-hand side of this expression give consumption out of income (including pension income and interest on government debt); the next four lines give consumption financed by the sale of inherited assets; the next three lines give consumption out of "annuity income"; the eleventh line covers consumption that occurs when a worker elects to withdraw DC pension assets; and the last two lines give consumption of health and long-term care services.

Household net saving is the difference between disposable income and consumption:

$$
NetSvngHH(t, age) = DispYHH(t, age) - PvtCons(t, age) .
$$

Adjusted net savings include savings captured by the private pension system:

$$AdjNetSvngHH(t, age) = AdjDispYHH(t, age) - PvtCons(t, age) \,.$$

Expressed in terms of unadjusted disposable income and change in pension wealth (see Section 4.1.11 of this annex),

$$
\begin{aligned}
AdjNetSvngHH(t, age) \quad = \quad & DispYHH(t, age) + \Delta K PvtPenSys(t, age) \\
+ \quad & BeqK PvtPenSys(t, age) - PvtCons(t, age) \,.
\end{aligned}
$$

In performing the accounting consistency check in Section 11 below, we will use this identity in the form

$$
\begin{aligned}
NetSvngHH(t, age) \quad = \quad & AdjNetSvngHH(t, age) - \Delta K PvtPenSys(t, age) \\
- \quad & BeqK PvtPenSys(t, age) \,.
\end{aligned}
$$

5. Income, Outlay, and Net Savings of Firms

Firms operate capital, earn profits, and pay out direct taxes and dividends.

5.1 Income

Earnings of firms consist of the return on capital owned by the three institutional claimants $[\bullet] = PvtPenSysDC, PvtPenSysDB, OthFinIns$:

$$ErngsFirmsK[\bullet](t, age) = r(t)K[\bullet](t, age) \,,$$

$$ErngsFirmsK[\bullet](age) = \sum_{age=0}^{MaxAge} ErngsFirmsK[\bullet](t, age) \,.$$

Recall that depreciation and indirect taxes have already been netted out.

5.2 Outlay

5.2.1 Direct taxes

Taxes on profits are described in Section 6.1 of this annex.

5.2.2 Dividends

Dividend distributions are made out of pre-tax earnings, and the proportion of earnings distributed is independent of the claimant by assumption. For the three claimants $[\bullet] = PvtPenSysDC, PvtPenSysDB, OthFinIns$,

$$DistErngsFirmsK[\bullet](t, age) = DividDistShare(t)ErngsFirmsK[\bullet](t, age) \,,$$

$$DistErngsFirmsK[\bullet](t) = \sum_{age=0}^{MaxAge} DistErngsFirmsK[\bullet](t, age) \,,$$

where the share of earnings distributed as dividends is an exogenous variable.

5.3 Net savings of firms

Net savings (retained earnings) of firms are

$$
\begin{aligned}
NetSvngErngsFirmsK[\bullet](t, age) \;=\; & ErngsFirmsK[\bullet](t, age) \\
- \; & DirTaxErngsFirmsK[\bullet](t, age) \\
- \; & DistErngsFirmsK[\bullet](t, age) \, .
\end{aligned}
$$

The sum over claimants is total net savings of firms:

$$
NetSvngFirms(t, age) = \sum_{[\bullet]} NetSvngErngsFirmsK[\bullet](t) \, .
$$

The sum over age groups gives total corporate savings:

$$
NetSvngFirms(t) = \sum_{age=0}^{MaxAge} NetSvngFirms(t, age) \, .
$$

6. Income, Outlay, and Net Savings of Government

Government consumes an exogenous share of GDP, collects taxes and social security contributions, and pays social security benefits.

6.1 Income

Government revenues are

$$
\begin{aligned}
GovRvn(t) \;=\; & IndTax(t) + DirTax(t) + ContPubPenSyst(t) \\
+ \; & ContHlthCareSys(t) + ContLngTrmCareSys(t) \, ,
\end{aligned}
$$

where

$$
IndTax(t) = IndTaxRate(t)GDP(t) \, ,
$$

$$
\begin{aligned}
DirTax(t) \;=\; & \sum_{age=15}^{MaxAge} DirTaxWageY(t, age) \\
+ \; & \sum_{age=15}^{MaxAge} DirTaxEntrY(t, age) \\
+ \; & \sum_{age=15}^{MaxAge} DirTaxRntlY(t, age) \\
+ \; & \sum_{age=EligAge}^{MaxAge} DirTaxBenPubPenSys(t, age)
\end{aligned}
$$

$$+ \sum_{age=0}^{MaxAge} DirTaxIntGovDebt(t,age)$$

$$+ \sum_{age=0}^{MaxAge} \sum_{[\bullet]} DirTaxErngsFirmsK[\bullet](t,age) ,$$

where $[\bullet] = PvtPenSysDC, PvtPenSysDB, OthFinIns$ and the direct tax streams are

$$DirTaxWageY(t,age) = DirTaxRate(t)WageY(t,age) ,$$

$$DirTaxRntlY(t,age) = DirTaxRate(t)RntlY(t,age) ,$$

$$DirTaxEntrY(t,age) = DirTaxRate(t)EntrY(t,age) ,$$

$$DirTaxBenPubPenSys(t,age) = DirTaxRate(t)BenPubPenSys(t,age) ,$$

$$DirTaxIntGovDebt(t,age) = DirTaxRate(t)IntGovDebt(t,age) ,$$

$$DirTaxErngsFirmsK[\bullet](t,age) = DirTaxRate(t)ErngsFirmsK[\bullet](t) .$$

Contributions to the public pension system are described in Section 7.1.1 of this annex.

6.2 Outlay

Government expenditure is

$$GovExp(t) = GovCons(t) + BenPubPenSys(t) + BenHlthCareSys(t)$$
$$+ BenLngTrmCareSys(t) + IntGovDebt(t) ,$$

where government consumption is taken simply as a fixed share of GDP:

$$GovCons(t) = GovConsShare(t)GDP(t) .$$

Benefits paid out by the public pension system are described in Section 7.1.2 of this annex. Interest on government debt is the sum over age groups

$$IntGovDebt(t) = \sum_{age=0}^{MaxAge} r(t)GovDebt(t,age) .$$

6.3 Net savings of government

Government net savings are

$$NetSvngGov(t) = GovRvn(t) - GovExp(t) .$$

Net savings of government are allocated across age groups using shares drawn from the age distribution of wealth:

$$NetSvngGov(t,age) = \frac{KTot(t,age)}{\sum_{age=0}^{MaxAge} KTot(t,age)} NetSvngGov(t) .$$

6.4 Government debt

Government debt is cumulated over time

$$GovDebt(t) = GovDebt(-1) - NetSvngGov(t)$$

and shared down over age groups

$$GovDebt(t, age) = \frac{KTot(t, age)}{\sum\limits_{age=0}^{MaxAge} KTot(t, age)} GovDebt(t).$$

6.5 Dynamic consistency

To enforce dynamic consistency, a target level of government debt as a proportion of GDP is set. If below (above) target, government consumption is adjusted up (down) until the target is reached.

7. Pension System

7.1 Public DB PAYG pension system

7.1.1 Income

Contributions to the public pension system out of wages are

$$ContPubPenSysWageY(t, age) =$$

$$[PartSharePubPenSys\ ContRatePubPenSys(t)\ TaxableWageYShare]$$

$$WageY(t, age),$$

where $PartSharePubPenSys$ is the proportion of the workforce participating in the public pension system and $TaxableWageYShare$ is the proportion of the wage bill that is subject to social security taxation. For simplicity, both of these parameters are assumed to be age independent. The social security contribution rate $ContRatePubPenSys(t)$ is also assumed to be age independent. Each year, it is calculated to ensure that total contributions to the system equal total payments of benefits. No distinction is made between employees' and employers' contributions. Social security contributions out of entrepreneurial income are calculated similarly:

$$ContPubPenSysEntrY(t, age) =$$

$$[PartSharePubPenSys\ ContRatePubPenSys(t)\ TaxableShareEntrY]$$

$$EntrY(t, age).$$

Contribution rates applying to wage and entrepreneurial income are assumed to be the same.

Total public pension system revenues out of each income stream are

$$ContPubPenSysWageY(t) = \sum_{age=15}^{MaxAge} ContPubPenSysWageY(t, age),$$

$$ContPubPenSysEntrY(t) = \sum_{age=15}^{MaxAge} ContPubPenSysEntrY(t, age),$$

and the system total is

$$ContPubPenSys(t) = ContPubPenSysWageY(t) + ContPubPenSysEntrY(t, age).$$

7.1.2 Outlay

The public pension system is assumed to be a DB system. Let the social security benefit entitlement for the average system participant aged age who retired $RtrmntDur$ years ago be $BenEntPubPenSys(t, age, RtrmntDur)$, where we assume that $BenEntPubPenSys(t, age, 0) = 0$. The pension for system participants entering retirement is computed according to the following formula:

$$BenEntPubPenSys(t, age, 1) =$$

$$WageRate(t - 1, age - 1)RplcmntRatioPubPenSys(t, age),$$

where

$$RplcmntRatioPubPenSys(t, age) =$$

$$YearsPartPubPenSys(t, age)AccrualRatePubPenSys(t),$$

in other words, the replacement ratio for members of a given cohort retiring in year t is equal to the accrual rate $AccrualRatePubPenSys(t)$ (an exogenous assumption) times the average number of years of labor force participation for members of the cohort retiring in that year. A major simplification is to calculate years spent in the labor force on a period basis, using age-specific rates from the year in which retirement occurs, instead of on a cohort basis over the life of the worker. For a system participant retiring at age age in year t, then

$$YearsPartPubPenSys(t, age) = \sum_{j=15}^{age} LabForcePartRate(t, j).$$

Once a system participant has retired, his or her pension is indexed to the average wage rate. For people who were already retired at $(t - 1)$, the pension is

$$BenEntPubPenSys(t, age, RtrmntDur) =$$

$$BenEntPubPenSys(t-1, age-1, RtrmntDur-1)$$

$$\left[1 + IndexRate(t)\frac{\overline{WageRate}(t) - \overline{WageRate}(t-1)}{\overline{WageRate}(t-1)}\right],$$

where $IndexRate$ is the rate of indexation of pensions to the average wage rate $\overline{WageRate}(t)$. When $IndexRate = 1$, pensions are fully indexed to wages; when $IndexRate = 0$, there is no indexation.

Social security system benefits paid out by age group of recipient are equal to the age and retirement-duration specific entitlement times the number of recipients, which reflects the rate of system participation (note that the latter is assumed to be time- and age-invariant for computational simplicity):

$$BenPubPenSys(t, age) = PartSharePubPenSys$$

$$\sum_{RtrmntDur=0}^{MaxAge-EligAge+1} BenEntPubPenSys(t, age, RtrmntDur)Pop(t, age, RtrmntDur),$$

where, making the simplifying assumption that once retired, persons stay retired,

$$Pop(t, age, RtrmntDur) =$$

$$Pop(t, age)\left[\begin{array}{l} LabForcePartRate(t - RtrmntDur, age - RtrmntDur) \\ -LabForcePartRate(t - RtrmntDur + 1, age - RtrmntDur + 1) \end{array}\right],$$

for $age = 1, \overline{age - RtrmntAge + 1}$. System-wide expenditures are equal to the summation over age groups

$$BenPubPenSys(t) = \sum_{age=EligAge}^{MaxAge} BenPubPenSys(t, age).$$

7.1.3 System balance

In a classic PAYG system (e.g., the German system), total contributions equal total benefits; there is neither accumulation of a return-generating surplus nor a deficit to be financed out of general government revenue. The default model solution option, corresponding to this case, is one in which the required contribution rate is calculated by setting contributions equal to expenditures.

7.2 Private DC pension system

7.2.1 Income

Income of the private DC pension system comprises (i) current contributions (zero for persons who have retired) and (ii) dividends. (i) is the sum over contributions out of wage and entrepreneurial income, each consisting of the share of the workforce participating times the proportion of total income contributed:

$$ContPvtPenSysDCWageY(t, age) =$$

$$[PartSharePvtPenSysDC\ ContRatePvtPenSysDCWageY(t, age)]$$

$$WageY(t, age)\ ,$$

$$ContPvtPenSysDCEntrY(t, age) =$$

$$[PartSharePvtPenSysDC\ ContRatePvtPenSysDCEntrY(t, age)]$$

$$EntrY(t, age)\ .$$

In the case of the private DC pension system (and the private DB pension system, as well) there is no term analogous to $TaxableWageYShare$. Total contributions and dividend earnings are

$$ContPvtPenSysDC(t, age) \quad = \quad ContPvtPenSysDCWageY(t, age)$$
$$+ \quad ContPvtPenSysDCEntrY(t, age)\ ,$$

and

$$DividPvtPenSysDC(t) = \sum_{age=15}^{MaxAge} DistErngsFirmsKPvtPenSysDC(t, age)\ ,$$

where the paying out of dividends was described in Section 5.2.2 of this annex.

7.2.2 Outlay

Expenditures of the private DC pension are (i) benefits paid, (ii) payout to heirs of the pension assets of system participants who die, and (iii) withdrawal of assets by job switchers who choose not to roll over their pension wealth into another plan. (i) is analogous to the "annuitization" of non-pension capital assets described in Section 4.2.1 of this annex. For those over the retirement age,

$$BenPvtPenSysDC(t, age) = \frac{KPvtPenSysDC(t, age)}{105 - age}\ , age \geq EligAge\ ,$$

where $age \geq EligAge$ and 105 is the maximum age to which a person expects to live. (ii) was described above in Section 4.2.2 of this annex. (iii) is calculated using an exogenously assumed withdrawal rate reflecting both the number of job changes and the proportion who choose not to roll over their assets:

$$WthdrwlPvtPenSysDC(t, age) =$$

$$WthdrwlRatePvtPenSysDC(t)\ KPvtPenSysDC(t, age)\ .$$

If, for example, 10 percent of system participants change jobs every year and half choose to withdraw their assets, $WthdrwlRatePvtPenSysDC = 0.05$.

7.3 Private DB pension system

7.3.1 Income

In the private DB pension system only wage income is taxed (i.e., entrepreneurs are not covered), in addition to which, all wage income is subject to contributions. Therefore,

$ContPvtPenSysDBWageY(t, age) =$

$[PartSharePvtPenSysDB\ ContRatePvtPenSysDB(t, age)]\ WageY(t, age)$,

$ContPvtPenSysDB(t, age) = ContPvtPenSysDB\ WageY(t, age)$.

Age-specific dividends are

$DividPvtPenSysDB(t, age) = DistErngsFirmsK PvtPenSysDB(t, age)$.

And total dividends are

$$DividPvtPenSysDB(t) = \sum_{age=15}^{MaxAge} DividPvtPenSysDB(t, age) \,.$$

7.3.2 Outlay

The approach taken is the same as in the case of the public DB pension system; in other words, the presentation in Section 7.1.2 applies in its entirety, with Pvt substituted for Pub in variable mnemonics.

7.3.3 System balance

As a general rule, private DB pension plans today are underfunded. On the assumption that these plans will be run effectively on a PAYG basis, the contribution rate is calculated to balance inflows and outflows.

7.4 Total private pension system contributions and benefits

Private pension system totals are

$ContPvtPenSysWageY(t) =$

$ContPvtPenSysDCWageY(t) + ContPvtPenSysDBWageY(t)$,

$ContPvtPenSysEntrY(t) =$

$ContPvtPenSysDCEntrY(t) + ContPvtPenSysDBEntrY(t)$,

$DividPvtPenSys(t) =$

$DividPvtPenSysDC(t) + DividPvtPenSysDB(t)$,

$BenPvtPenSys(t) =$

$BenPvtPenSysDB(t) + BenPvtPenSysDC(t)$.

8. Health and Long-Term Care Systems

8.1 Income

The health care and long-term care systems, assumed to be financed on a PAYG basis like the public pension system, are structurally identical. For $[\bullet] = Hlth, LngTrm$, we have contributions out of wage and entrepreneurial income:

$$Cont[\bullet]CareSysWageY(t) = \sum_{age=0}^{MaxAge} ContRate[\bullet]CareSys(t, age)\, WageY(t, age)\,,$$

$$Cont[\bullet]CareSysEntrY(t) = \sum_{age=0}^{MaxAge} ContRate[\bullet]CareSys(t, age)\, EntrY(t, age)\,.$$

Total contributions are

$$\begin{aligned} Cont[\bullet]CareSys(t) &= Cont[\bullet]CareSysWageY(t) \\ &+ Cont[\bullet]CareSysEntrY(t)\,. \end{aligned}$$

As in the case of the public pension system, each of the two contribution rates is calculated to balance its corresponding system.

8.2 Outlay

There are two sources of growth in health and long-term care expenditure, one related to demographic change (both the size of the population and its age structure) and the second related to technological change, development of new treatments, labor costs, age-specific coverage and service utilization rates, and so on. We treat the second, "underlying" rate of growth as an exogenous assumption and concentrate on modeling the first.

Let $h(age)$ be the relative cost (i.e., expenditure per capita) of health care at age age with the numéraire being, say, the cost of health care between age 0 and 1; let $l(age)$ be the analogous index for long-term care. Then, indices of demographically induced growth in consumption of health and long-term care are

$$ConsHlthCareIndex(t) = \frac{\displaystyle\sum_{age=0}^{MaxAge(t)} Pop(t, age)\, h(t, age)}{\displaystyle\sum_{age,0}^{MaxAge(t)} Pop(0, age)\, h(0, age)}\,,$$

$$ConsLngTrmCareIndex(t) = \frac{\displaystyle\sum_{age=0}^{MaxAge(t)} Pop(t, age)\, l(t, age)}{\displaystyle\sum_{age,0}^{MaxAge(t)} Pop(0, age)\, l(0, age)}\,,$$

where 0 represents the base year. These indices contain both volume effects related to population growth and composition effects related to the age structure of the population.

Then, total health and long-term care expenditures are equal to themselves lagged one year times growth in the index times the underlying growth rate:

$$Cons[\bullet]Care(t) = Cons[\bullet]Care(t-1)$$

$$\times [1 + UnderGrowthRateCons[\bullet]Care(t-1,t)]$$

$$\times \left[\frac{Cons[\bullet]CareIndex(t)}{Cons[\bullet]CareIndex(t-1)} \right].$$

The situation is especially simple when, as we assume here, the underlying rate of expenditure growth is equal to the rate of GDP growth. In that case, change in the share of health or long-term care expenditure in GDP is entirely a function of change in the age structure of the population.

Total expenditure is shared down by age group:

$$Cons[\bullet]Care(t,age) = Cons[\bullet]Care(t)\,Cons[\bullet]AgeShare(t,age)\,,$$

where age shares are implicit in the expenditure indices introduced above:

$$ConsHlthCareAgeShare(t,age) = \frac{h(age)Pop(t,age)}{\displaystyle\sum_{age=0}^{MaxAge} h(age)Pop(t,age)},$$

$$ConsLngTrmCareAgeShare(age,t) = \frac{l(age)Pop(t,age)}{\displaystyle\sum_{age=0}^{MaxAge} l(age)Pop(t,age)}.$$

Note that we implicitly assume that the underlying growth rates of health and long-term care expenditure are age neutral.

We split age-specific spending into components covered by social insurance and private co-payments, assuming that these exogenous shares are constant over the age spectrum; this residual is then equal to system benefits:

$$Ben[\bullet]CareSys(t,age) =$$

$$(1 - [\bullet]CareCoPayShare(t,age))\,Cons[\bullet]Care(t,age)\,,$$

and total benefits are the sum over age groups:

$$Ben[\bullet]CareSys(t) = \sum_{age=0}^{MaxAge} Ben[\bullet]CareSys(t,age)\,.$$

9. The Life-Cycle Dynamics of Capital Accumulation

Corresponding to each of the asset classes $KPvtPenSysDC$, $KPvtPenSysDB$, $KRsdntial$, $KPvtUnincorpEnt$, and $KOthFinIns$ is an age-specific capital accumulation identity.

9.1 DC private pension system

Change in age-specific private DC pension wealth is

$$
\begin{aligned}
\Delta KPvtPenSysDC(t,age) \;=\;\; & ContPvtPenSysDC(t,age)\\
+\;\; & DividPvtPenSysDC(t,age)\\
-\;\; & BenPvtPenSysDC(t,age)\\
-\;\; & BeqKPvtPenSysDC(t,age)\\
-\;\; & WthdrwlKPvtPenSysDC(t,age)\,.
\end{aligned}
$$

The most important characteristic of the private DC pension system is that there is a fixed relationship between the amount a cohort pays in during its working life and the amount it receives after retirement. For an individual cohort born in year $t = 0$ whose last members die in year $t = 105$, lifetime pension contributions plus lifetime earnings on pension assets minus lifetime pension benefits received equals bequest of pension wealth. Expressing this differently,

$$
\sum_{t=0}^{90}\sum_{age=15}^{105}\Delta KPvtPenSysDC(t,age)=
$$

$$
\sum_{t=0}^{90}\sum_{age=15}^{105}
\left[
\begin{array}{l}
ContPvtPenSysDC(t,age)\\
+\;DividPvtPenSysDC(t,age)\\
-\;BenPvtPenSysDC(t,age)\\
-\;BeqKPvtPenSysDC(t,age)\\
-\;WthdrwlKPvtPenSysDC(t,age)
\end{array}
\right]
=0\,.
$$

9.2 DB private pension system

Contributions to the private DC pension system purchase an asset, which is owned by the system participant who made the contribution. Contributions to the private DB pension system, by contrast, purchase a claim on a future pension to be paid by the firm, which is in turn backed by assets belonging to the firm. The question of whether assets backing a DB pension scheme belong to system participants or to the firm is a complicated one, and legal regimes differ from country to country. For accounting purposes, however, we treat assets of the DB pension system the same way we treat assets of the DC pension system:

$$
\begin{aligned}
\Delta KPvtPenSysDB(t,age) \;=\;\; & ContPvtPenSysDB(t,age)\\
+\;\; & DividPvtPenSysDB(t,age)\\
-\;\; & BenPvtPenSysDB(t,age)\\
-\;\; & BeqKPvtPenSysDB(t,age)\,.
\end{aligned}
$$

9.3 Other assets

For $[\bullet] = Rsdntial, PvtUnincorpEnt, OthFinIns$, the age-specific accumulation equations are

$$
\begin{aligned}
\Delta K[\bullet](t, age) \;=\; & K[\bullet]Share(t) \\
& [NetSvngHH(t, age) + NetSvngFirms(t, age) \\
& + NetSvngGovt(t, age)] \\[4pt]
- \; & AnnYK[\bullet](t, age) + K[\bullet]Share(t) \sum_{[\bullet]} AnnYK[\bullet] \\[4pt]
- \; & BeqK[\bullet](t, age) + InhK[\bullet](t, age) - SaleInhK[\bullet](t, age) \\
+ \; & K[\bullet]Share(t) \sum_{[\bullet]} SaleInhK[\bullet] \\[4pt]
+ \; & K[\bullet]Share(t)[SaleInhKPvtPenSysDC(t, age) \\
+ \; & SaleInhKPvtPenSysDB(t, age)] \,.
\end{aligned}
$$

The following are the components of change, in order:

- In the first term on the right-hand side of the identity, a share variable $K[\bullet]Share(t)$ summing to unity across the three forms of non-pension wealth is used to apportion unadjusted household net savings plus the imputed age-specific savings of firms and government between $\Delta K Rsdntial$, $\Delta K PvtUnincorpEnt$, and $\Delta K OthFinIns$.[5]
- The second set of terms on the right-hand side is of relevance only for elderly households. The first term in the line subtracts dissaving in the form of annuitization of assets, as described in Section 4.2.1 of this annex. The second term in the line, when combined with the consumption from annuity income implicit in net household savings in the first line, has the effect of distributing savings from annuity income among the non-pension asset classes.
- The third set of terms on the right-hand side subtracts net bequests (the first two items) and distributes that portion of inherited wealth not converted into consumption among asset classes. Consumption financed by the sale of inherited assets is not accounted for here because, like consumption from annuity income, it has already been subtracted off in calculating net household savings.
- The fourth set of terms on the right-hand side distributes inheritance of pension assets among the non-pension asset classes.[6] Again, associated consumption has already been accounted for when net household savings in the first line is calculated.

10. Macroeconomic Identities

10.1 Gross domestic product

GDP is the sum of wages, net profits, indirect taxes, and depreciation:

$$
\begin{aligned}
GDP(t) \;=\;& WageY(t) + EntrY(t) + RntlY(t) \\
+\;& ErngsFirmsKPvtPenSysDB(t) \\
+\;& ErngsFirmsKPvtPenSysDC(t) + ErngsFirmsKOthFinIns(t) \\
+\;& \left[\frac{IndTaxRate(t)GDP(t)}{KTot(t)} + DeprRate(t) \right] KTot(t) \,.
\end{aligned}
$$

Since

$$
\begin{aligned}
KTot(t) \;=\;& KRsdntial(t) + KPvtUnincorpEnt(t) \\
+\;& KPvtPenSysDB(t) + KPvtPenSysDC(t) + KOthFinIns(t) \,,
\end{aligned}
$$

it is clear without further checking that GDP thus expressed will be equal to GDP calculated using the production function in Section 3.1 of this annex.

10.2 National disposable income

National disposable income is GDP adjusted for depreciation:

$$
NatDispY(t) = GDP(t) - DeprRate(t)KTot(t) \,.
$$

10.3 Net national savings

Net national savings are equal to national disposable income minus consumption:

$$
NetNatSvng(t) = NatDispY(t) - PvtCons(t) - GovCons(t) \,.
$$

We show in the next section that net national savings thus calculated are equal to the sum of net savings of households, firms, and government.

11. Accounting Consistency Checks

We apply two accounting consistency checks, the first to confirm that the sum of net savings over age groups equals total capital formation, and the second to confirm that net savings calculated by summing across households, firms, and government equal net savings calculated by subtracting consumption from GDP.

11.1 Net savings equals capital formation

First, adding across the accumulation equations given in Section 9.3 of this annex for the three non-pension forms of wealth, and remembering that the $K[\bullet]Share(t)$ variables sum to unity across the three non-pension asset classes,

$$\Delta K\,Rsdntial(t, age) \quad + \quad \Delta K\,PvtUnincorpEnt(t, age) + \Delta K\,OthFinIns(t, age) =$$

$$[NetSvngHH(t, age) + NetSvngFirms(t, age)$$
$$+NetSvngGovt(t, age)]$$
$$- \quad AnnYK\,Rsdntial(t, age)$$
$$- \quad AnnYK\,PvtUnincorpEnt(t, age)$$
$$- \quad AnnYK\,OthFinIns(t, age)$$
$$+ \quad AnnYK\,Rsdntial(t, age)$$
$$+ \quad AnnYK\,PvtUnincorpEnt(t, age)$$
$$+ \quad AnnYK\,OthFinIns(t, age)$$
$$- \quad BeqK\,Rsdntial(t, age)$$
$$- \quad BeqK\,PvtUnincorpEnt(t, age)$$
$$- \quad BeqK\,OthFinIns(t, age)$$
$$+ \quad InhK\,Rsdntial(t, age)$$
$$+ \quad InhK\,PvtUnincorpEnt(t, age)$$
$$+ \quad InhK\,OthFinIns(t, age)$$
$$- \quad SaleInhK\,Rsdntial(t, age)$$
$$- \quad SaleInhK\,PvtUnincorpEnt(t, age)$$
$$- \quad SaleInhK\,OthFinIns(t, age)$$
$$+ \quad SaleInhK\,Rsdntial(t, age)$$
$$+ \quad SaleInhK\,PvtUnincorpEnt(t, age)$$
$$+ \quad SaleInhK\,OthFinIns(t, age)$$
$$+ \quad SaleInhK\,PvtPenSys(t, age)\,.$$

Making cancellations and remembering that

$$InhK\,PvtPenSys(t, age) = SaleK\,PvtPenSys(t, age)\,,$$

we arrive at

$$\Delta K\,Rsdntial(t, age) \quad + \quad \Delta K\,PvtUnincorpEnt(t, age) + \Delta K\,OthFinIns(t, age) =$$

$$[NetSvngHH(t, age) + NetSvngFirms(t, age)$$
$$+NetSvngGovt(t, age)]$$
$$- \quad BeqK\,Rsdntial(t, age) - BeqK\,PvtUnincorpEnt(t, age)$$
$$- \quad BeqK\,OthFinIns(t, age) + InhK\,Rsdntial(t, age)$$
$$+ \quad InhK\,PvtUnincorpEnt(t, age) + InhK\,OthFinIns(t, age)$$
$$+ \quad InhK\,PvtPenSys(t, age)\,.$$

Adding pension wealth, change in total wealth is

$$
\begin{aligned}
\Delta KTot(t, age) \quad = \quad & \Delta K PvtPenSys(t, age) \\
+ \quad & [NetSvngHH(t, age) + NetSvngFirms(t, age) \\
& + NetSvngGovt(t, age)] \\
- \quad & BeqK Rsdntial(t, age) - BeqK PvtUnincorpEnt(t, age) \\
- \quad & BeqK OthFinIns(t, age) + InhK Rsdntial(t, age) \\
+ \quad & InhK PvtUnincorpEnt(t, age) + InhK OthFinIns(t, age) \\
+ \quad & InhK PvtPenSys(t, age) \, .
\end{aligned}
$$

Based on the definition of adjusted net household savings given in Section 4.4 of this annex,

$$NetSvngHH(t, age) =$$

$$AdjNetSvngHH(t, age) - \Delta K PvtPenSys(t, age) - BeqK PvtPenSys(t, age) \, ,$$

so

$$\Delta KTot(t, age) = \Delta K PvtPenSys(t, age)$$

$$
+ \left[
\begin{array}{l}
AdjNetSvgHH(t, age) - \Delta K PvtPenSys(t, age) - BeqK PvtPenSys(t, age) \\
+ NetSvngFirms(t, age) + NetSvngGovt(t, age)
\end{array}
\right]
$$

$$- BeqK Rsdntial(t, age) - BeqK PvtUnincorpEnt(t, age) - BeqK OthFinIns(t, age)$$

$$+ InhK Rsdntial(t, age) + InhK PvtUnincorpEnt(t, age) + InhK OthFinIns(t, age)$$

$$+ InhK PvtPenSys(t, age) \, .$$

$\Delta K PvtPenSys(t, age)$ cancels, leaving the result

$$
\begin{aligned}
\Delta KTot(t, age) \quad = \quad & [AdjNetSvgHH(t, age) + NetSvngFirms(t, age) \\
& + NetSvngGovt(t, age)] \\
+ \quad & InhK Rsdntial(t, age) + InhK PvtUnincorpEnt(t, age) \\
+ \quad & InhK OthFinIns(t, age) + InhK PvtPenSys(t, age) \\
- \quad & BeqK Rsdntial(t, age) - BeqK PvtUnincorpEnt(t, age) \\
- \quad & BeqK PvtPenSys(t, age) - BeqK OthFinIns(t, age) \, .
\end{aligned}
$$

In other words, change in wealth for members of a given cohort in a given year is equal to

- their net savings, adjusted to include net savings through the private pension system,
- plus their imputed share of the net savings of firms and government,
- plus the sum across all asset classes (pension and non-pension alike) of inheritance minus bequests.

Summing over age groups, inheritance and bequests cancel out, leaving

$$\Delta KTot(t) = AdjNetSvngHH(t) + NetSvngFirms(t) + NetSvngGovt(t) \, ,$$

which is the desired result.

11.2 Net savings calculated "bottom up" equal net savings calculated "top down"

In this section, we confirm that net national savings calculated "top down" as national disposable income minus consumption are equal to net national savings calculated "bottom up" by summing net savings across households, firms, and government.

11.2.1 " Bottom up"

We start by summing across sectors.

11.2.1.1 Households

Combining the first two expressions in Section 4.4 of this annex and summing over age groups,

$$
\begin{aligned}
AdjDispYHH(t) \;=\; & DispWageY(t) + DispRntlY(t) + DispEntrY(t) \\
+\; & DispDividY(t) + DispIntGovDebt(t) \\
+\; & DispPensionY(t) + BenHlthCareSys(t) \\
+\; & BenLngTrmCareSys(t) + ContPvtPenSys(t) \\
-\; & BenPvtPenSys(t) + DividPvtPenSys(t) \\
-\; & WthdrwlKPvtPenSysDC(t)\,.
\end{aligned}
$$

By expanding this expression and subtracting consumption, we obtain adjusted net saving:

$$
\begin{aligned}
AdjNetSvngHH(t) \;=\; & WageY(t) - DirTaxWageY(t) \\
-\; & ContPubPenSysWageY(t) \\
-\; & ContPvtPenSysWageY(t) - ContHlthCareSysWageY(t) \\
-\; & ContLngTrmCareSysWageY(t) + RntlY(t) \\
-\; & DirTaxRntlY(t) + EntrY(t) \\
-\; & DirTaxEntrY(t) - ContPubPenSysEntrY(t) \\
-\; & ContPvtPenSysEntrY(t) - ContHlthCareSysEntrY(t) \\
-\; & ContLngTrmCareSysEntrY(t) + DividY(t) \\
+\; & IntGovDebt(t) - DirTaxIntGovDebt(t) \\
+\; & BenPubPenSys(t) \\
-\; & DirTaxBenPubPenSys(t) + BenPvtPenSys(t, age) \\
+\; & WthdrwlKPvtPenSysDC(t) + ContPvtPenSys(t) \\
+\; & DividPvtPenSys(t) - BenPvtPenSys(t, age) \\
-\; & WthdrwlKPvtPenSys(t) - PvtCons(t)\,.
\end{aligned}
$$

Making cancellations and substituting dividends paid out by firms for dividends received by households, the expression is written as

$$
\begin{aligned}
AdjNetSvngHH(t) =\ & WageY(t) - DirTaxWageY(t) \\
-\ & ContPubPenSysWageY(t) - ContHlthCareSysWageY(t) \\
-\ & ContLngTrmCareSysWageY(t) + RntlY(t) \\
-\ & DirTaxRntlY(t) + EntrY(t) - DirTaxEntrY(t) \\
-\ & ContPubPenSysEntrY(t) - ContHlthCareSysEntrY(t) \\
-\ & ContLngTrmCareSysEntrY(t) \\
+\ & IntGovDebt(t) - DirTaxIntGovDebt(t) \\
+\ & DistErngsFirmsKOthFinIns(t) \\
+\ & BenPubPenSys(t) - DirTaxBenPubPenSys(t) \\
+\ & BenHlthCareSyst(t) + BenLngTrmCareSys(t) \\
+\ & DistErngsFirmsKPvtPenSys(t) - PvtCons(t)\,.
\end{aligned}
$$

11.2.1.2 Firms

$$
\begin{aligned}
NetSvngFirms(t) =\ & NetSvngErngsFirmsKPvtPenSys(t) \\
+\ & NetSvngErngsFirmsKOthFinIns(t)\,,
\end{aligned}
$$

which expands to

$$
\begin{aligned}
NetSvngFirms(t) =\ & ErngsFirmsKPvtPenSys(t) \\
-\ & DirTaxErngsFirmsKPvtPenSys(t) \\
-\ & DistErngsFirmsKPvtPenSys(t) \\
+\ & ErngsFirmsKOthFinIns(t) \\
-\ & DirTaxErngsFirmsKOthFinIns(t) \\
-\ & DistErngsFirmsKOthFinIns(t)\,.
\end{aligned}
$$

11.2.1.3 Government

$$
\begin{aligned}
NetSvngGov(t) =\ & IndTax(t) + DirTax(t) + ContPubPenSys(t) \\
-\ & GovCons(t) - BenPubPenSys(t) - IntGovDebt(t)\,,
\end{aligned}
$$

which expands to

$$
\begin{aligned}
NetSvngGov(t) =\ & IndTax(t) + DirTaxWageY(age, t) \\
+\ & DirTaxEntrY(age, t) + DirTaxRntlY(age, t) \\
+\ & DirTaxIntGovDebt(t) + DirTaxBenPubPenSys(t) \\
+\ & DirTaxErngsFirmsKPvtPenSys(t) \\
+\ & DirTaxErngsFirmsKOthFinIns(t) \\
+\ & ContPubPenSysWageY(t) + ContPubPenSysEntrY(t) \\
-\ & GovCons(t) - BenPubPenSys(t) - IntGovDebt(t)\,.
\end{aligned}
$$

11.2.1.4 Total

Adding across sectors and making cancellations, net national savings are

$$
\begin{aligned}
NetNatSvng(t) \;=\;& WageY(t) + EntrY(t) + RntlY(t) \\
+\;& ErngsFirmsKPvtPenSys(t) \\
+\;& ErngsFirmsKOthFinIns(t) + IndTax(t) \\
-\;& PvtCons(t) - GovCons(t)\,.
\end{aligned}
$$

11.2.2 "Top down"

Net national savings are given by the expression

$$NetNatSvng(t) = NatDispY(t) - PvtCons(t) - GovCons(t)\,.$$

First, we express national disposable income in terms of GDP

$$NatDispY(t) = GDP(t) - DeprRate(t)KTot(t)\,,$$

and then expand GDP using the expression from Section 10.1 of this annex:

$$
\begin{aligned}
NetNatSvng(t) \;=\;& WageY(t) + EntrY(t) + RntlY(t) \\
+\;& ErngsFirmsKPvtPenSys(t) \\
+\;& ErngsFirmsKOthFinIns(t) \\
+\;& IndTax(t) + DeprRate(t)KTot \\
-\;& DeprRate(t)KTot(t) - PvtCons(t) - GovCons(t)\,.
\end{aligned}
$$

Depreciation cancels, leaving

$$
\begin{aligned}
NetNatSvng(t) \;=\;& WageY(t) + EntrY(t) + RntlY(t) \\
+\;& ErngsFirmsKPvtPenSys(t) \\
+\;& ErngsFirmsKOthFinIns(t) + IndTax(t) \\
-\;& PvtCons(t) - GovCons(t)\,.
\end{aligned}
$$

This is the same as the expression at the end of Section 11.2.1.4.

Notes

[1] Hereafter, we use "firms" to designate "incorporated enterprises."

[2] The logic behind this assumption is that, on retirement, the benefit entitlement from the private DB pension scheme is calculated on the basis of years of participation and earnings. If we were to allow withdrawal of assets, it would be necessary to "restart the clock" every time assets were withdrawn, or to link benefits with accumulated assets (as in the private DC pension system) rather than earnings.

[3] From the standpoint of calculating individual wealth, the bequest term is irrelevant, because the individual must die in order to bequeath. In calculating cohort wealth, however, bequests must be taken into account.

[4] One expedient way to solve this problem is to assume that only persons under some age, say 65, inherit wealth, but this runs the danger of failing to account for significant intra-elderly age group spousal bequests. Ultimately, a vector of age-specific share coefficients should be applied to allocate bequests from persons of a given age group over heirs by age group.

[5] For computational simplicity, allocation shares are not indexed by age.

[6] Early withdrawals from the private DC pension system, as well as consumption financed by such withdrawals, are included in net household savings in the first line.

Annex 3.2:
Initializing Assumptions

In this annex, we list the baseline exogenous assumptions for Japan. The relevant textual discussion is in Section 3.3 of the chapter. Assumptions for all regions are listed in MacKellar *et al.* (2002).

Assumptions

Macroeconomic parameters

GDP per capita, initial year (1995)	US$36,617
Capital : GDP, initial year (1995)	2.6
Capital coefficient in Cobb-Douglas production function	0.333
Labor coefficient in Cobb-Douglas production function	0.667
Depreciation rate (% per year)	5%
Rate of total factor productivity growth (% per year)	1%
Government consumption (% of GDP; adjusted to respect debt ceiling)	15%
Debt ceiling (% of GDP)	30%
Direct tax rate	12%
Indirect tax rate (% of GDP)	5%
Share of earnings distributed as dividends	15%
Unemployment rate	4%

Average propensities to consume

Wage income	90%
Entrepreneurial income	60%
Imputed residential rents	100%
Dividends	50%
Interest on government debt	60%
Public pension benefits	100%
Private defined-contribution (DC) pension benefits	100%
Private defined-benefit (DB) pension benefits	100%
Annuity income	60%
Inheritance (proportion converted to consumption)	10%
Withdrawals from the private defined-contribution (DC) pension system	30%

Allocation of net savings to capital formation

Residential	14%

Nonresidential	86%
Capital operated by private unincorporated enterprises	33%
Capital operated by firms	67%

International allocation of savings
Private earnings-related (DB) pay-as-you-go (PAYG) pension system

Domestic	90%
Foreign	10%
Private DC pension system	
Domestic	90%
Foreign	10%
Other financial institutions	
Domestic	85%
Foreign	15%
Share of foreign assets consisting of foreign direct investment (FDI)	50%
Share of earnings on FDI repatriated	50%
Share of repatriated earnings distributed as dividends	15%

Age-specific labor force participation rates by age
(males and females combined)

15–19	16.4%
20–24	70.3%
25–29	81.0%
30–34	76.0%
35–39	78.0%
40–44	82.1%
45–49	82.9%
50–54	80.5%
55–59	74.6%
60–64	54.6%
65–69	37.1%
70–74	24.8%
75–79	16.1%
80–84	9.0%
85+	4.2%

Pension, health and long-term care systems

Pensionable age	60 (65 by 2015)
Public earnings-related (DB) PAYG pension scheme	
Proportion of workers participating	90%
Share of wage income subject to contributions	80%
Proportion of self-employed participating	90%
Share of entrepreneurial income subject to contributions	80%
Accrual rate	0.71%
Indexation factor (%-change pension : %-change average wage)	0.20
Flat rate public pension	
Proportion of population participating	60%
Flat rate pension : average wage	10%

Private earnings-related (DB) PAYG pension scheme
  Proportion of workers participating   45%
  Share of wage income subject to contributions   100%
  Accrual rate   0.33%
  Indexation factor (%-change pension : %-change average wage)   0.10
Private DC pension scheme
  Proportion of workers participating   30%
  Share of wage income subject to contributions   100%
  Contribution rate, wage income   5%
  Proportion of self-employed participating   30%
  Share of entrepreneurial income subject to contributions   100%
  Contribution rate, entrepreneurial income   5%
  Proportion of DC pension assets withdrawn every year   3%

Health care system
  Share of health care spending in GDP, initial year (1995)   6%
  Proportion of population covered   100%
  Patient co-payment rate   20%

Long-term care system
  Share of long-term care spending in GDP, initial year (1995)   2%
  Proportion of population covered   100%
  Patient co-payment rate   20%

Annex 3.3:
Comparison of IIASA Model Baseline Projections for Japan, 2000–2050, with the Projections of Other Models

The baseline scenario presented in Chapter 3 foresees that rapid ageing of the Japanese population over the next half century will be accompanied by a slowing of economic growth, a decline in saving rates, and a decline in the current account balance. The model also projects that contribution rates for public pensions and the health and long-term care systems will rise and that these expenditures will account for a steeply increasing share of gross domestic product (GDP). As a way of assessing the "reasonableness" of the projections of the baseline scenario of the IIASA model, the projections of that model have been compared with the projections of other models. Not all of the recent studies using models of the Japanese population and economy have published the values corresponding to their reference scenario.[1] However, enough information exists to make possible a number of comparisons with respect to nine variables: two demographic, five economic, and two dealing with the social security system.

1. Population Growth Rates

Model scenarios will inevitably be sensitive to the underlying demographic assumptions. The IIASA model scenario is based on the assumption of a continuing decline in population growth rates over the next half century, with negative population growth after 2010. The projections underlying the scenarios of Mason et al. (1994),[2] Ogawa (1995), Takayama (1996),[3] and Turner et al. (1998) are quite similar to those of the IIASA model. They also follow a downward course, but in the IIASA baseline scenario, the growth rate turns negative sooner and the declines are greater.

Table A3.3.1. Rate of population growth (% per annum), Japan, 2000–2050.

Year	IIASA	Turner	Mason	Ogawa	Takayama
2000	0.17	0.20	0.48	0.28	0.30
2010	−0.10	0.00	0.09	0.05	0.23
2020	−0.40	−0.40	−0.25	−0.04	
2030	−0.53	−0.40			−0.29
2040	−0.59	−0.40			
2050	−0.65	−0.40			

148

2. The Old-Age Dependency Ratio

IIASA uses as its old-age dependency ratio the ratio of persons aged 60 and older to the number of persons aged 15–59. The old-age dependency rates for Japan calculated from the study by Chauveau and Loufir (1997)[4] are very close to the IIASA rates. The models of McMorrow and Roeger (1999)[5] and Turner *et al.* (1998) project old-age dependency for the years 2000 and 2050. Although the trends in their numbers match those of the IIASA figures, their old-age dependency ratios are consistently lower.

Table A3.3.2. Population 60+ : population 15–59 (%), 2000–2050.

Year	IIASA	Chauveau	McMorrow	Turner
2000	35.2	37.2	29.6	21.3
2010	50.0	52.2		
2020	57.1	59.1		
2030	61.9	64.1		
2040	73.2	72.3		
2050	74.9	70.1	65.4	55.6

Five studies made projections of the old-age dependency ratio using other definitions of that ratio but did not include the data needed to make them comparable with the IIASA figures. Takayama (1996) defined the old-age dependency ratio as the population aged 65 and older divided by the population aged 20–64. Horioka (1989) did the same, as did Heller (1989). Meredith (1995) defined the old-age dependency ratio as the population aged 65 and older divided by the population aged 15–64.

Though the dependency ratios in these studies are not directly comparable with the IIASA figures, they are presented in *Table A3.3.3*. Since the dependent group in the five studies is smaller than in the IIASA study, the old-age dependency ratios are smaller. However, the Takayama and Horioka projections are very closely aligned with each other and follow the same trend as the IIASA projections.

Table A3.3.3. Alternative measures of the old-age dependency ratio, Japan, 2000–2050.

Year	IIASA	Takayama	Horioka	Heller	Meredith
2000	35.2	27.4	27.1	24.2	
2010	50.0	37.0	35.8	31.5	
2020	57.1	47.8	44.0	40.0	40.0
2030	61.9	47.7	42.6		
2040	73.2	54.0	46.4		
2050	74.9	55.7	44.3		

3. Rate of Growth of Per Capita Output

Only Mason *et al.* (1994) and Turner *et al.* (1998) present their results for the growth rate of per capita output. Mason *et al.* foresee a growth rate that generally accelerates. While Turner *et al.* foresee a lower growth rate of per capita GDP than does the IIASA model, they also project that the growth rate of per capita output will decline over time.

Table A3.3.4. The growth rate of per capita GDP (% per annum), Japan, 2000–2050.

Year	IIASA	Mason	Turner
2000	1.7	3.1	1.5
2010	1.4	3.8	1.3
2020	1.6	4.1	1.3
2030	1.5		1.4
2040	1.2		0.8
2050	1.4		0.9

4. The Capital-Output Ratio

The IIASA model projects that Japan's capital-output ratio will rise modestly over the next 50 years, from roughly 2.6 to 3.5. This implies a gradual decline in the average productivity of the capital stock (see *Table A3.3.5*). The model of Mason *et al.* (1994) presents data on "Private Capital,"[6] and hence it is not surprising that their figures for the initial capital-output ratio are below those assumed by IIASA.[7] It is striking that, in spite of continued accumulation, their capital-output ratio declines significantly over the projection period, implying a continuing improvement in the productivity of capital. Turner *et al.* (1998) have only a point estimate of the capital-output ratio in the year 2000. Not shown are estimates of the ratio of net worth to income by Ando *et al.* (1995): they are 6.7 for 2020 and 8.7 for 2050.[8]

Table A3.3.5. The capital-output ratio, Japan, 2000–2050.

Year	IIASA	Mason	Turner
2000	2.6	2.1	2.2
2010	2.9	1.7	
2020	3.1	1.2	
2030	3.3		
2040	3.4		
2050	3.5		

5. The Rate of Return to Capital

The IIASA model projects steady decline in the rate of return to capital. The model of Mason *et al.* (1994) projects a decline until 2010, followed by an increase over the following decade. Yashiro *et al.* (1997)[9] project a sharp rise in the rate of return between 1995 and 2000 followed by a decline through mid-century. Their projection roughly tracks that of the IIASA model. Though the rate-of-return projection for 2000 of Turner *et al.* (1998) (5 percent) is close to IIASA's figure,[10] they project a rise in the rate of return to capital to 5.4 percent by 2050, a figure almost twice that of the IIASA model projection. Thus, the Turner *et al.* and IIASA model solution results differ both in estimated level and projected trend.

Table A3.3.6. Rate of return to capital (%), Japan, 2000–2050.

Year	IIASA	Mason	Yashiro	Turner
2000	5.6	4.6	4.6	5.00
2010	4.8	3.6		
2020	4.0	4.4		
2030	3.4			
2040	2.9			
2050	2.6		3.0	5.42

6. Net National Savings as a Percentage of GDP

It is widely believed that the ageing of the Japanese population will bring with it a decline in the proportion of income that is saved. Though this decline is reflected in the IIASA projections, it is considerably less rapid than is forecast by other models of the Japanese economy. The study by Kato (1998) uses the national savings concept, as does the IIASA model, and the projected saving rates are similar. Kato's rate begins in 1995 at a slightly lower level than the rate derived from the IIASA model. From that point on, Kato's saving rates fall more rapidly than those generated by the IIASA model.

The saving rates projected by Horioka (1989)[11] show a higher initial value and a more rapid rate of decline than Kato's rates, thus, a much more rapid rate of decline than those projected by the IIASA model. The steep decline reflects Horioka's view that life cycle considerations are the determinant of saving rates in Japan. Like Horioka, Higgins (1997) also projects a substantially negative saving rate by 2010 (–6.2 percent).

Table A3.3.7. Net national savings[a] as a percentage of GDP, Japan, 2000–2050.

Year	IIASA	Kato	Horioka	Higgins
2000	7.2	5.17	6.70	
2010	6.6	3.16	–3.80	–6.2
2020	5.6	0.53	–12.2	
2030	4.6	–0.70	–10.2	–9.3(2025)
2040	3.5	–1.72	–15.4	
2050	2.6	–2.65	–12.9	

[a]The IIASA model relates net national saving to GDP. A case could be made for relating net national savings, a figure that does not include depreciation allowances, to net national product or net domestic product.

7. Change in Net Foreign Assets as a Percentage of GDP

The IIASA model projects that change in the ratio of net foreign assets to GDP[12] will be extremely small though positive in 2000 (0.32 percent), then decline slightly over the projection period, ending up at –0.16 percent of GDP. Turner *et al.* (1998) projected that, in the years 2000–2015, Japan's current account surplus will remain stable at 2 percent of its GDP. However, Turner *et al.* project that by 2050 Japan's stock of external assets will be exhausted, a projection consistent with the IIASA model's projection of a decline in external assets from 2030 on. The projections of Horioka (1996) are not very different from those of Turner *et al.* He projects that the ratio of the current account to GDP will be zero in 2020 and will fall to −1.0 percent in 2025. Meredith (1995a) projected that the ratio of current account to GDP will fall to −15.0 percent in 2020, and Yashiro *et al.* (1997) projected that the current account balance would be −5.7 percent by 2025 and would be −17.0 percent by 2050. These results are considerably more dramatic than those of the IIASA scenario.

Table A3.3.8. Change in net foreign assets as a percentage of GDP, Japan, 2000–2050.

Year	IIASA	Higgins	Meredith	Yashiro	Horioka	Turner
2000	0.4		2.0	0.0		2.0
2010	0.3	−1.3				2.0
2020	0.1		−15.0		0.0	2.0
2030	0.1			−5.7(2025)	−1.0(2025)	
2040	0.0					
2050	−0.1			−17.0		

8. Public Pension Contribution as a Percentage of Covered Wages

The IIASA model projects that the proportion of covered wages contributed to public pensions will increase from 22.6 percent in 2000 to 25.4 percent in 2020. This is less dramatic than the projection of the Ogawa (1995) model, which did not assume an increase in the retirement age.

Table A3.3.9. Public pension contributions as a percentage of covered wages, Japan, 2000–2020.

Year	IIASA	Ogawa
2000	22.6	18.9
2010	24.6	22.0
2020	25.4	30.9
2030	25.7	
2040	29.3	
2050	32.3	

9. Public Pension Contributions as a Percentage of GDP

The IIASA model projects that, as a result of population ageing, the proportion of Japanese GDP contributed to the public pension funds will grow from 8.4 percent in 2000 to 11.7 percent in 2050. The Roseveare *et al.* (1996) projections closely track those made by the IIASA model.[13] Takayama (1996) also projects a rapidly rising share of output going to public pensions. His projection for 2025 for the proportion of national income going to public pensions[14] is 15 percent, which is greater than the IIASA projection for 2050.

Table A3.3.10. Public pension plan contributions as a percent of output, Japan, 2000–2050.

Year	IIASA	Roseveare	Takayama
2000	8.4	7.5	10.5
2010	9.1	9.6	14.0
2020	9.3	12.4	
2030	9.4	13.4	15.0(2025)
2040	10.7	14.9	
2050	11.7	16.5	

10. Conclusion

This annex compared the IIASA model's projections of Japan's population, economy, and pension system with those of a number of other individual researchers and research teams. Because many studies present only deviations from a baseline, surprisingly few results can be directly compared. Among those that can, there is no unanimity. Thus, for example, IIASA and Turner *et al.* (1998) predict deceleration of economic growth, while Mason *et al.* (1994) predict an acceleration, IIASA and Yashiro *et al.* (1997) predict a decline in the rate of return to capital, and Turner *et al.* (1998) predict an increase. The diversity of results reflects the diversity of approaches and assumptions, demonstrating concretely the importance of adequate documentation. Areas in which there appears to be agreement, however, are (i) declining net national savings relating to GDP, (ii) a move toward deficit in the current account, and (iii) rising public pension contributions as a share of covered wages and GDP.

Notes

[1] Hviding and Mérette (1998) present, in their Table 4, the effects of policy reform on the national saving rate. In Table 5, they show its effect on the real return on capital. In Table 6, they show its effect on per capita GDP. However all these figures are given as percent differences from the baseline values, and the baseline values are not given, making it impossible to compare their projections with those of the IIASA model. Turner *et al.* (1998) provide some very limited information about their reference scenario. Their Table 5 (p. 49) provides projections of the growth rates of GDP per capita (adjusted for changes in the terms of trade). Table A2 (p. 105) gives initial values for the capital-output ratio, the real interest rate, and the trade balance as a percentage of GDP. However, all projections for 2010, 2020, 2030, 2040, and 2050 are presented in tables as differences from the reference case. Since the reference case projections are not given, the projections of Turner *et al.* cannot be systematically compared with those of the IIASA model. McMorrow and Roeger (1999) present their demographic projections in their Table 1 (p. 9). However, their economic projections are generally expressed as changes relative to the baseline.

[2] Mason *et al.* gave figures for total population in five-year intervals. Growth rates were calculated from that data (Mason *et al.*, 1994, Table 7.8). The Mason *et al.* projections were based on a 1986 projection by Ogawa (1986) and thus did not fully capture the effect of the continuing decline in Japanese fertility that occurred during the 1990s (Mason *et al.*, 1994, p. 176).

[3] Takayama's projections (Table 6) were based on Ministry of Health projections published in 1992.

[4] Chauveau and Loufir (1997) disaggregated the Japanese population into three age groups: under 20, 20–59, and 60 and older. To make their distribution comparable with the IIASA distribution, 25 percent of their under-20 group was added to their 20–59 age group.

[5] McMorrow and Roeger (1999) disaggregated the Japanese population into three age groups: under 15, 15–64, and 65 and older. To make their distribution comparable with the IIASA distribution, 10 percent of their 15–64 age group was subtracted from that group and added to their 65 and older age group.

[6] Thus investments in public capital such as roads, bridges, port facilities, and school buildings are omitted from this measure.

[7] Hayashi (1991) also estimated an extremely low capital-output ratio for Japan. For the year 1989, his estimated capital-output ratio was 1.54.

[8] The fact that the ratio of net worth to income is two or more times the capital-output ratio may be due to the inclusion of land wealth and foreign assets.

[9] Yashiro *et al.* (1997) project long-term interest rates (Table 1, p. 38).

[10] The figures presented by Turner *et al.* (1998) refer to the real interest rate rather than the return to capital. In a state of macroeconomic equilibrium, the two figures should be equal.

[11] Horioka's saving rates refer to personal saving calculated on the basis of replacement cost rather than historical cost. Horioka (1991) projected saving rates for 1995, 2000, and 2010 that were almost identical to his 1989 projections.

[12] The change in net foreign assets should be approximately equal to the balance on current account or the negative of the balance on the capital account.

[13] Roseveare *et al.* (1996) and Takayama (1996) projected public pension expenditures as a percentage of GDP, rather than contributions.

[14] Takayama (1996) projected public pension expenditures as a percentage of national income rather than GDP.

Chapter 4

Economic Impacts of Alternative Demographic Scenarios

4.1 Introduction

In this chapter, we investigate the sensitivity of the baseline scenario presented in Chapter 3 to alternative demographic scenarios involving low fertility and low mortality. We concentrate on lower than expected fertility and greater than expected longevity, because history suggests that forecasts are more likely to err in these directions, not only in Japan, but in other developed countries as well. We do not simulate the impact of high net migration because there is no evidence that Japanese policy makers would consider a more liberal migration regime in response to population ageing.[1]

4.2 How Important is Demographic Uncertainty?

Perhaps the uncertainties most often cited in the social security field are those arising from uncertain mortality and fertility rates (Lee and Tuljapurkar, 1994). *Figure 4.1* displays paths of selected variables under three demographic scenarios: the central fertility–central mortality–central migration (CCC) scenario, a low fertility–central mortality–central migration (LCC) scenario, and a central fertility–low mortality–central migration (CLC) scenario. These demographic scenarios are analyzed in detail in Section 4.3, and their construction is described in Annex 4.1.[2]

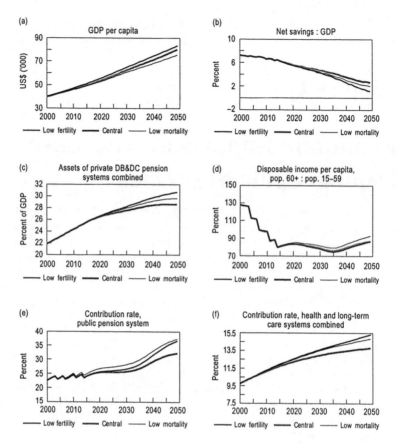

Figure 4.1. Three demographic scenarios: Baseline or central (CCC), low fertility (LCC), low mortality (CLC).

The variables illustrated are gross domestic product (GDP) per capita, the aggregate saving rate (net savings as a percentage of GDP), assets of the private defined-benefit (DB) and private defined-contribution (DC) pension systems combined (as a percentage of GDP), the ratio of the disposable income per capita of the elderly population relative to that of the working-age population (expressed as a percentage), and the payroll tax rates needed to balance the public pension and combined health and long-term care systems.

The most important conclusion to be drawn from examining *Figure 4.1* is that overall trends in these selected variables are, practically speaking, insensitive to the choice of demographic scenario. Low fertility slightly accelerates growth in GDP per capita and low mortality slightly decelerates it, but the impacts, amounting to 3–5 percent after 50 years, are hardly decisive (see *Figure 4.1a*). Both low fertility and low mortality have the effect of reducing the aggregate saving rate by increasing the share of the adult population in the dissaving elderly age bracket as well as through increases in social contribution rates (thereby reducing disposable income, out of which household savings are drawn). The impact of low fertility, which in the long run has the greater effect on the elderly dependency ratio, is the more significant of the two (*Figure 4.1b*). The increases in social contribution rates are illustrated in *Figures 4.1e* and *4.1f*. As described in Chapter 3, the share of health and long-term care spending in GDP is purely a function of age structure. With low fertility having a greater impact on age structure than low mortality, low fertility increases the combined health and long-term care contribution rate slightly more than low mortality does (see *Figure 4.1f*). The mechanism for calculating pension expenditure is more complicated, and with low fertility increasing the wage rate and low mortality reducing it, the impact of low mortality on contribution rates is more significant than that of low fertility (see *Figure 4.1e*). In the long run, however, the impact of low fertility approaches that of low mortality because of its more significant impact on the dependency ratio, and it can be seen in the figure that if the situation were extended, low fertility would eventually have the greater impact.

Low fertility has no discernible impact on the ratio of the disposable income of the elderly relative to that of the young (see *Figure 4.1d*), because the ratio of the average pension to the average wage is not significantly affected; moreover, while payroll contribution rates are higher for the young, so is the wage rate. By contrast, low mortality increases the disposable income of the elderly relative to that of the working-age population. This is because it increases payroll contribution rates by increasing the number of beneficiaries while decreasing the wage rate (and, less significantly, increasing the rate of return on the assets held predominantly by the elderly). Finally, in both alternative demographic scenarios, total private pension system assets are higher relative to GDP (*Figure 4.1c*). This reflects the fact that GDP is a fast-reacting flow variable whereas assets are a slow-reacting stock variable. An interpretation is that, since the population is older, on average, in each of the two alternative scenarios than it is in the baseline, the ratio of pension wealth to income is higher. In this interpretation, low fertility has a greater impact than low mortality because it has the greater impact on average age.

These results tell us that even if fertility is much lower than expected, and even if longevity is much greater than expected, the general evolution of the economy will be more or less as in the baseline (CCC) scenario. Since our model is essentially linear, the symmetric conclusion also follows: even if, unlikely as it seems based on past forecasts, demographers have underestimated future fertility and overestimated future mortality, Japan is likely to experience what we termed "demographic stagnation."

4.3   A Decomposition Analysis

In the remainder of this chapter, we apply a standard technique by which differences between the alternative and baseline demographic scenarios are decomposed into a composition effect (impact of the new population age distribution, holding the baseline total population size constant) and a volume effect (impact of the new population size, holding the baseline age structure constant). It is virtually impossible to discuss the effects of demographic trends without keeping this distinction in mind. The same approach has been implemented by Masson and Tryon (1990), Turner *et al.* (1998), and others. Up to terms of higher order (insignificant given the simplicity of the model), the two effects add up to give the total difference between the baseline (CCC) and alternative scenarios (LCC and CLC).

Whenever we use language such as "greater than," "less than," "older than," etc., we are speaking in baseline versus alternative terms, where the baseline is the CCC scenario. Level variables (GDP per capita, etc.) are compared in percentage difference terms ("The impact of higher than expected mortality is to reduce GDP per capita by x percent vis-à-vis the baseline," etc.). Differences in ratio variables (social insurance contribution rates, the dependency ratio, etc.) are given in absolute percentage point terms (i.e., "The impact of lower than expected fertility is to raise the dependency ratio by y percentage points," etc.). An exception is the capital-output ratio, changes in which we describe in proportional terms. To keep the number of figures manageable, we consider two points in time: 2025, corresponding to the medium term, and 2050, corresponding to the long term.[3]

Low Fertility (LCC) Population Scenario

The difference between the baseline (CCC) and the LCC alternative population projections for Japan is analyzed in *Table 4.1*. Line 1 gives the baseline. Line 2 gives the figure resulting when the LCC alternative population age structure is applied to the baseline total population (in the case of the total population variable, of course, line 2 is the same as line 1). What we in line 3 label the "pure effect of population age structure" and often refer to as "the age-structure (or composition) effect" is the difference between line 1 and line 2. In the case of the population aged 0–14, the age-structure effect of lower fertility is to reduce the number of persons (vis-à-vis the baseline) in both the medium (2025) and long (2050) terms. In the medium term, the age-structure impact of lower fertility is to increase the

Table 4.1. Baseline (CCC) versus low-fertility alternative (LCC) scenario: Population and labor force (billions).

		2000	Average annual change	2025	Average annual change	2050
Total	1. Base	0.125	-0.13%	0.120	-0.55%	0.105
population	2. New age structure, same total pop.	0.125	-0.13%	0.120	-0.55%	0.105
	3. Diff. from 1 (pure effect of pop. age structure)	0.00%	0.00%	0.00%	0.00%	0.00%
	4. New age structure, new total population	0.125	-0.31%	0.114	-0.79%	0.090
	5. Diff. from 2 (pure effect of pop. size)	-0.22%	-0.17%	-5.32%	-0.24%	-14.26%
	6. Diff. from 1 (sum of 3 and 5)	-0.22%	-0.17%	-5.32%	-0.24%	-14.26%
Population	1. Base	0.018	-0.44%	0.016	-0.36%	0.014
aged 0–14	2. New age structure, same total pop.	0.018	-1.08%	0.013	-0.83%	0.010
	3. Diff. from 1 (pure effect of pop. age structure)	-1.34%	-0.64%	-18.63%	-0.46%	-29.26%
	4. New age structure, new total population	0.018	-1.25%	0.012	-1.15%	0.009
	5. Diff. from 2 (pure effect of pop. size)	-0.23%	-0.17%	-5.27%	-0.33%	-14.23%
	6. Diff. from 1 (sum of 3 and 5)	-1.57%	-0.81%	-22.92%	-0.79%	-39.33%
Population	1. Base	0.080	-0.63%	0.066	-0.95%	0.052
aged 15–59	2. New age structure, same total pop.	0.080	-0.60%	0.067	-1.18%	0.050
	3. Diff. from 1 (pure effect of pop. age structure)	0.23%	0.03%	1.11%	-0.23%	-4.53%
	4. New age structure, new total population	0.080	-0.77%	0.063	-1.31%	0.042
	5. Diff. from 2 (pure effect of pop. size)	-0.21%	-0.17%	-5.33%	-0.13%	-14.26%
	6. Diff. from 1 (sum of 3 and 5)	0.01%	-0.15%	-4.28%	-0.36%	-18.15%
Population	1. Base	0.028	1.13%	0.039	0.01%	0.039
aged 60+	2. New age structure, same total pop.	0.028	1.31%	0.041	0.34%	0.045
	3. Diff. from 1 (pure effect of pop. age structure)	0.22%	0.18%	5.63%	0.33%	16.61%
	4. New age structure, new total population	0.028	1.13%	0.039	0.01%	0.039
	5. Diff. from 2 (pure effect of pop. size)	-0.22%	-0.18%	-5.33%	-0.33%	-14.27%
	6. Diff. from 1 (sum of 3 and 5)	0.00%	0.00%	0.00%	0.00%	-0.03%
Population 60+ :	1. Base	34.74%		58.78%		74.87%
population	2. New age structure, same total pop.	34.73%		61.41%		91.46%
15–59 (%)	3. Diff. from 1 (pure effect of pop. age structure)	0.00%		2.63%		16.58%
	4. New age structure, new total population	34.73%		61.41%		91.45%
	5. Diff. from 2 (pure effect of pop. size)	0.00%		0.00%		-0.01%
	6. Diff. from 1 (sum of 3 and 5)	0.00%		2.63%		16.57%
Labor force	1. Base	0.064	-0.45%	0.056	-0.70%	0.045
	2. New age structure, same total pop.	0.064	-0.36%	0.057	-0.77%	0.046
	3. Diff. from 1 (pure effect of pop. age structure)	0.22%	0.10%	3.18%	-0.07%	1.15%
	4. New age structure, new total population	0.064	-0.53%	0.054	-1.09%	0.039
	5. Diff. from 2 (pure effect of pop. size)	-0.22%	-0.17%	-5.33%	-0.33%	-14.26%
	6. Diff. from 1 (sum of 3 and 5)	0.00%	-0.08%	-2.32%	-0.39%	-13.27%

Note: Differences between percents are given in percentage points.

number of persons in both the adult (15–59) and elderly (60 and older) age groups. Over the long term, however, the age-structure impact of lower fertility in the early years of the scenario "moves up the age ladder." The result, in 2050, is that both the population aged 0–14 and the population aged 15–59 are lower than in the baseline, the balancing entry being a sharply increased elderly population. Note also that, while the age-structure effect concentrates the population aged 15–59 into the years of highest labor force participation (and highest earning power), it has no impact on the age distribution of the elderly population (low fertility beginning in year 0 does not begin affecting the age distribution of the population aged 60 and older until year 60).

The "pure effect of population size"—or, more simply, the "population-size (or volume) effect"—is calculated as a residual (thus, higher-order interaction effects are lumped together with the population-size effect; however, as mentioned above, these are insignificant) by comparing the LCC alternative scenario figures in line 4 with the figures in line 2, which varied only age structure while maintaining the baseline scenario total population. In all age groups in both the medium and long terms, the population-size effect of lower fertility is naturally a smaller population: by 5.32 percent in 2025 and by 14.26 percent in 2050. Since the volume effect holds the age structure of the population constant, it is equal (in proportional terms) for each of the three age groups. The population-size and age-structure effects are precisely offsetting for the population aged 60 and older. This must be the case, because a change in fertility beginning in 1995 (the initial solution year) can have no impact on the absolute number of persons aged 60 and older in 2025 or 2050; such persons have already been born by 1995.

The penultimate block of figures in *Table 4.1* decomposes the difference in the dependency ratio (population aged 60 and older relative to population aged 15–59). The total difference between dependency ratios in the two scenarios is 2.63 percentage points in 2025 (CCC dependency ratio of 58.78 percent and LCC dependency ratio of 61.41 percent) and 16.58 percentage points in 2050 (CCC dependency ratio of 74.87 percent and LCC dependency ratio of 91.45 percent). Here, the difference between the two scenarios holding age structure constant (the volume effect) is zero, and the entire difference is accounted for by the age-structure effect.

The last block of figures gives labor force on the assumption that age-specific labor force participation rates (LFPRs) remain constant. The pure effect of population size in the LCC scenario is to reduce labor force (relative to the baseline) across the board in every age group and in every year. The age-structure effect increases both the populations aged 15–59 and 60 and older in the medium term, translating into a larger labor force despite the higher dependency ratio. In the long term, while the age-structure effect reduces the population aged 15–59, it redistributes population in this age group toward peak labor supply years. In addition, the significantly increased elderly population is, in Japan, characterized by a relatively high LFPR, hence the counterintuitive insight that in Japan the pure age-structure effect of lower fertility is to increase labor force throughout the simulation period (provided, of course, that age-specific LFPRs do not decline). However, the total (population size and age structure combined) effect of low fertility is, as expected, to reduce the size of the labor force.

Table 4.2. Baseline (CCC) versus low-mortality alternative (CLC) scenario: Population and labor force (billions).

		2000	Average annual change	2025	Average annual change	2050
Total	1. Base	0.125	-0.16%	0.120	-0.55%	0.105
population	2. New age structure, same total pop.	0.125	-0.16%	0.120	-0.55%	0.105
	3. Diff. from 1 (pure effect of pop. age structure)	0.00%	0.00%	0.00%	0.00%	0.00%
	4. New age structure, new total population	0.125	-0.05%	0.124	-0.39%	0.112
	5. Diff. from 2 (pure effect of pop. size)	0.09%	0.11%	2.90%	0.16%	7.10%
	6. Diff. from 1 (sum of 3 and 5)	0.09%	0.11%	2.90%	0.16%	7.10%
Population	1. Base	0.018	-0.53%	0.016	-0.43%	0.014
aged 0–14	2. New age structure, same total pop.	0.018	-0.62%	0.015	-0.57%	0.013
	3. Diff. from 1 (pure effect of pop. age structure)	-0.11%	-0.08%	-2.18%	-0.14%	-5.50%
	4. New age structure, new total population	0.018	-0.51%	0.016	-0.41%	0.014
	5. Diff. from 2 (pure effect of pop. size)	0.11%	0.11%	2.88%	0.16%	7.10%
	6. Diff. from 1 (sum of 3 and 5)	0.00%	0.03%	0.64%	0.02%	1.21%
Population	1. Base	0.080	-0.75%	0.066	-0.95%	0.052
aged 15–59	2. New age structure, same total pop.	0.080	-0.84%	0.064	-1.09%	0.049
	3. Diff. from 1 (pure effect of pop. age structure)	-0.05%	-0.09%	-2.17%	-0.14%	-5.46%
	4. New age structure, new total population	0.080	-0.73%	0.066	-0.93%	0.053
	5. Diff. from 2 (pure effect of pop. size)	0.09%	0.11%	2.90%	0.16%	7.10%
	6. Diff. from 1 (sum of 3 and 5)	0.04%	0.02%	0.67%	0.02%	1.25%
Population	1. Base	0.028	1.36%	0.039	0.01%	0.039
aged 60+	2. New age structure, same total pop.	0.028	1.53%	0.040	0.19%	0.042
	3. Diff. from 1 (pure effect of pop. age structure)	0.22%	0.17%	4.57%	0.18%	9.27%
	4. New age structure, new total population	0.028	1.64%	0.042	0.35%	0.045
	5. Diff. from 2 (pure effect of pop. size)	0.07%	0.11%	2.89%	0.16%	7.09%
	6. Diff. from 1 (sum of 3 and 5)	0.29%	0.29%	7.59%	0.34%	17.02%
Population 60+ :	1. Base	34.74%		58.78%		74.87%
population	2. New age structure, same total pop.	34.83%		62.83%		86.54%
15–59 (%)	3. Diff. from 1 (pure effect of pop. age structure)	0.09%		4.05%		11.66%
	4. New age structure, new total population	34.82%		62.82%		86.54%
	5. Diff. from 2 (pure effect of pop. size)	-0.01%		-0.01%		0.00%
	6. Diff. from 1 (sum of 3 and 5)	0.09%		4.04%		11.66%
Labor force	1. Base	0.064	-0.54%	0.056	-0.84%	0.045
	2. New age structure, same total pop.	0.064	-0.60%	0.055	-0.95%	0.043
	3. Diff. from 1 (pure effect of pop. age structure)	-0.03%	-0.06%	-1.47%	-0.11%	-4.13%
	4. New age structure, new total population	0.064	-0.49%	0.056	-0.79%	0.046
	5. Diff. from 2 (pure effect of pop. size)	0.09%	0.11%	2.90%	0.16%	7.08%
	6. Diff. from 1 (sum of 3 and 5)	0.06%	0.05%	1.38%	0.05%	2.66%

Note: Differences between percents are given in percentage points.

Low Mortality (CLC) Population Scenario

The data in *Table 4.2* perform the same decomposition for differences between the CCC and CLC scenarios. Here, we would expect the alternative scenario to be characterized by a larger population (due to greater survival) and an older age structure (because mortality reductions are likely to be greater at older ages). In the event, the total population is 2.9 percent greater in 2025 and 7.1 percent greater in 2050. The dependency ratio is 4.04 percentage points higher in 2025 (62.82

percent as opposed to 58.78 percent) and 11.66 percentage points higher in 2050 (86.54 percent as opposed to 74.87 percent). In the medium term, then, the dependency ratio is more sensitive to low mortality than to low fertility, but in the long term it is more sensitive to low fertility. This is because low fertility climbs up the age ladder only gradually, but as it does, it has a cumulative ratchet effect on the dependency ratio—fewer adults having children at lower rates—that low mortality does not. To the extent that demographic impacts on pension and health systems are a function of population age structure rather than size, this shows that in the near term, the main demographic risk is greater than expected old-age survival, but in the long term, the main risk is lower than expected fertility. There is a hint of this in *Figures 4.1e* and *4.1f*. Health and long-term care contribution rates, which are functions exclusively of the age distribution in our model, are clearly more sensitive to low fertility than to low mortality after 2030 or so. The public pension system contribution rate, whose determination is more complicated, is more sensitive to low mortality than to low fertility throughout the simulation period, but as mentioned above, it is evident from *Figure 4.1e* that this ranking would be reversed if the simulation were extended another 10 years.[4] As previously, population age-structure impacts on total population size are zero by definition, as are population-size effects on the dependency ratio. Looking at population by age group, as one would expect, lower than expected mortality has relatively little impact on the number of persons under age 60, because mortality over this portion of the life span is very low already. Few women die before completing childbearing, so there is no significant upward ratchet effect of lower mortality on the number of births. The main effect of lower mortality is on the number of persons over age 60, which is 7.59 percent higher in 2025 and 17.02 percent higher in 2050.

Whereas the population-size effect of low fertility is to reduce labor force, the population size effect of low mortality is to increase it. Since mortality in the prime working ages is already low, however, the effect is modest in magnitude (labor force increased by 2.90 percent in 2025 and by 7.08 percent in 2050). In contrast to low fertility, low mortality has the age-structure effect of reducing labor force in both the medium (by 1.47 percent) and long (by 4.13 percent) terms. As would be expected, the total impact of lower mortality is to increase the size of the labor force (1.38 percent in the medium term, 2.66 in the long term).

4.4   Economic Impacts

The population-size effect/age-structure effect decomposition approach can be applied to all variables, not just demographic ones. In *Tables 4.3* and *4.4* and *Figures 4.2* and *4.3*, we summarize the decomposed economic impacts of the alternative demographic scenarios on Japan. Much more detail is given in the tables in Annexes 4.2 (CCC versus LCC) and 4.3 (CCC versus CLC).

Low Fertility

In the medium term (2025), the age-structure effect of low fertility increases per capita GDP by 2.53 percent owing to the larger labor force (see bottom of *Table 4.1*); since the population-size effect is also acting to boost GDP per capita, the total impact of low fertility is a fairly substantial 3.81 percent increase (see *Table 4.3* and *Table A4.2.1* in Annex 4.2). In the long run (2050), the age-structure effect is weaker (although still positive) and the population-size effect is stronger; as a result, the net impact on GDP per capita is essentially the same (a 3.83 percent increase). The long-run results are illustrated in *Figure 4.2b*.

Again referring to *Table 4.3* (and *Table A4.2.1* in Annex 4.2), it can be seen that the age-structure effect of low fertility, operating through increased labor force (see discussion in Section 4.3), is to reduce the capital-output ratio by 1.28 percent in the medium term and by 0.70 percent in the long term. The population-size effect, which reduces labor force in both 2025 and 2050, increases the capital-output ratio. Since the sum of the age-structure and population-size effects is a reduced labor force, their combined impact is a higher capital-output ratio, which increases by 1.24 percent in the medium term and by 5.46 percent in the long term.

In the medium term (2025), differences in saving rates in the two scenarios are small. In the long term (2050), however, the aggregate saving rate is 1.50 percentage points lower in the LCC alternative than in the CCC baseline scenario (1.14 percent of GDP as opposed to 2.63 percent of GDP; see also *Figure 4.2b*); this impact is due in roughly equal proportion to the age-structure and population-size effects. The former (responsible for 0.63 percentage points of the decline) represents the redistribution of population and disposable income from working-age adults to the elderly (see *Table 4.1* for population and *Tables A4.2.3* and *A4.2.4* in Annex 4.2 for total disposable income). The latter (responsible for 0.87 percentage points of the decrease) represents the fact that, when total GDP is decreased by the population-size impact of low fertility, consumption corresponding to decumulation of assets by the elderly remains fixed, therefore the aggregate saving rate is reduced. This is the reverse of the impact described in the first simulation of Section 3.5; note, however, that whereas in that case the shock to population size was uniform across time periods, here it starts off small and grows. Hence, whereas the population-size impact in Section 3.5 diminished in absolute value over time (i.e., the aggregate saving rate gradually returned to baseline), in this more realistic case the population-size impact grows (i.e., the aggregate saving rate gradually diverges from baseline).

Table 4.3. Baseline (CCC) versus low-fertility alternative (LCC) scenario: Summary presentation.

		2000	Average annual change	2025	Average annual change	2050
Demography						
Total population	1. Base	0.125	-0.16%	0.120	-0.55%	0.105
(billions)	2. New age structure, same total pop.	0.125	-0.16%	0.120	-0.55%	0.105
	3. Diff. from 1 (pure effect of pop. age structure)	0.00%	0.00%	0.00%	0.00%	0.00%
	4. New age structure, new total population	0.125	-0.37%	0.114	-0.94%	0.090
	5. Diff. from 2 (pure effect of pop. size)	-0.22%	-0.21%	-5.32%	-0.39%	-14.26%
	6. Diff. from 1 (sum of 3 and 5)	-0.22%	-0.21%	-5.32%	-0.39%	-14.26%
Dependency ratio,	1. Base	34.74%		58.78%		74.87%
% (pop. 60+ :	2. New age structure, same total pop.	34.73%		61.41%		91.46%
pop. 15–59)	3. Diff. from 1 (pure effect of pop. age structure)	0.00%		2.63%		16.58%
	4. New age structure, new total population	34.73%		61.41%		91.45%
	5. Diff. from 2 (pure effect of pop. size)	0.00%		0.00%		-0.01%
	6. Diff. from 1 (sum of 3 and 5)	0.00%		2.63%		16.57%
Macro-economy						
GDP per capita	1. Base	39,943	1.49%	57,813	1.32%	80,249
(US$)	2. New age structure, same total pop.	40,002	1.59%	59,273	1.25%	80,894
	3. Diff. from 1 (pure effect of pop. age structure)	0.15%	0.10%	2.53%	-0.07%	0.80%
	4. New age structure, new total population	40,028	1.63%	60,015	1.32%	83,325
	5. Diff. from 2 (pure effect of pop. size)	0.07%	0.05%	1.25%	0.07%	3.01%
	6. Diff. from 1 (sum of 3 and 5)	0.21%	0.14%	3.81%	0.00%	3.83%
Capital-output ratio	1. Base	2.64	0.78%	3.20	0.36%	3.50
	2. New age structure, same total pop.	2.63	0.73%	3.16	0.38%	3.48
	3. Diff. from 1 (pure effect of pop. age structure)	-0.13%	-0.05%	-1.28%	0.02%	-0.70%
	4. New age structure, new total population	2.64	0.83%	3.24	0.52%	3.69
	5. Diff. from 2 (pure effect of pop. size)	0.13%	0.10%	2.56%	0.14%	6.20%
	6. Diff. from 1 (sum of 3 and 5)	0.00%	0.05%	1.24%	0.16%	5.46%
Net savings	1. Base	7.21%		5.09%		2.63%
(% of GDP)	2. New age structure, same total pop.	7.17%		5.21%		2.01%
	3. Diff. from 1 (pure effect of pop. age structure)	-0.04%		0.12%		-0.63%
	4. New age structure, new total population	7.21%		4.86%		1.14%
	5. Diff. from 2 (pure effect of pop. size)	0.04%		-0.35%		-0.87%
	6. Diff. from 1 (sum of 3 and 5)	0.00%		-0.23%		-1.50%
Social insurance						
Public pension	1. Base	22.56%		25.47%		32.26%
system	2. New age structure, same total pop.	22.57%		26.03%		36.76%
contribution rate	3. Diff. from 1 (pure effect of pop. age structure)	0.01%		0.56%		4.50%
(%)	4. New age structure, new total population	22.56%		25.98%		36.71%
	5. Diff. from 2 (pure effect of pop. size)	-0.01%		-0.05%		-0.06%
	6. Diff. from 1 (sum of 3 and 5; total effect)	0.00%		0.51%		4.45%
Public pension	1. Base	8.42%		9.32%		11.71%
system	2. New age structure, same total pop.	8.43%		9.53%		13.34%
contributions	3. Diff. from 1 (pure effect of pop. age structure)	0.00%		0.21%		1.64%
(% of GDP)	4. New age structure, new total population	8.42%		9.49%		13.27%
	5. Diff. from 2 (pure effect of pop. size)	0.00%		-0.03%		-0.07%
	6. Diff. from 1 (sum of 3 and 5; total effect)	0.00%		0.18%		1.56%

Note: Differences between percents are given in percentage points.

Table 4.3. *Continued.*

		2000	2025	2050
Health care system	1. Base	7.28%	9.47%	10.36%
contribution rate	2. New age structure, same total pop.	7.29%	9.82%	11.45%
(%)	3. Diff. from 1 (pure effect of pop. age structure)	0.00%	0.35%	1.09%
	4. New age structure, new total population	7.29%	9.83%	11.49%
	5. Diff. from 2 (pure effect of pop. size)	0.00%	0.02%	0.04%
	6. Diff. from 1 (sum of 3 and 5)	0.00%	0.36%	1.14%
Health care	1. Base	5.23%	6.66%	7.23%
contributions	2. New age structure, same total pop.	5.23%	6.91%	7.99%
(% of GDP)	3. Diff. from 1 (pure effect of pop. age structure)	0.00%	0.25%	0.76%
	4. New age structure, new total population	5.23%	6.91%	7.99%
	5. Diff. from 2 (pure effect of pop. size)	0.00%	0.00%	0.00%
	6. Diff. from 1 (sum of 3 and 5; total effect)	0.00%	0.25%	0.76%
Long-term care	1. Base	2.43%	3.16%	3.45%
contribution rate	2. New age structure, same total pop.	2.43%	3.27%	3.82%
(%)	3. Diff. from 1 (pure effect of pop. age structure)	0.00%	0.12%	0.37%
	4. New age structure, new total population	2.43%	3.28%	3.83%
	5. Diff. from 2 (pure effect of pop. size)	0.00%	0.01%	0.01%
	6. Diff. from 1 (sum of 3 and 5)	0.00%	0.12%	0.38%
Long-term care	1. Base	1.74%	2.22%	2.41%
contributions	2. New age structure, same total pop.	1.74%	2.16%	2.39%
(% of GDP)	3. Diff. from 1 (pure effect of pop. age structure)	0.00%	-0.05%	-0.02%
	4. New age structure, new total population	1.74%	2.26%	2.71%
	5. Diff. from 2 (pure effect of pop. size)	0.00%	0.09%	0.32%
	6. Diff. from 1 (sum of 3 and 5)	0.00%	0.04%	0.30%
Intergenerational distribution				
Disposable income	1. Base	127.6%	81.8%	86.6%
per capita, %	2. New age structure, same total pop.	127.7%	81.5%	87.1%
(pop. 60+ : pop. 15–59)	3. Diff. from 1 (pure effect of pop. age structure)	0.1%	-0.3%	0.5%
	4. New age structure, new total population	127.7%	80.9%	86.1%
	5. Diff. from 2 (pure effect of pop. size)	0.0%	-0.6%	-1.0%
	6. Diff. from 1 (sum of 3 and 5)	0.1%	-0.9%	-0.5%
Non-health-related	1. Base	134.5%	87.1%	95.2%
consumption	2. New age structure, same total pop.	134.6%	86.0%	94.8%
per capita, %	3. Diff. from 1 (pure effect of pop. age structure)	0.1%	-1.1%	-0.5%
(pop. 60+ : pop. 15–59)	4. New age structure, new total population	134.5%	85.6%	94.3%
	5. Diff. from 2 (pure effect of pop. size)	-0.1%	-0.4%	-0.4%
	6. Diff. from 1 (sum of 3 and 5)	0.0%	-1.5%	-0.9%

Note: Differences between percents are given in percentage points.

The next block in *Table 4.3* shows social insurance contribution rates. In all cases, we would expect the population-size effect to be insignificant—in a pay-as-you-go (PAYG) system, there is no reason to think that scaling all age groups up or down by the same factor would significantly change contribution rates (or contributions as a share of GDP), although the absolute size of contributions would of course change. Furthermore, we would expect age-structure effects to track changes in the dependency ratio, which, given constant LFPRs and a fixed retirement age, is practically the same thing as the system dependency ratio.

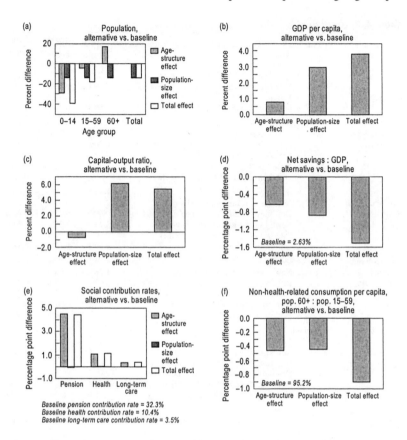

Figure 4.2. Baseline (CCC) versus low-fertility alternative (LCC) scenario: Summary results, 2050.

From *Table 4.3*, the long-term (2050) impact of lower fertility is to increase the public pension, health care, and long-term care contribution rates by 4.45, 1.14, and 0.38 percentage points, respectively (relative to baseline values of 32.26 percent, 10.36 percent, and 3.45 percent, respectively). As illustrated for 2050 in *Figure 4.2e*, these increases consist almost entirely of age-structure effects. Impacts on contributions as a share of GDP do not differ greatly from impacts on contribution rates.

The age distribution of disposable income is roughly the same in the CCC and LCC scenarios (see *Figure 4.1d* and the last block of *Table 4.3*). This is worth analyzing, since it apparently contradicts what one would expect to be the main impact of lower fertility, namely, a higher wage rate. There are a number of factors to be considered. Focusing on the final year (2050), the population-size effect of low fertility is, as expected, to increase the wage rate, by 3.01 percent (see *Table A4.2.1* in Annex 4.2). Since those aged 15–59 derive a higher proportion of their disposable income from wages than do those aged 60 and older, this volume effect reduces the ratio of the disposable income of the elderly to the disposable income of those aged 15–59 by 1 percentage point (see *Table 4.3*). The age-structure effect is to decrease the average wage rate throughout the simulation because it increases the labor force (see *Table 4.1* for labor force and *Table A4.2.1* in Annex 4.2 for the wage rate impact). Because it also increases social contribution rates (by over 10 percent in proportional terms by the end of the simulation), the net impact of the age-structure effect is to reduce disposable wage income per capita, with a greater proportional impact on the population aged 15–59 than on the population aged 60 and older.[5] When the population-size effect, which favors the population aged 15–59, is balanced against the age-structure effect, which favors the population aged 60 and older, income distribution is largely unaffected. This explains, in detail, the results observed in *Figure 4.1d*. Note, however, that all these shifts are small in absolute magnitude, much smaller than those observed in the case of low mortality analyzed in the next section. Shifts in relative non-health-related consumption (*Figure 4.2f*) are also small.

While we have devoted little attention to regions other than Japan, it is worth referring in passing to international impacts. "Low fertility" in this simulation means low fertility in *all* regions of the world, yet clearly uncertainty—and room for age-specific fertility rates to fall further than they already have—is greater in some regions than others. Uncertainty regarding fertility is greatest in the less developed countries (LDCs); therefore, it is not surprising that the relative impact of low fertility is greater in that region than others. (As shown in *Table A4.2.10* in Annex 4.2, in LDCs, GDP per capita in the LCC scenario is 7.76 percent higher than in the baseline scenario by 2050, the end of the simulation period.) Net factor income from abroad (the difference between GDP and gross national product) is reduced for non-LDC regions and increased for the LDCs; this is mostly because of the effect of changing relative GDP sizes on net foreign assets (also shown in *Table A4.2.10* in Annex 4.2). Impacts on current account balances, to the extent that these can be inferred from changes in net foreign assets, are not very significant: +US$18 billion in LDCs in 2050, –US$19 billion for the other three regions of the world combined (the slight discrepancy reflects rounding error). However, the baseline scenario already includes substantial ageing, so that these results should not be confused with estimates of the total impact of population ageing on international capital flows.

Table 4.4. Baseline (CCC) versus low-mortality alternative (CLC) scenario: Summary presentation.

		2000	Average annual change	2025	Average annual change	2050
Demography						
Total population	1. Base	0.125	-0.16%	0.12	-0.55%	0.105
(billions)	2. New age structure, same total pop.	0.125	-0.16%	0.12	-0.55%	0.105
	3. Diff. from 1 (pure effect of pop. age structure)	0.00%	0.00%	0.00%	0.00%	0.00%
	4. New age structure, new total population	0.125	-0.05%	0.124	-0.39%	0.112
	5. Diff. from 2 (pure effect of pop. size)	0.09%	0.11%	2.90%	0.16%	7.10%
	6. Diff. from 1 (sum of 3 and 5)	0.09%	0.11%	2.90%	0.16%	7.10%
Dependency ratio,	1. Base	34.74%		58.78%		74.87%
% (pop. 60+ :	2. New age structure, same total pop.	34.83%		62.83%		86.54%
pop. 15–59)	3. Diff. from 1 (pure effect of pop. age structure)	0.09%		4.05%		11.66%
	4. New age structure, new total population	34.82%		62.82%		86.54%
	5. Diff. from 2 (pure effect of pop. size)	-0.01%		-0.01%		0.00%
	6. Diff. from 1 (sum of 3 and 5)	0.09%		4.04%		11.66%
Macro-economy						
GDP per capita	1. Base	39,943	1.49%	57,813	1.32%	80,249
(US$)	2. New age structure, same total pop.	39,936	1.44%	57,040	1.19%	76,592
	3. Diff. from 1 (pure effect of pop. age structure)	-0.02%	-0.05%	-1.34%	-0.13%	-4.56%
	4. New age structure, new total population	39,925	1.41%	56,644	1.16%	75,622
	5. Diff. from 2 (pure effect of pop. size)	-0.03%	-0.03%	-0.69%	-0.02%	-1.27%
	6. Diff. from 1 (sum of 3 and 5)	-0.04%	-0.08%	-2.02%	-0.16%	-5.77%
Capital-output ratio	1. Base	2.64	0.78%	3.20	0.36%	3.50
	2. New age structure, same total pop.	2.64	0.79%	3.21	0.31%	3.47
	3. Diff. from 1 (pure effect of pop. age structure)	0.02%	0.01%	0.27%	-0.05%	-0.89%
	4. New age structure, new total population	2.63	0.73%	3.16	0.27%	3.38
	5. Diff. from 2 (pure effect of pop. size)	-0.05%	-0.05%	-1.40%	-0.05%	-2.55%
	6. Diff. from 1 (sum of 3 and 5)	-0.04%	-0.04%	-1.14%	-0.09%	-3.42%
Net savings	1. Base	7.21%		5.09%		2.63%
(% of GDP)	2. New age structure, same total pop.	7.21%		4.75%		1.70%
	3. Diff. from 1 (pure effect of pop. age structure)	0.00%		-0.34%		-0.94%
	4. New age structure, new total population	7.22%		4.94%		2.00%
	5. Diff. from 2 (pure effect of pop. size)	0.01%		0.19%		0.30%
	6. Diff. from 1 (sum of 3 and 5)	0.01%		-0.15%		-0.64%
Social insurance						
Public pension	1. Base	22.56%		25.47%		32.26%
system	2. New age structure, same total pop.	22.61%		27.31%		37.32%
contribution rate	3. Diff. from 1 (pure effect of pop. age structure)	0.05%		1.84%		5.06%
(%)	4. New age structure, new total population	22.61%		27.35%		37.33%
	5. Diff. from 2 (pure effect of pop. size)	0.00%		0.04%		0.00%
	6. Diff. from 1 (sum of 3 and 5; total effect)	0.05%		1.88%		5.07%
Public pension	1. Base	8.42%		9.32%		11.71%
system	2. New age structure, same total pop.	8.44%		9.99%		13.55%
contributions	3. Diff. from 1 (pure effect of pop. age structure)	0.02%		0.67%		1.84%
(% of GDP)	4. New age structure, new total population	8.44%		10.01%		13.57%
	5. Diff. from 2 (pure effect of pop. size)	0.00%		0.02%		0.02%
	6. Diff. from 1 (sum of 3 and 5; total effect)	0.02%		0.69%		1.86%

Note: Differences between percents are given in percentage points.

Table 4.4. *Continued.*

		2000	2025	2050
Health care system	1. Base	7.28%	9.47%	10.36%
contribution rate	2. New age structure, same total pop.	7.29%	9.77%	11.16%
(%)	3. Diff. from 1 (pure effect of pop. age structure)	0.01%	0.30%	0.80%
	4. New age structure, new total population	7.29%	9.76%	11.14%
	5. Diff. from 2 (pure effect of pop. size)	0.00%	-0.01%	-0.02%
	6. Diff. from 1 (sum of 3 and 5)	0.01%	0.29%	0.79%
Health care	1. Base	5.23%	6.66%	7.23%
contributions	2. New age structure, same total pop.	5.23%	6.87%	7.79%
(% of GDP)	3. Diff. from 1 (pure effect of pop. age structure)	0.00%	0.21%	0.56%
	4. New age structure, new total population	5.23%	6.87%	7.79%
	5. Diff. from 2 (pure effect of pop. size)	0.00%	0.00%	0.00%
	6. Diff. from 1 (sum of 3 and 5; total effect)	0.00%	0.21%	0.56%
Long-term care	1. Base	2.43%	3.16%	3.45%
contribution rate	2. New age structure, same total pop.	2.43%	3.26%	3.72%
(%)	3. Diff. from 1 (pure effect of pop. age structure)	0.00%	0.10%	0.27%
	4. New age structure, new total population	2.43%	3.25%	3.71%
	5. Diff. from 2 (pure effect of pop. size)	0.00%	0.00%	-0.01%
	6. Diff. from 1 (sum of 3 and 5)	0.00%	0.10%	0.26%
Long-term care	1. Base	1.74%	2.22%	2.41%
contributions	2. New age structure, same total pop.	1.74%	2.25%	2.52%
(% of GDP)	3. Diff. from 1 (pure effect of pop. age structure)	0.00%	0.03%	0.12%
	4. New age structure, new total population	1.74%	2.20%	2.39%
	5. Diff. from 2 (pure effect of pop. size)	0.00%	-0.05%	-0.14%
	6. Diff. from 1 (sum of 3 and 5)	0.00%	-0.02%	-0.02%
Intergenerational distribution				
Disposable income	1. Base	127.6%	81.8%	86.6%
per capita, %	2. New age structure, same total pop.	127.6%	83.3%	91.9%
(pop. 60+ : pop. 15–59)	3. Diff. from 1 (pure effect of pop. age structure)	0.0%	1.6%	5.3%
	4. New age structure, new total population	127.6%	83.7%	92.4%
	5. Diff. from 2 (pure effect of pop. size)	0.0%	0.4%	0.5%
	6. Diff. from 1 (sum of 3 and 5)	0.0%	1.9%	5.8%
Non-health-related	1. Base	134.5%	87.1%	95.2%
consumption	2. New age structure, same total pop.	134.5%	88.9%	101.6%
per capita, %	3. Diff. from 1 (pure effect of pop. age structure)	0.0%	1.8%	6.4%
(pop. 60+ : pop. 15–59)	4. New age structure, new total population	134.5%	89.2%	101.8%
	5. Diff. from 2 (pure effect of pop. size)	0.1%	0.3%	0.2%
	6. Diff. from 1 (sum of 3 and 5)	0.0%	2.1%	6.6%

Note: Differences between percents are given in percentage points.

Low Mortality

In the CLC scenario, GDP per capita is significantly reduced (by 2.02 percent in 2025 and by 5.77 percent in 2050; see *Table 4.4* and *Table A4.3.1* in Annex 4.3), because of capital dilution in the case of the population-size effect and because the age-structure effect reduces the number of workers while increasing the number of elderly. Most of the impact is due to the age-structure effect. The capital-output ratio is reduced by 1.14 percent in 2025 and by 3.42 percent in 2050; most of this change consists of the population-size effect. The impact on the saving rate is modest in the near term but quite significant in the long term (–0.15 percentage points

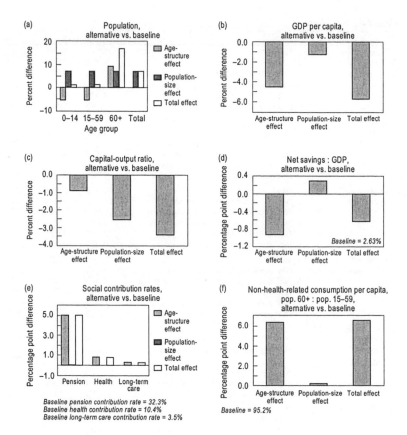

Figure 4.3. Baseline (CCC) versus low-mortality alternative (CLC) scenario: Summary results, 2050.

in 2025 and –0.64 percentage points in 2050, relative to baseline levels of 5.09 percent and 2.63 percent, respectively). The negative direction would be expected of a change redistributing population (proportionally speaking) from the saving years to the dissaving years while simultaneously increasing social contribution rates. A modest population-size effect increases the saving rate; reasons for this are discussed in Chapter 3.

Concentrating on the long term (2050), public pension, health, and long-term care contribution rates increase by 5.07, 0.79, and 0.26 percentage points, respectively, compared with the CCC scenario levels of 32.3, 10.4, and 3.5 percent, respectively. The increase in the pension contribution rate is slightly greater than in the LCC scenario, while the ranking of the two scenarios is reversed for health and long-term care contribution rates. As noted above, alternative demographic assumptions affect health and long-term care contribution rates in our model entirely through their impact on population age structure.

Whether measured in terms of relative disposable income or relative non-health-related consumption, the distributional impact of low mortality is in favor of the elderly population, as the wage rate is reduced (see *Table A4.3.1* in Annex 4.3) while social contribution rates are increased. The absolute impact is much more significant (in fact, an order of magnitude greater) than in the case of low fertility: whereas the total impact of low fertility is to reduce the disposable income of the elderly relative to that of the population aged 15–59 by only 0.5 percentage points (relative to a baseline of 86.6 percent; see *Table 4.3*), the impact of low mortality is to increase it by 5.8 percentage points (see *Figure 4.1d* and *Table 4.4*). The mortality impact on relative disposable income consists almost entirely of the age-structure component (see *Table 4.4*). Population-size impacts on social contribution rates are close to zero, given our model structure, and the population-size impacts of reduced mortality on labor force and through it the wage rate, while significant, are modest. Shifts in relative non-health-related consumption (*Figure 4.3f* and *Table A4.3.5* in Annex 4.3) closely track shifts in relative disposable income.

Looking at regions other than Japan, dominant population-size impacts lead to reductions in GDP per capita in all regions (see *Table A4.3.10* in Annex 4.3). This effect is least pronounced in the LDCs because only in this region is mortality significant in the 0–14 and 15–59 age groups; thus, lower mortality in the CLC scenario translates into a higher number of workers in the medium and long terms. The current account of the LDC region is estimated to move toward surplus by US$13 billion, balanced by an identical move in the opposite direction by the three industrial regions of the world combined. It is worth pointing out that the low-mortality scenarios make no provision for productivity gains associated with the accompanying lower morbidity.

4.5 Conclusion

In this chapter, we have used the model presented in Chapter 3 to analyze the economic impacts on the Japanese economy of two alternative demographic scenarios, namely, lower than expected fertility and greater than expected longevity (i.e., lower than expected mortality). The relative insensitivity to changes in demographic assumptions indicates that, among the many sources of uncertainty regarding the economic impact of population ageing on Japan, uncertain demography probably ranks rather low. In large part because of demographic inertia, significant economic impacts are already "baked in the cake."

Despite the stability of the outlook, a few alternative versus baseline scenario comparisons are worth encapsulating:

- Lower than expected fertility might increase per capita GDP on the order of 4 percent after 50 years; lower than expected mortality might reduce it on the order of 5 percent. Given the long time frame, these results might be described as significant but modest.
- Both lower than expected fertility and lower than expected mortality are esti- mated to have the effect of reducing the net saving rate, more significantly in the case of mortality than fertility.
- Lower than expected fertility and lower than expected mortality have the po- tential to increase social contribution rates, in proportional terms, by roughly 10–15 percent after 50 years.
- The age distribution of disposable income and non-health-related consumption is much more sensitive to lower than expected mortality (which moves the dis- tribution in favor of the elderly) than to lower than expected fertility (which moves the distribution in favor of the young).
- Since the model is linear, symmetric conclusions also follow. In particular, hopes that an upturn in fertility might have significant impact appear misplaced.

While policy makers are naturally interested in the total effect of various demo- graphic trends, from an analytical point of view, it is only possible to understand this total effect by examining the constituent impacts—those impacts due to ageing per se (change in population age structure holding size constant) and those due to the deceleration of aggregate population growth (change in population size holding age structure constant)—separately. As often as not, age-structure and population- size effects are opposite in sign and of differing absolute magnitudes. In working through the decomposed impacts step-by-step, we have increased our confidence in our model and the conclusions that emerge from it. We describe the latter in a brief afterword at the end of this volume

Notes

[1] In addition, simulation of alternative migration scenarios involves a number of judg- ments that are not straightforward. For example, do in-migrants assume the same pro- ductivity profile as existing workers? Do they save at the same rate? What proportion of their earnings is remitted to countries of origin? How many remain in Japan after retirement, and how many years have they participated in the pension system?

[2] The low fertility (LCC) and low mortality (CLC) scenarios were designed to corre- spond to experts' subjective 95 percent confidence intervals. Since the model simula- tions themselves are deterministic, however, we cannot attach a rigorous probabilistic

interpretation to the results in *Figure 4.1*. Hence our rather imprecise language: "Even if fertility/mortality is much lower than expected ...." Since the scenarios are symmetric and the model is linear, high fertility and high mortality scenarios would simply be mirror images of those in *Figure 4.1*.

[3] Since the initial year of the model solution is 1995 and demographic variables are slow moving, differences for 2000 are zero or trivially small. Note that changes between 2025 and 2050 cannot be extrapolated into the second half of the century. In fact, simplifying the story considerably, the unfavorable demographic trends of the first half of the century are generally expected to be reversed in the second half, although forecast uncertainty is massive.

[4] Low mortality decreases the wage rate over the entire simulation period, thus increasing the contribution rate necessary to balance the pension system, all else being equal. Low fertility increases the wage rate starting in about year 15 of the simulation (2010), thus reducing the necessary contribution rate, all else being equal.

[5] Referring to *Tables A4.3.3* and *A4.3.4* in Annex 4.3, the age-structure effect is to reduce the per capita disposable wage income of the population aged 15–59 by 7.80 percent in 2050, as opposed to by 15.59 percent for the population aged 60 and older. The milder proportional impact on the young reflects the fact that the age-structure effect, in addition to reducing the average wage rate, redistributes the population aged 15–59 into the peak labor force participation and earning power years. However, wages account for over three-quarters of the total disposable income of those aged 15–59, as opposed to less than one-quarter for the population aged 60 and older; hence the greater overall impact on disposable income of the young (–7.35% as opposed to –1.69% for the population aged 60 and older). Note that the population-size impact on per capita disposable wage income is equiproportional across the age spectrum.

Annex 4.1: Demographic Scenarios

The demographic scenarios used here result from combining United Nations (UN) Population Division (UN Population Division, 1998) projections and projections from the Population Project at the International Institute for Applied Systems Analysis (IIASA; Lutz, 1996). This approach is necessary because each of the two sets of projections offers something different. The UN does projections on an individual-country basis, but provides only a single low-fertility alternative scenario. IIASA provides alternative scenarios for mortality as well as fertility, but does projections only by region, rather then by individual country. Combining the two sets of projections makes it possible to produce globally consistent baseline and alternative fertility and mortality scenarios for Japan, the United States, Other Industrial Countries, and Less Developed Countries (LDCs).

The UN projections were produced using point-estimates of demographic parameters (fertility, mortality, and migration) based on expert judgment. The IIASA projections were also produced on the basis of expert opinion, but using a slightly different approach. Panels of experts were asked to construct high–low scenarios for the total fertility rate, life expectancy, and net international migration in 13 world regions so that their high–low bounds corresponded to subjective 90 percent confidence intervals (i.e., 5 percent of probability mass lies above the high and 5 percent below the low). The central scenario for each of these three basic demographic parameters was then taken as the arithmetic average of the high–low bounds. Since this scenario combines central assumptions for fertility, mortality, and international migration, it is referred to as the CCC scenario. Alternative scenarios are referred to as LCC (low fertility–central mortality–central migration) and CLC (central fertility–low mortality–central migration).

Baseline scenario

To produce our baseline scenario, we have used the UN central projections for Japan and the United States, calculated Other Industrial Countries as the IIASA Industrial Countries region baseline minus the UN Japan and United States baselines, and calculated LDCs as IIASA's world total baseline minus Japan, the United States, and Other Industrial Countries. By construction, Industrial Countries (i.e., Japan plus the United States plus Other Industrial Countries), Less Developed Countries, and the world total are the same in our baseline and in the IIASA baseline.

174

Alternative scenarios

To construct alternative scenarios, in each year we scaled our baseline population by single year age group up or down according to the ratio of the IIASA alternative to the IIASA central (i.e., CCC) projections, as follows:

alternative Japan population in age group i = baseline Japan population in age group i × (IIASA alternative Industrial Countries region population in age group i / IIASA baseline Industrial Countries region population in age group i)

alternative U.S. population in age group i = baseline U.S. population in age group i × (IIASA alternative Industrial Countries region population in age group i / IIASA baseline Industrial Countries region population in age group i)

alternative Other Industrial Countries population in age group i = baseline Other Industrial Countries population in age group i × (IIASA alternative Industrial Countries region population in age group i / IIASA baseline Industrial Countries region population in age group i)

alternative Less Developed Countries population in age group i = baseline Less Developed Countries population in age group i × (IIASA alternative Less Developed Countries region population in age group i / IIASA baseline Less Developed Countries region population in age group i)

There is no doubt that this ad hoc scaling procedure is less defensible the further out it goes, but out to 2050, it is an acceptable expedient.

The two alternative demographic scenarios analyzed in Chapter 4 are a low fertility–central mortality–central migration (LCC) scenario and a central fertility–low mortality–central migration (CLC) scenario. What we refer to as the "Older age structure" or "Maximum Population Ageing" scenario in *Table 3.2* is constructed on the basis of IIASA LLL scenario, that is, low fertility, low mortality, and low migration. Among the IIASA variants, this is characterized by the oldest population age structure.

Annex 4.2: CCC versus LCC

Table A4.2.1. Baseline (CCC) versus low-fertility alternative (LCC) scenario: GDP, GNP, and rates of return to factors.

		2000	Average annual change	2025	Average annual change	2050
GDP per capita	1. Base	39,943	1.49%	57,813	1.32%	80,249
(US$)	2. New age structure, same total pop.	40,002	2.66%	59,273	1.25%	80,894
	3. Diff. from 1 (pure effect of pop. age structure)	0.15%	1.17%	2.53%	-0.07%	0.80%
	4. New age structure, new total population	40,028	1.63%	60,015	1.32%	83,325
	5. Diff. from 2 (pure effect of pop. size)	0.07%	-1.02%	1.25%	0.07%	3.01%
	6. Diff. from 1 (sum of 3 and 5)	0.21%	0.14%	3.81%	0.00%	3.83%
GNP per capita	1. Base	40,228	1.52%	58,602	1.33%	81,481
(US$)	2. New age structure, same total pop.	40,288	1.61%	60,073	1.26%	82,130
	3. Diff. from 1 (pure effect of pop. age structure)	0.15%	0.09%	2.51%	-0.07%	0.80%
	4. New age structure, new total population	40,315	1.66%	60,827	1.33%	84,591
	5. Diff. from 2 (pure effect of pop. size)	0.07%	0.05%	1.26%	0.07%	3.00%
	6. Diff. from 1 (sum of 3 and 5)	0.21%	0.14%	3.80%	0.00%	3.82%
Net factor income	1. Base	286	4.15%	789	1.80%	1,232
from abroad	2. New age structure, same total pop.	286	4.20%	800	1.76%	1,237
per capita	3. Diff. from 1 (pure effect of pop. age structure)	0.12%	0.05%	1.37%	-0.04%	0.34%
(US$)	4. New age structure, new total population	286	4.26%	812	1.79%	1,266
	5. Diff. from 2 (pure effect of pop. size)	0.09%	0.06%	1.52%	0.04%	2.40%
	6. Diff. from 1 (sum of 3 and 5)	0.21%	0.11%	2.92%	-0.01%	2.74%
Capital-output	1. Base	2.64	0.78%	3.20	0.36%	3.50
ratio	2. New age structure, same total pop.	2.64	0.73%	3.16	0.38%	3.48
	3. Diff. from 1 (pure effect of pop. age structure)	-0.13%	-0.05%	-1.28%	0.02%	-0.70%
	4. New age structure, new total population	2.64	0.83%	3.24	0.52%	3.69
	5. Diff. from 2 (pure effect of pop. size)	0.13%	0.10%	2.56%	0.14%	6.20%
	6. Diff. from 1 (sum of 3 and 5)	0.00%	0.05%	1.24%	0.16%	5.46%
Average wage	1. Base	52,458	1.89%	83,673	1.62%	124,927
(US$)	2. New age structure, same total pop.	52,424	1.86%	83,143	1.63%	124,497
	3. Diff. from 1 (pure effect of pop. age structure)	-0.07%	-0.02%	-0.63%	0.01%	-0.34%
	4. New age structure, new total population	52,458	1.91%	84,184	1.70%	128,239
	5. Diff. from 2 (pure effect of pop. size)	0.07%	0.05%	1.25%	0.07%	3.01%
	6. Diff. from 1 (sum of 3 and 5)	0.00%	0.02%	0.61%	0.08%	2.65%
Rate of return to	1. Base	5.62%		3.75%		2.99%
capital (net of	2. New age structure, same total pop.	5.64%		3.86%		3.05%
indirect taxes and	3. Diff. from 1 (pure effect of pop. age structure)	0.01%		0.11%		0.06%
depreciation, %)	4. New age structure, new total population	5.62%		3.64%		2.58%
	5. Diff. from 2 (pure effect of pop. size)	-0.01%		-0.22%		-0.47%
	6. Diff. from 1 (sum of 3 and 5)	0.00%		-0.11%		-0.41%

Note: Differences between percents are given in percentage points.

Table A4.2.2. Baseline (CCC) versus low-fertility alternative (LCC) scenario: Saving rates (% of GDP).

		2000	2025	2050
Net savings	1. Base	7.21%	5.09%	2.63%
	2. New age structure, same total pop.	7.17%	5.21%	2.01%
	3. Diff. from 1 (pure effect of pop. age structure)	3.77%	0.12%	-0.63%
	4. New age structure, new total population	7.21%	4.86%	1.14%
	5. Diff. from 2 (pure effect of pop. size)	0.04%	-0.35%	-0.87%
	6. Diff. from 1 (sum of 3 and 5)	3.81%	-0.23%	-1.50%
Households	1. Base	3.40%	0.25%	-2.08%
(adjusted	2. New age structure, same total pop.	3.43%	0.21%	-2.84%
for change in	3. Diff. from 1 (pure effect of pop. age structure)	0.03%	-0.04%	-0.75%
pension wealth)	4. New age structure, new total population	3.40%	0.01%	-3.35%
	5. Diff. from 2 (pure effect of pop. size)	-0.03%	-0.20%	-0.51%
	6. Diff. from 1 (sum of 3 and 5)	0.00%	-0.24%	-1.27%
Population	1. Base	6.44%	5.66%	5.37%
aged 15–59	2. New age structure, same total pop.	6.46%	5.70%	5.33%
	3. Diff. from 1 (pure effect of pop. age structure)	0.02%	0.03%	-0.03%
	4. New age structure, new total population	6.44%	5.60%	5.14%
	5. Diff. from 2 (pure effect of pop. size)	-0.02%	-0.10%	-0.19%
	6. Diff. from 1 (sum of 3 and 5)	0.00%	-0.07%	-0.23%
Population	1. Base	-3.04%	-5.41%	-7.45%
aged 60+	2. New age structure, same total pop.	-3.03%	-5.48%	-8.17%
	3. Diff. from 1 (pure effect of pop. age structure)	0.00%	-0.07%	-0.72%
	4. New age structure, new total population	-3.04%	-5.58%	-8.49%
	5. Diff. from 2 (pure effect of pop. size)	-0.01%	-0.10%	-0.32%
	6. Diff. from 1 (sum of 3 and 5)	0.00%	-0.17%	-1.04%
Firms	1. Base	4.40%	5.22%	4.98%
	2. New age structure, same total pop.	4.40%	5.30%	5.04%
	3. Diff. from 1 (pure effect of pop. age structure)	0.00%	0.07%	0.07%
	4. New age structure, new total population	4.40%	5.13%	4.53%
	5. Diff. from 2 (pure effect of pop. size)	0.00%	-0.17%	-0.51%
	6. Diff. from 1 (sum of 3 and 5)	0.00%	-0.09%	-0.45%
Government	1. Base	-0.59%	-0.38%	-0.26%
	2. New age structure, same total pop.	-0.66%	-0.30%	-0.20%
	3. Diff. from 1 (pure effect of pop. age structure)	-0.07%	0.08%	0.06%
	4. New age structure, new total population	-0.59%	-0.29%	-0.04%
	5. Diff. from 2 (pure effect of pop. size)	0.07%	0.01%	0.16%
	6. Diff. from 1 (sum of 3 and 5)	0.00%	0.09%	0.22%

Note: Differences between percents are given in percentage points.

Table A4.2.3. Baseline (CCC) versus low-fertility alternative (LCC) scenario: Disposable income, consumption, and savings, population aged 15–59.

		2000	Average annual change	2025	Average annual change	2050
Disposable income per capita (US$)	1. Base	29,513	1.77%	45,775	1.21%	61,819
	2. New age structure, same total pop.	29,487	1.79%	45,899	1.07%	59,862
	3. Diff. from 1 (pure effect of pop. age structure)	-0.09%	0.01%	0.27%	-0.14%	-3.17%
	4. New age structure, new total population	29,505	1.83%	46,399	1.13%	61,388
	5. Diff. from 2 (pure effect of pop. size)	0.06%	0.04%	1.09%	0.06%	2.55%
	6. Diff. from 1 (sum of 3 and 5; total effect)	-0.03%	0.06%	1.36%	-0.08%	-0.70%
Wages (US$)	1. Base	23,526	1.68%	35,696	1.23%	48,417
	2. New age structure, same total pop.	23,504	1.68%	35,620	1.01%	45,842
	3. Diff. from 1 (pure effect of pop. age structure)	-0.09%	0.00%	-0.21%	-0.21%	-5.32%
	4. New age structure, new total population	23,521	1.73%	36,079	1.08%	47,217
	5. Diff. from 2 (pure effect of pop. size)	0.07%	0.05%	1.29%	0.07%	3.00%
	6. Diff. from 1 (sum of 3 and 5; total effect)	-0.02%	0.04%	1.07%	-0.14%	-2.48%
Entrepreneurial income, rents, dividends, interest, etc. (US$)	1. Base	3,385	-0.37%	3,086	0.22%	3,259
	2. New age structure, same total pop.	3,386	-0.31%	3,131	-0.04%	3,098
	3. Diff. from 1 (pure effect of pop. age structure)	0.01%	0.06%	1.46%	-0.26%	-4.94%
	4. New age structure, new total population	3,385	-0.36%	3,097	-0.17%	2,970
	5. Diff. from 2 (pure effect of pop. size)	-0.03%	-0.04%	-1.10%	-0.13%	-4.15%
	6. Diff. from 1 (sum of 3 and 5; total effect)	-0.02%	0.01%	0.35%	-0.39%	-8.88%
Health and long-term care benefits (US$)	1. Base	2,194	2.38%	3,952	1.37%	5,554
	2. New age structure, same total pop.	2,190	2.49%	4,055	1.47%	5,842
	3. Diff. from 1 (pure effect of pop. age structure)	-0.16%	0.11%	2.59%	0.10%	5.19%
	4. New age structure, new total population	2,192	2.54%	4,106	1.54%	6,018
	5. Diff. from 2 (pure effect of pop. size)	0.06%	0.05%	1.26%	0.07%	3.01%
	6. Diff. from 1 (sum of 3 and 5; total effect)	-0.10%	0.16%	3.87%	0.17%	8.35%
Adjusted disposable income per capita (US$)	1. Base	31,065	1.79%	48,454	1.27%	66,419
	2. New age structure, same total pop.	31,038	1.81%	48,652	1.17%	65,080
	3. Diff. from 1 (pure effect of pop. age structure)	-0.08%	0.02%	0.41%	-0.10%	-2.02%
	4. New age structure, new total population	31,056	1.86%	49,172	1.23%	66,714
	5. Diff. from 2 (pure effect of pop. size)	0.06%	0.04%	1.07%	0.06%	2.51%
	6. Diff. from 1 (sum of 3 and 5; total effect)	-0.03%	0.06%	1.48%	-0.04%	0.44%
Early withdrawals from private DC pension system, per capita (US$)	1. Base	150	3.14%	325	1.42%	462
	2. New age structure, same total pop.	150	3.28%	335	1.54%	491
	3. Diff. from 1 (pure effect of pop. age structure)	-0.02%	0.13%	3.24%	0.12%	6.35%
	4. New age structure, new total population	150	3.30%	337	1.58%	499
	5. Diff. from 2 (pure effect of pop. size)	0.01%	0.02%	0.57%	0.04%	1.67%
	6. Diff. from 1 (sum of 3 and 5; total effect)	-0.01%	0.16%	3.82%	0.16%	8.12%

Note: Differences between percents are given in percentage points.

Table A4.2.3. *Continued.*

		2000	Average annual change	2025	Average annual change	2050
Consumption per capita (US$)	1. Base	27,023	1.83%	42,478	1.23%	57,726
	2. New age structure, same total pop.	26,986	1.84%	42,559	1.10%	55,961
	3. Diff. from 1 (pure effect of pop. age structure)	-0.14%	0.01%	0.19%	-0.13%	-3.06%
	4. New age structure, new total population	27,015	1.89%	43,110	1.17%	57,661
	5. Diff. from 2 (pure effect of pop. size)	0.11%	0.05%	1.29%	0.07%	3.04%
	6. Diff. from 1 (sum of 3 and 5)	-0.03%	0.06%	1.49%	-0.06%	-0.11%
Health and long-term care (US$)	1. Base	2,742	2.38%	4,941	1.37%	6,942
	2. New age structure, same total pop.	2,738	2.49%	5,068	1.47%	7,303
	3. Diff. from 1 (pure effect of pop. age structure)	-0.16%	0.11%	2.59%	0.10%	5.19%
	4. New age structure, new total population	2,740	2.54%	5,132	1.54%	7,522
	5. Diff. from 2 (pure effect of pop. size)	0.06%	0.05%	1.26%	0.07%	3.01%
	6. Diff. from 1 (sum of 3 and 5)	-0.10%	0.16%	3.87%	0.17%	8.35%
Other (US$)	1. Base	24,281	1.76%	37,538	1.22%	50,784
	2. New age structure, same total pop.	24,248	1.76%	37,491	1.05%	48,658
	3. Diff. from 1 (pure effect of pop. age structure)	-0.13%	0.00%	-0.13%	-0.17%	-4.19%
	4. New age structure, new total population	24,276	1.81%	37,978	1.12%	50,139
	5. Diff. from 2 (pure effect of pop. size)	0.11%	0.05%	1.30%	0.07%	3.04%
	6. Diff. from 1 (sum of 3 and 5)	-0.02%	0.05%	1.17%	-0.10%	-1.27%
Saving rate (% of disposable income, unadjusted for changes in pension wealth)	1. Base	8.44%		7.20%		6.62%
	2. New age structure, same total pop.	8.48%		7.28%		6.52%
	3. Diff. from 1 (pure effect of pop. age structure)	0.05%		0.07%		-0.10%
	4. New age structure, new total population	8.44%		7.09%		6.07%
	5. Diff. from 2 (pure effect of pop. size)	-0.04%		-0.19%		-0.45%
	6. Diff. from 1 (sum of 3 and 5)	0.00%		-0.11%		-0.55%
Disposable income (billion US$)	1. Base	2,347	1.01%	3,015	0.25%	3,206
	2. New age structure, same total pop.	2,351	1.06%	3,056	-0.12%	2,964
	3. Diff. from 1 (pure effect of pop. age structure)	0.14%	0.05%	1.38%	-0.37%	-7.55%
	4. New age structure, new total population	2,347	0.88%	2,925	-0.46%	2,606
	5. Diff. from 2 (pure effect of pop. size)	-0.15%	-0.17%	-4.30%	-0.34%	-12.07%
	6. Diff. from 1 (sum of 3 and 5; total effect)	-0.01%	-0.12%	-2.98%	-0.71%	-18.72%
Savings (billion US$, unadjusted for changes in pension wealth)	1. Base	198	0.37%	217	-0.09%	212
	2. New age structure, same total pop.	199	0.44%	222	-0.56%	193
	3. Diff. from 1 (pure effect of pop. age structure)	0.69%	0.07%	2.44%	-0.47%	-9.00%
	4. New age structure, new total population	198	0.18%	207	-1.08%	158
	5. Diff. from 2 (pure effect of pop. size)	-0.67%	-0.25%	-6.77%	-0.51%	-18.10%
	6. Diff. from 1 (sum of 3 and 5)	0.01%	-0.18%	-4.50%	-0.99%	-25.47%

Note: Differences between percents are given in percentage points.

Table A4.2.3. *Continued.*

		2000	Average annual change	2025	Average annual change	2050
Savings per capita	1. Base	2,489	1.13%	3,297	0.87%	4,093
(US$, unadjusted	2. New age structure, same total pop.	2,501	1.16%	3,340	0.62%	3,902
for changes in	3. Diff. from 1 (pure effect of pop. age structure)	0.46%	0.03%	1.31%	-0.25%	-4.68%
pension wealth)	4. New age structure, new total population	2,489	1.12%	3,289	0.50%	3,727
	5. Diff. from 2 (pure effect of pop. size)	-0.46%	-0.04%	-1.52%	-0.12%	-4.48%
	6. Diff. from 1 (sum of 3 and 5)	0.00%	-0.01%	-0.23%	-0.37%	-8.95%
Adjusted disposable	1. Base	2,471	1.03%	3,191	0.31%	3,445
income	2. New age structure, same total pop.	2,474	1.08%	3,240	-0.02%	3,222
(billion US$)	3. Diff. from 1 (pure effect of pop. age structure)	0.14%	0.06%	1.52%	-0.33%	-6.46%
	4. New age structure, new total population	2,471	0.91%	3,100	-0.36%	2,832
	5. Diff. from 2 (pure effect of pop. size)	-0.16%	-0.17%	-4.32%	-0.34%	-12.11%
	6. Diff. from 1 (sum of 3 and 5; total effect)	-0.01%	-0.12%	-2.86%	-0.67%	-17.78%
Saving rate	1. Base	13.01%		12.33%		13.09%
(% of disposable	2. New age structure, same total pop.	13.06%		12.52%		14.01%
income, adjusted	3. Diff. from 1 (pure effect of pop. age structure)	0.05%		0.19%		0.92%
for changes in	4. New age structure, new total population	13.01%		12.33%		13.57%
pension wealth)	5. Diff. from 2 (pure effect of pop. size)	-0.04%		-0.19%		-0.44%
	6. Diff. from 1 (sum of 3 and 5)	0.00%		0.00%		0.48%
Savings	1. Base	321	0.81%	394	0.55%	451
(billion US$,	2. New age structure, same total pop.	323	0.92%	406	0.43%	452
adjusted for	3. Diff. from 1 (pure effect of pop. age structure)	0.50%	0.10%	3.10%	-0.12%	0.15%
changes in	4. New age structure, new total population	321	0.69%	382	0.02%	384
pension wealth)	5. Diff. from 2 (pure effect of pop. size)	-0.49%	-0.22%	-5.80%	-0.41%	-14.88%
	6. Diff. from 1 (sum of 3 and 5)	0.01%	-0.12%	-2.89%	-0.52%	-14.76%
Savings per capita	1. Base	4,041	1.58%	5,975	1.51%	8,694
(billion US$,	2. New age structure, same total pop.	4,052	1.64%	6,093	1.63%	9,120
adjusted for	3. Diff. from 1 (pure effect of pop. age structure)	0.27%	0.07%	1.97%	0.12%	4.90%
changes in	4. New age structure, new total population	4,041	1.64%	6,063	1.62%	9,053
pension wealth)	5. Diff. from 2 (pure effect of pop. size)	-0.27%	-0.01%	-0.50%	-0.01%	-0.73%
	6. Diff. from 1 (sum of 3 and 5)	-0.01%	0.06%	1.46%	0.11%	4.14%
Change in pension	1. Base	1,552		2,679		4,600
wealth per capita	2. New age structure, same total pop.	1,551		2,753		5,218
(US$)	3. Diff. from 1 (pure effect of pop. age structure)	-0.03%		2.77%		13.43%
	4. New age structure, new total population	1,552		2,773		5,327
	5. Diff. from 2 (pure effect of pop. size)	0.02%		0.74%		2.08%
	6. Diff. from 1 (sum of 3 and 5)	-0.01%		3.53%		15.78%

Note: Differences between percents are given in percentage points.

Table A4.2.4. Baseline (CCC) versus low-fertility alternative (LCC) scenario: Disposable income, consumption, and savings, population aged 60 and older.

		2000	Average annual change	2025	Average annual change	2050
Disposable income per capita (US$)	1. Base	37,655	-0.02%	37,426	1.44%	53,556
	2. New age structure, same total pop.	37,658	-0.03%	37,395	1.34%	52,168
	3. Diff. from 1 (pure effect of pop. age structure)	0.01%	0.00%	-0.08%	-0.10%	-2.59%
	4. New age structure, new total population	37,668	-0.01%	37,534	1.38%	52,881
	5. Diff. from 2 (pure effect of pop. size)	0.03%	0.01%	0.37%	0.04%	1.37%
	6. Diff. from 1 (sum of 3 and 5; total effect)	0.03%	0.01%	0.29%	-0.06%	-1.26%
Wages (US$)	1. Base	8,418	0.46%	9,447	1.05%	12,257
	2. New age structure, same total pop.	8,411	0.35%	9,170	0.78%	11,125
	3. Diff. from 1 (pure effect of pop. age structure)	-0.09%	-0.12%	-2.93%	-0.27%	-9.24%
	4. New age structure, new total population	8,418	0.39%	9,288	0.84%	11,459
	5. Diff. from 2 (pure effect of pop. size)	0.08%	0.05%	1.29%	0.07%	3.01%
	6. Diff. from 1 (sum of 3 and 5; total effect)	-0.01%	-0.07%	-1.68%	-0.20%	-6.51%
Entrepreneurial income, rents, dividends, interest, etc. (US$)	1. Base	7,338	-1.16%	5,485	0.30%	5,906
	2. New age structure, same total pop.	7,341	-1.15%	5,498	-0.08%	5,384
	3. Diff. from 1 (pure effect of pop. age structure)	0.05%	0.01%	0.24%	-0.38%	-8.85%
	4. New age structure, new total population	7,337	-1.31%	5,280	-0.37%	4,813
	5. Diff. from 2 (pure effect of pop. size)	-0.06%	-0.16%	-3.95%	-0.29%	-10.59%
	6. Diff. from 1 (sum of 3 and 5; total effect)	0.00%	-0.15%	-3.73%	-0.67%	-18.50%
Public pension benefits (US$)	1. Base	13,751	0.40%	15,201	1.68%	23,039
	2. New age structure, same total pop.	13,747	0.37%	15,088	1.65%	22,708
	3. Diff. from 1 (pure effect of pop. age structure)	-0.03%	-0.03%	-0.74%	-0.03%	-1.44%
	4. New age structure, new total population	13,751	0.41%	15,227	1.71%	23,271
	5. Diff. from 2 (pure effect of pop. size)	0.03%	0.04%	0.92%	0.06%	2.48%
	6. Diff. from 1 (sum of 3 and 5; total effect)	0.00%	0.01%	0.17%	0.03%	1.01%
Private DB pension benefits (US$)	1. Base	2,806	0.08%	2,861	1.67%	4,325
	2. New age structure, same total pop.	2,806	0.05%	2,838	1.62%	4,244
	3. Diff. from 1 (pure effect of pop. age structure)	-0.01%	-0.03%	-0.79%	-0.04%	-1.87%
	4. New age structure, new total population	2,806	0.07%	2,859	1.68%	4,338
	5. Diff. from 2 (pure effect of pop. size)	0.01%	0.03%	0.75%	0.06%	2.20%
	6. Diff. from 1 (sum of 3 and 5; total effect)	0.00%	0.00%	-0.05%	0.01%	0.29%
Private DC pension benefits (US$)	1. Base	233	2.13%	395	2.47%	727
	2. New age structure, same total pop.	233	2.13%	395	2.43%	719
	3. Diff. from 1 (pure effect of pop. age structure)	-0.02%	0.00%	0.08%	-0.04%	-1.00%
	4. New age structure, new total population	233	2.12%	394	2.43%	718
	5. Diff. from 2 (pure effect of pop. size)	0.02%	-0.01%	-0.19%	0.00%	-0.20%
	6. Diff. from 1 (sum of 3 and 5; total effect)	0.00%	0.00%	-0.11%	-0.04%	-1.20%
Health and long-term care benefits (US$)	1. Base	6,282	1.54%	9,212	1.52%	13,431
	2. New age structure, same total pop.	6,292	1.64%	9,444	1.45%	13,542
	3. Diff. from 1 (pure effect of pop. age structure)	0.15%	0.10%	2.52%	-0.07%	0.83%
	4. New age structure, new total population	6,296	1.69%	9,563	1.52%	13,950
	5. Diff. from 2 (pure effect of pop. size)	6.84%	0.05%	1.26%	0.07%	3.01%
	6. Diff. from 1 (sum of 3 and 5; total effect)	21.45%	0.14%	3.81%	0.00%	3.87%

Note: Differences between percents are given in percentage points.

Table A4.2.4. *Continued.*

		2000	Average annual change	2025	Average annual change	2050
Adjusted dispos-able income per capita (US$)	1. Base	35,020	-0.06%	34,499	1.42%	49,023
	2. New age structure, same total pop.	35,023	-0.06%	34,492	1.31%	47,758
	3. Diff. from 1 (pure effect of pop. age structure)	0.01%	0.00%	-0.02%	-0.11%	-2.58%
	4. New age structure, new total population	35,032	-0.05%	34,607	1.35%	48,374
	5. Diff. from 2 (pure effect of pop. size)	0.03%	0.01%	0.33%	0.04%	1.29%
	6. Diff. from 1 (sum of 3 and 5; total effect)	0.04%	0.01%	0.31%	-0.07%	-1.32%
Annuity income per capita (US$)	1. Base	6,101	2.05%	10,144	2.02%	16,740
	2. New age structure, same total pop.	6,096	1.94%	9,867	1.78%	15,328
	3. Diff. from 1 (pure effect of pop. age structure)	-0.07%	-0.11%	-2.73%	-0.25%	-8.43%
	4. New age structure, new total population	6,101	2.03%	10,093	1.93%	16,271
	5. Diff. from 2 (pure effect of pop. size)	0.07%	0.09%	2.29%	0.15%	6.15%
	6. Diff. from 1 (sum of 3 and 5; total effect)	0.00%	-0.02%	-0.50%	-0.10%	-2.80%
Consumption per capita (US$)	1. Base	40,509	0.35%	44,216	1.56%	65,143
	2. New age structure, same total pop.	40,500	0.34%	44,046	1.44%	63,036
	3. Diff. from 1 (pure effect of pop. age structure)	-0.02%	-0.01%	-0.38%	-0.12%	-3.24%
	4. New age structure, new total population	40,525	0.37%	44,453	1.51%	64,728
	5. Diff. from 2 (pure effect of pop. size)	6.29%	0.03%	0.92%	0.07%	2.68%
	6. Diff. from 1 (sum of 3 and 5)	3.93%	0.02%	0.54%	-0.05%	-0.64%
Health and long-term care (US$)	1. Base	7,853	1.54%	11,515	1.52%	16,788
	2. New age structure, same total pop.	7,865	1.64%	11,805	1.45%	16,927
	3. Diff. from 1 (pure effect of pop. age structure)	0.15%	0.10%	2.52%	-0.07%	0.83%
	4. New age structure, new total population	7,870	1.69%	11,954	1.52%	17,437
	5. Diff. from 2 (pure effect of pop. size)	6.84%	0.05%	1.26%	0.07%	3.01%
	6. Diff. from 1 (sum of 3 and 5)	21.45%	0.14%	3.81%	0.00%	3.87%
Other (US$)	1. Base	32,656	0.01%	32,700	1.58%	48,355
	2. New age structure, same total pop.	32,635	-0.05%	32,240	1.44%	46,109
	3. Diff. from 1 (pure effect of pop. age structure)	-0.06%	-0.05%	-1.41%	-0.14%	-4.65%
	4. New age structure, new total population	32,655	-0.02%	32,499	1.51%	47,290
	5. Diff. from 2 (pure effect of pop. size)	6.16%	0.03%	0.80%	0.07%	2.56%
	6. Diff. from 1 (sum of 3 and 5)	-0.28%	-0.02%	-0.61%	-0.07%	-2.20%
Saving rate (% of dispos-able income, unadjusted for changes in pension wealth)	1. Base	-7.58%		-18.14%		-21.64%
	2. New age structure, same total pop.	-7.55%		-17.78%		-20.83%
	3. Diff. from 1 (pure effect of pop. age structure)	0.03%		0.36%		0.80%
	4. New age structure, new total population	-7.59%		-18.44%		-22.40%
	5. Diff. from 2 (pure effect of pop. size)	-0.04%		-0.65%		-1.57%
	6. Diff. from 1 (sum of 3 and 5)	-0.01%		-0.29%		-0.77%
Disposable income (billion US$)	1. Base	1,040	1.33%	1,449	1.46%	2,080
	2. New age structure, same total pop.	1,043	1.54%	1,529	1.75%	2,362
	3. Diff. from 1 (pure effect of pop. age structure)	0.22%	0.21%	5.54%	0.30%	13.59%
	4. New age structure, new total population	1,040	1.33%	1,449	1.46%	2,080
	5. Diff. from 2 (pure effect of pop. size)	-0.22%	-0.21%	-5.25%	-0.30%	-11.96%
	6. Diff. from 1 (sum of 3 and 5; total effect)	0.00%	0.00%	0.00%	0.00%	0.00%

Note: Differences between percents are given in percentage points.

Table A4.2.4. *Continued.*

		2000	Average annual change	2025	Average annual change	2050
Savings	1. Base	-79	4.93%	-263	2.17%	-450
(billion US$,	2. New age structure, same total pop.	-79	5.09%	-272	2.40%	-492
unadjusted for	3. Diff. from 1 (pure effect of pop. age structure)	-0.21%	0.15%	3.47%	0.23%	9.37%
changes in	4. New age structure, new total population	-79	5.01%	-268	2.19%	-460
pension wealth)	5. Diff. from 2 (pure effect of pop. size)	0.33%	-0.08%	-1.50%	-0.22%	-6.55%
	6. Diff. from 1 (sum of 3 and 5)	0.12%	0.07%	1.92%	0.01%	2.21%
Savings per capita	1. Base	-2,854	3.53%	-6,789	2.16%	-11,587
(US$, unadjusted	2. New age structure, same total pop.	-2,842	3.46%	-6,650	1.98%	-10,868
for changes in	3. Diff. from 1 (pure effect of pop. age structure)	-0.42%	-0.07%	-2.05%	-0.18%	-6.21%
pension wealth)	4. New age structure, new total population	-2,857	3.60%	-6,919	2.17%	-11,846
	5. Diff. from 2 (pure effect of pop. size)	0.55%	0.14%	4.04%	0.19%	9.00%
	6. Diff. from 1 (sum of 3 and 5)	0.12%	0.07%	1.92%	0.01%	2.24%
Adjusted dispos-	1. Base	968	1.30%	1335	1.43%	1904
able income	2. New age structure, same total pop.	970	1.51%	1,410	1.72%	2,162
(billion US$)	3. Diff. from 1 (pure effect of pop. age structure)	0.23%	0.21%	5.61%	0.30%	13.60%
	4. New age structure, new total population	968	1.31%	1,340	1.36%	1,878
	5. Diff. from 2 (pure effect of pop. size)	-0.19%	-0.20%	-5.02%	-0.36%	-13.16%
	6. Diff. from 1 (sum of 3 and 5; total effect)	0.04%	0.01%	0.31%	-0.07%	-1.35%
Saving rate	1. Base	-15.67%		-28.16%		-32.88%
(% of disposable	2. New age structure, same total pop.	-15.64%		-27.70%		-31.99%
income, adjusted	3. Diff. from 1 (pure effect of pop. age structure)	0.04%		0.46%		0.89%
for changes in	4. New age structure, new total population	-15.68%		-28.45%		-33.81%
pension wealth)	5. Diff. from 2 (pure effect of pop. size)	-0.04%		-0.75%		-1.82%
	6. Diff. from 1 (sum of 3 and 5)	0.00%		-0.29%		-0.93%
Savings	1. Base	-152	3.70%	-376	2.06%	-626
(billion US$,	2. New age structure, same total pop.	-152	3.86%	-391	2.31%	-692
adjusted for	3. Diff. from 1 (pure effect of pop. age structure)	-0.01%	0.16%	3.87%	0.25%	10.52%
changes in	4. New age structure, new total population	-152	3.75%	-381	2.06%	-635
pension wealth)	5. Diff. from 2 (pure effect of pop. size)	0.07%	-0.11%	-2.43%	-0.25%	-8.23%
	6. Diff. from 1 (sum of 3 and 5)	0.06%	0.05%	1.34%	0.00%	1.43%
Savings per capita	1. Base	-5,489	2.31%	-9,717	2.05%	-16,120
(US$, adjusted	2. New age structure, same total pop.	-5,477	2.25%	-9,554	1.90%	-15,278
for changes in	3. Diff. from 1 (pure effect of pop. age structure)	-0.23%	-0.06%	-1.67%	-0.15%	-5.23%
pension wealth)	4. New age structure, new total population	-5,493	2.36%	-9,847	2.05%	-16,354
	5. Diff. from 2 (pure effect of pop. size)	0.29%	0.11%	3.06%	0.15%	7.05%
	6. Diff. from 1 (sum of 3 and 5)	0.06%	0.05%	1.34%	0.00%	1.45%
Change in pension	1. Base	-2,635		-2,927		-4,533
wealth per capita	2. New age structure, same total pop.	-2,635		-2,904		-4,410
(US$)	3. Diff. from 1 (pure effect of pop. age structure)	-0.02%		-0.80%		-2.72%
	4. New age structure, new total population	-2,635		-2,927		-4,508
	5. Diff. from 2 (pure effect of pop. size)	0.02%		0.80%		2.22%
	6. Diff. from 1 (sum of 3 and 5)	0.00%		0.00%		-0.56%

Note: Differences between percents are given in percentage points.

Table A4.2.5. Baseline (CCC) versus low-fertility alternative (LCC) scenario: Distribution (%).

		2000	2025	2050
Disposable income per capita (pop. 60+ : pop. 15–59)	1. Base	127.6%	81.8%	86.6%
	2. New age structure, same total pop.	127.7%	81.5%	87.1%
	3. Diff. from 1 (pure effect of pop. age structure)	0.1%	-0.3%	0.5%
	4. New age structure, new total population	127.7%	80.9%	86.1%
	5. Diff. from 2 (pure effect of pop. size)	0.0%	-0.6%	-1.0%
	6. Diff. from 1 (sum of 3 and 5)	0.1%	-0.9%	-0.5%
Consumption per capita (pop. 60+ : pop. 15–59)	1. Base	149.9%	104.1%	112.8%
	2. New age structure, same total pop.	150.1%	103.5%	112.6%
	3. Diff. from 1 (pure effect of pop. age structure)	0.2%	-0.6%	-0.2%
	4. New age structure, new total population	150.0%	103.1%	112.3%
	5. Diff. from 2 (pure effect of pop. size)	-0.1%	-0.4%	-0.4%
	6. Diff. from 1 (sum of 3 and 5)	0.1%	-1.0%	-0.6%
Excluding health and long-term care	1. Base	134.5%	87.1%	95.2%
	2. New age structure, same total pop.	134.6%	86.0%	94.8%
	3. Diff. from 1 (pure effect of pop. age structure)	0.1%	-1.1%	-0.5%
	4. New age structure, new total population	134.5%	85.6%	94.3%
	5. Diff. from 2 (pure effect of pop. size)	-0.1%	-0.4%	-0.4%
	6. Diff. from 1 (sum of 3 and 5)	0.0%	-1.5%	-0.9%

Note: Differences between percents are given in percentage points.

Table A4.2.6. Baseline (CCC) versus low-fertility alternative (LCC) scenario: Assets (US$).

		2000	Average annual change	2025	Average annual change	2050
Assets per capita	1. Base	99,323	2.62%	189,717	1.49%	274,916
(pop. 15–59)	2. New age structure, same total pop.	99,093	2.59%	187,591	1.44%	268,128
	3. Diff. from 1 (pure effect of pop. age structure)	-0.23%	-0.04%	-1.12%	-0.06%	-2.47%
	4. New age structure, new total population	99,311	2.78%	197,055	1.73%	302,544
	5. Diff. from 2 (pure effect of pop. size)	0.22%	0.19%	5.05%	0.29%	12.84%
	6. Diff. from 1 (sum of 3 and 5; total effect)	-0.01%	0.16%	3.87%	0.23%	10.05%
Private DC	1. Base	5,157	3.87%	13,323	1.56%	19,622
pension system	2. New age structure, same total pop.	5,150	4.00%	13,735	1.78%	21,333
assets	3. Diff. from 1 (pure effect of pop. age structure)	-0.13%	0.13%	3.09%	0.22%	8.72%
	4. New age structure, new total population	5,156	4.03%	13,847	1.83%	21,783
	5. Diff. from 2 (pure effect of pop. size)	0.12%	0.03%	0.81%	0.05%	2.11%
	6. Diff. from 1 (sum of 3 and 5; total effect)	-0.01%	0.16%	3.93%	0.27%	11.01%
Private DB	1. Base	3,091	-2.70%	1,560	1.97%	2,540
pension system	2. New age structure, same total pop.	3,084	-2.72%	1,548	2.80%	3,084
assets	3. Diff. from 1 (pure effect of pop. age structure)	-0.22%	-0.02%	-0.78%	0.83%	21.42%
	4. New age structure, new total population	3,091	-2.53%	1,629	2.42%	2,960
	5. Diff. from 2 (pure effect of pop. size)	0.21%	0.19%	5.20%	-0.38%	-4.03%
	6. Diff. from 1 (sum of 3 and 5; total effect)	-0.01%	0.17%	4.38%	0.45%	16.53%
Non-pension	1. Base	91,075	2.64%	174,834	1.49%	252,753
wealth	2. New age structure, same total pop.	90,858	2.59%	172,308	1.40%	243,711
	3. Diff. from 1 (pure effect of pop. age structure)	-0.24%	-0.05%	-1.44%	-0.09%	-3.58%
	4. New age structure, new total population	91,064	2.80%	181,580	1.72%	277,801
	5. Diff. from 2 (pure effect of pop. size)	0.23%	0.21%	5.38%	0.32%	13.99%
	6. Diff. from 1 (sum of 3 and 5; total effect)	-0.01%	0.16%	3.86%	0.23%	9.91%
Assets per capita	1. Base	202,026	1.15%	269,182	1.68%	408,315
(pop. 60+)	2. New age structure, same total pop.	201,671	1.04%	261,495	1.43%	372,880
	3. Diff. from 1 (pure effect of pop. age structure)	-0.18%	-0.11%	-2.86%	-0.25%	-8.68%
	4. New age structure, new total population	202,024	1.14%	268,090	1.59%	397,818
	5. Diff. from 2 (pure effect of pop. size)	0.17%	0.09%	2.52%	0.16%	6.69%
	6. Diff. from 1 (sum of 3 and 5; total effect)	0.00%	-0.02%	-0.41%	-0.09%	-2.57%
Private DC	1. Base	7,095	1.70%	10,817	2.19%	18,601
pension system	2. New age structure, same total pop.	7,086	1.70%	10,790	2.13%	18,288
assets	3. Diff. from 1 (pure effect of pop. age structure)	-0.13%	-0.01%	-0.25%	-0.06%	-1.68%
	4. New age structure, new total population	7,095	1.70%	10,807	2.15%	18,387
	5. Diff. from 2 (pure effect of pop. size)	0.13%	0.00%	0.16%	0.02%	0.54%
	6. Diff. from 1 (sum of 3 and 5; total effect)	0.00%	0.00%	-0.09%	-0.04%	-1.15%
Private DB	1. Base	8,787	1.42%	12,490	0.39%	13,764
pension system	2. New age structure, same total pop.	8,768	1.22%	11,878	0.05%	12,015
assets	3. Diff. from 1 (pure effect of pop. age structure)	-0.22%	-0.20%	-4.91%	-0.34%	-12.71%
	4. New age structure, new total population	8,787	1.41%	12,483	0.39%	13,750
	5. Diff. from 2 (pure effect of pop. size)	0.22%	0.19%	5.10%	0.34%	14.44%
	6. Diff. from 1 (sum of 3 and 5; total effect)	0.00%	0.00%	-0.06%	0.00%	-0.10%
Non-pension	1. Base	186,144	1.12%	245,874	1.71%	375,951
wealth	2. New age structure, same total pop.	185,817	1.01%	238,827	1.45%	342,577
	3. Diff. from 1 (pure effect of pop. age structure)	-0.18%	-0.11%	-2.87%	-0.26%	-8.88%
	4. New age structure, new total population	186,142	1.10%	244,800	1.62%	365,680
	5. Diff. from 2 (pure effect of pop. size)	0.17%	0.09%	2.50%	0.16%	6.74%
	6. Diff. from 1 (sum of 3 and 5; total effect)	0.00%	-0.02%	-0.44%	-0.09%	-2.73%

Note: Differences between percents are given in percentage points.

Table A4.2.7. Baseline (CCC) versus low-fertility alternative (LCC) scenario: Public pension, health, and long-term care expenditure.

		2000	Average annual change	2025	Average annual change	2050
Public pension	1. Base	420.6	1.74%	647.3	1.69%	983.5
system benefits /	2. New age structure, same total pop.	421.4	1.92%	678.6	2.06%	1130.0
contributions	3. Diff. from 1 (pure effect of pop. age structure)	0.19%	0.18%	4.84%	0.37%	14.89%
(billion US$)	4. New age structure, new total population	420.6	1.75%	648.3	1.72%	992.6
	5. Diff. from 2 (pure effect of pop. size)	-0.19%	-0.18%	-4.47%	-0.34%	-12.16%
	6. Diff. from 1 (sum of 3 and 5; total effect)	0.00%	0.01%	0.15%	0.03%	0.93%
% of GDP	1. Base	8.42%		9.32%		11.71%
	2. New age structure, same total pop.	8.43%		9.53%		13.34%
	3. Diff. from 1 (pure effect of pop. age structure)	0.00%		0.21%		1.64%
	4. New age structure, new total population	8.42%		9.49%		13.27%
	5. Diff. from 2 (pure effect of pop. size)	0.00%		-0.03%		-0.07%
	6. Diff. from 1 (sum of 3 and 5; total effect)	0.00%		0.18%		1.56%
Public pension	1. Base	22.56%		25.47%		32.26%
contribution rate	2. New age structure, same total pop.	22.57%		26.03%		36.76%
(%)	3. Diff. from 1 (pure effect of pop. age structure)	0.01%		0.56%		4.50%
	4. New age structure, new total population	22.56%		25.98%		36.71%
	5. Diff. from 2 (pure effect of pop. size)	-0.01%		-0.05%		-0.06%
	6. Diff. from 1 (sum of 3 and 5; total effect)	0.00%		0.51%		4.45%
Health system	1. Base	261.1	2.32%	462.7	1.09%	607.1
benefits /	2. New age structure, same total pop.	261.6	2.56%	492.1	1.28%	676.8
contributions	3. Diff. from 1 (pure effect of pop. age structure)	0.21%	0.24%	6.36%	0.19%	11.47%
(billion US$)	4. New age structure, new total population	261.2	2.39%	471.8	0.95%	597.7
	5. Diff. from 2 (pure effect of pop. size)	-0.15%	-0.17%	-4.14%	-0.33%	-11.68%
	6. Diff. from 1 (sum of 3 and 5)	0.07%	0.08%	1.96%	-0.14%	-1.55%
% of GDP	1. Base	5.23%		6.66%		7.23%
	2. New age structure, same total pop.	5.23%		6.91%		7.99%
	3. Diff. from 1 (pure effect of pop. age structure)	0.00%		0.25%		0.76%
	4. New age structure, new total population	5.23%		6.91%		7.99%
	5. Diff. from 2 (pure effect of pop. size)	0.00%		0.00%		0.00%
	6. Diff. from 1 (sum of 3 and 5; total effect)	0.00%		0.25%		0.76%
Health care	1. Base	7.28%		9.47%		10.36%
contribution rate	2. New age structure, same total pop.	7.29%		9.82%		11.45%
(%)	3. Diff. from 1 (pure effect of pop. age structure)	0.00%		0.35%		1.09%
	4. New age structure, new total population	7.29%		9.83%		11.49%
	5. Diff. from 2 (pure effect of pop. size)	0.00%		0.02%		0.04%
	6. Diff. from 1 (sum of 3 and 5)	0.00%		0.36%		1.14%
Long-term care	1. Base	87.0	2.32%	154.2	1.09%	202.4
system contri-	2. New age structure, same total pop.	87.2	2.56%	164.0	1.28%	225.6
butions / benefits	3. Diff. from 1 (pure effect of pop. age structure)	0.21%	0.24%	6.36%	0.19%	11.47%
(billion US$)	4. New age structure, new total population	87.1	2.39%	157.3	0.95%	199.2
	5. Diff. from 2 (pure effect of pop. size)	-0.15%	-0.17%	-4.14%	-0.33%	-11.68%
	6. Diff. from 1 (sum of 3 and 5)	0.07%	0.08%	1.96%	-0.14%	-1.55%
% of GDP	1. Base	1.74%		2.22%		2.41%
	2. New age structure, same total pop.	1.74%		2.16%		2.39%
	3. Diff. from 1 (pure effect of pop. age structure)	0.00%		-0.05%		-0.02%
	4. New age structure, new total population	1.74%		2.26%		2.71%
	5. Diff. from 2 (pure effect of pop. size)	0.00%		0.09%		0.32%
	6. Diff. from 1 (sum of 3 and 5)	0.00%		0.04%		0.30%

Note: Differences between percents are given in percentage points.

Table A4.2.7. *Continued.*

		2000	Average annual change	2025	Average annual change	2050
Long-term care contribution rate (%)	1. Base	2.43%		3.16%		3.45%
	2. New age structure, same total pop.	2.43%		3.27%		3.82%
	3. Diff. from 1 (pure effect of pop. age structure)	0.00%		0.12%		0.37%
	4. New age structure, new total population	2.43%		3.28%		3.83%
	5. Diff. from 2 (pure effect of pop. size)	0.00%		0.01%		0.01%
	6. Diff. from 1 (sum of 3 and 5)	0.00%		0.12%		0.38%

Note: Differences between percents are given in percentage points.

The Economic Impacts of Population Ageing in Japan

Table A4.2.8. Baseline (CCC) versus low-fertility alternative (LCC) scenario: Health care expenditure.

		2000	Average annual changes	2025	Average annual changes	2050
Health system expenditure (US$ per capita)	1. Base	2,610	2.48%	4,812	1.65%	7,249
	2. New age structure, same total pop.	2,616	2.72%	5,118	1.84%	8,080
	3. Diff. from 1 (pure effect of pop. age structure)	0.21%	0.24%	6.36%	0.19%	11.47%
	4. New age structure, new total population	2,617	2.77%	5,182	1.91%	8,323
	5. Diff. from 2 (pure effect of pop. size)	0.07%	0.05%	1.25%	0.07%	3.01%
	6. Diff. from 1 (sum of 3 and 5; total effect)	0.28%	0.29%	7.69%	0.26%	14.82%
Population aged 0–59	1. Base	1,680	2.34%	2,995	1.26%	4,099
	2. New age structure, same total pop.	1,682	2.60%	3,192	1.44%	4,564
	3. Diff. from 1 (pure effect of pop. age structure)	0.13%	0.26%	6.57%	0.18%	11.33%
	4. New age structure, new total population	1,683	2.64%	3,232	1.51%	4,700
	5. Diff. from 2 (pure effect of pop. size)	0.07%	0.05%	1.25%	0.07%	3.00%
	6. Diff. from 1 (sum of 3 and 5; total effect)	0.19%	0.30%	7.90%	0.25%	14.67%
Population aged 60+	1. Base	5,890	1.54%	8,636	1.52%	12,591
	2. New age structure, same total pop.	5,898	1.64%	8,854	1.45%	12,695
	3. Diff. from 1 (pure effect of pop. age structure)	0.15%	0.10%	2.52%	-0.07%	0.83%
	4. New age structure, new total population	5,902	1.69%	8,965	1.52%	13,078
	5. Diff. from 2 (pure effect of pop. size)	0.07%	0.05%	1.26%	0.07%	3.01%
	6. Diff. from 1 (sum of 3 and 5; total effect)	0.21%	0.14%	3.81%	0.00%	3.87%
Health system expenditure (billion US$)	1. Base	326	2.32%	578	1.09%	759
	2. New age structure, same total pop.	327	2.56%	615	1.28%	846
	3. Diff. from 1 (pure effect of pop. age structure)	0.21%	0.24%	6.36%	0.19%	11.47%
	4. New age structure, new total population	327	2.39%	590	0.95%	747
	5. Diff. from 2 (pure effect of pop. size)	-0.15%	-0.17%	-4.14%	-0.33%	-11.68%
	6. Diff. from 1 (sum of 3 and 5; total effect)	0.07%	0.08%	1.96%	-0.14%	-1.55%
Population aged 0–59	1. Base	164	1.61%	244	0.41%	270
	2. New age structure, same total pop.	164	1.76%	253	0.28%	271
	3. Diff. from 1 (pure effect of pop. age structure)	0.07%	0.15%	3.72%	-0.13%	0.43%
	4. New age structure, new total population	163	1.59%	243	-0.05%	239
	5. Diff. from 2 (pure effect of pop. size)	-0.15%	-0.17%	-4.14%	-0.33%	-11.68%
	6. Diff. from 1 (sum of 3 and 5; total effect)	-0.08%	-0.02%	-0.57%	-0.46%	-11.31%
Population aged 60+	1. Base	163	2.92%	334	1.53%	489
	2. New age structure, same total pop.	163	3.24%	362	1.87%	575
	3. Diff. from 1 (pure effect of pop. age structure)	0.36%	0.31%	8.29%	0.33%	17.57%
	4. New age structure, new total population	163	3.07%	347	1.53%	508
	5. Diff. from 2 (pure effect of pop. size)	-0.15%	-0.17%	-4.14%	-0.33%	-11.68%
	6. Diff. from 1 (sum of 3 and 5; total effect)	0.21%	0.15%	3.81%	0.00%	3.84%
Health system expenditure (% of GDP)	1. Base	6.53%		8.32%		9.03%
	2. New age structure, same total pop.	6.54%		8.63%		9.99%
	3. Diff. from 1 (pure effect of pop. age structure)	0.00%		0.31%		0.96%
	4. New age structure, new total population	6.54%		8.63%		9.99%
	5. Diff. from 2 (pure effect of pop. size)	0.00%		0.00%		0.00%
	6. Diff. from 1 (sum of 3 and 5; total effect)	0.00%		0.31%		0.96%

Note: Differences between percents are given in percentage points.

Table A4.2.9. Baseline (CCC) versus low-fertility alternative (LCC) scenario: Long-term care expenditure.

		2000	Average annual change	2025	Average annual change	2050
Long-term care expenditure (US$ per capita)	1. Base	870	2.48%	1,604	1.65%	2,416
	2. New age structure, same total pop.	872	2.72%	1,706	1.84%	2,693
	3. Diff. from 1 (pure effect of pop. age structure)	0.21%	0.24%	6.36%	0.19%	11.47%
	4. New age structure, new total population	872	2.77%	1,727	1.91%	2,774
	5. Diff. from 2 (pure effect of pop. size)	0.07%	0.05%	1.25%	0.07%	3.01%
	6. Diff. from 1 (sum of 3 and 5; total effect)	0.28%	0.29%	7.69%	0.26%	14.82%
Population aged 0–59	1. Base	560	2.34%	998	1.26%	1,366
	2. New age structure, same total pop.	561	2.60%	1,064	1.44%	1,521
	3. Diff. from 1 (pure effect of pop. age structure)	0.13%	0.26%	6.57%	0.18%	11.33%
	4. New age structure, new total population	561	2.64%	1,077	1.51%	1,567
	5. Diff. from 2 (pure effect of pop. size)	0.07%	0.05%	1.25%	0.07%	3.00%
	6. Diff. from 1 (sum of 3 and 5; total effect)	0.19%	0.30%	7.90%	0.25%	14.67%
Population aged 60+	1. Base	1,963	1.54%	2,879	1.52%	4,197
	2. New age structure, same total pop.	1,966	1.64%	2,951	1.45%	4,232
	3. Diff. from 1 (pure effect of pop. age structure)	0.15%	0.10%	2.52%	-0.07%	0.83%
	4. New age structure, new total population	1,967	1.69%	2,988	1.52%	4,359
	5. Diff. from 2 (pure effect of pop. size)	0.07%	0.05%	1.26%	0.07%	3.01%
	6. Diff. from 1 (sum of 3 and 5; total effect)	0.21%	0.14%	3.81%	0.00%	3.87%
Long-term care expenditure (billion US$)	1. Base	109	2.32%	193	1.09%	253
	2. New age structure, same total pop.	109	2.56%	205	1.28%	282
	3. Diff. from 1 (pure effect of pop. age structure)	0.21%	0.24%	6.36%	0.19%	11.47%
	4. New age structure, new total population	109	2.39%	197	0.95%	249
	5. Diff. from 2 (pure effect of pop. size)	-0.15%	-0.17%	-4.14%	-0.33%	-11.68%
	6. Diff. from 1 (sum of 3 and 5; total effect)	0.07%	0.08%	1.96%	-0.14%	-1.55%
Population aged 0–59	1. Base	54	1.61%	81	0.41%	90
	2. New age structure, same total pop.	55	1.76%	84	0.28%	90
	3. Diff. from 1 (pure effect of pop. age structure)	0.07%	0.15%	3.72%	-0.13%	0.43%
	4. New age structure, new total population	54	1.59%	81	-0.05%	80
	5. Diff. from 2 (pure effect of pop. size)	-0.15%	-0.17%	-4.14%	-0.33%	-11.68%
	6. Diff. from 1 (sum of 3 and 5; total effect)	-0.08%	-0.02%	-0.57%	-0.46%	-11.31%
Population aged 60+	1. Base	54	2.92%	111	1.53%	163
	2. New age structure, same total pop.	54	3.24%	121	1.87%	192
	3. Diff. from 1 (pure effect of pop. age structure)	0.36%	0.31%	8.29%	0.33%	17.57%
	4. New age structure, new total population	54	3.07%	116	1.53%	169
	5. Diff. from 2 (pure effect of pop. size)	-0.15%	-0.17%	-4.14%	-0.33%	-11.68%
	6. Diff. from 1 (sum of 3 and 5; total effect)	0.21%	0.15%	3.81%	0.00%	3.84%
Long-term care expenditure (% of GDP)	1. Base	1.74%		2.22%		2.41%
	2. New age structure, same total pop.	1.74%		2.30%		2.66%
	3. Diff. from 1 (pure effect of pop. age structure)	0.00%		0.08%		0.25%
	4. New age structure, new total population	1.74%		2.30%		2.66%
	5. Diff. from 2 (pure effect of pop. size)	0.00%		0.00%		0.00%
	6. Diff. from 1 (sum of 3 and 5; total effect)	0.00%		0.08%		0.25%

Note: Differences between percents are given in percentage points.

Table A4.2.10. Baseline (CCC) versus low-fertility alternative (LCC) scenario: Global summary.

			2000	2025	2050
GDP per capita (US$)	Japan	Base	39,943	57,813	80,249
		Alternative	40,028	60,015	83,325
		Difference	0.21%	3.81%	3.83%
	United States	Base	31,144	44,287	62,198
		Alternative	31,242	46,176	64,393
		Difference	0.31%	4.26%	3.53%
	Other Industrial Countries	Base	27,791	42,710	58,591
		Alternative	27,855	44,213	59,629
		Difference	0.23%	3.52%	1.77%
	LDCs	Base	2,266	3,686	5,389
		Alternative	2,273	3,887	5,807
		Difference	0.27%	5.47%	7.76%
	World	Base	7,257	9,340	11,726
		Alternative	7,277	9,806	12,540
		Difference	0.27%	4.99%	6.95%
GNP per capita (US$)	Japan	Base	40,228	58,602	81,481
		Alternative	40,315	60,827	84,591
		Difference	0.21%	3.80%	3.82%
	United States	Base	31,233	44,433	62,456
		Alternative	31,331	46,329	64,650
		Difference	0.31%	4.27%	3.51%
	Other Industrial Countries	Base	27,869	42,986	59,042
		Alternative	27,933	44,500	60,102
		Difference	0.23%	3.52%	1.79%
	LDCs	Base	2,244	3,639	5,330
		Alternative	2,250	3,838	5,743
		Difference	0.27%	5.47%	7.75%
Net factor income from abroad (billion US$)	Japan	Base	36	95	129
		Alternative	36	92	114
		Difference	0	-2	-15
	United States	Base	24	47	89
		Alternative	24	46	74
		Difference	0	-1	-15
	Other Industrial Countries	Base	61	212	318
		Alternative	61	208	283
		Difference	0	-4	-35
	LDCs	Base	-120	-353	-536
		Alternative	-120	-346	-470
		Difference	0	7	66

Note: Differences between percents are given in percentage points; LDCs = Less Developed Countries.

Table A4.2.10. *Continued.*

			2000	2025	2050
Net foreign assets (billion US$)	Japan	Base	317	670	678
		Alternative	317	666	653
		Difference	0	-4	-26
	United States	Base	49	117	528
		Alternative	49	110	433
		Difference	0	-7	-95
	Other Industrial Countries	Base	384	1,461	2,177
		Alternative	384	1,449	2,029
		Difference	0	-12	-148
	LDCs	Base	-750	-2,248	-3,383
		Alternative	-750	-2,225	-3,115
		Difference	0	22	268
Acquisition of gross foreign assets (billion US$)	Japan	Base	295	282	166
		Alternative	295	269	84
		Difference	0	-13	-82
	United States	Base	397	597	645
		Alternative	397	564	422
		Difference	0	-33	-224
	Other Industrial Countries	Base	1,482	1,765	1,091
		Alternative	1,482	1,671	566
		Difference	0	-95	-525
	LDCs	Base	615	1,142	1,200
		Alternative	616	1,098	828
		Difference	1	-44	-373
Sales of domestic assets to rest of world (billion US$)	Japan	Base	277	276	173
		Alternative	277	263	92
		Difference	0	-13	-81
	United States	Base	402	586	616
		Alternative	403	554	400
		Difference	0	-33	-216
	Other Industrial Countries	Base	1,452	1,714	1,080
		Alternative	1,452	1,622	565
		Difference	0	-92	-515
	LDCs	Base	658	1,210	1,234
		Alternative	659	1,163	843
		Difference	1	-48	-391
Change in net foreign assets (billion US$)	Japan	Base	19	6	-7
		Alternative	19	6	-8
		Difference	0	0	-1
	United States	Base	-6	11	29
		Alternative	-6	10	22
		Difference	0	-1	-8
	Other Industrial Countries	Base	30	51	11
		Alternative	30	48	1
		Difference	0	-3	-10
	LDCs	Base	-43	-68	-34
		Alternative	-43	-64	-15
		Difference	0	4	18

Note: Differences between percents are given in percentage points; LDCs = Less Developed Countries.

Annex 4.3: CCC versus CLC

Table A4.3.1. Baseline (CCC) versus low-mortality alternative (CLC) scenario: GDP, GNP, and rates of return to factors.

		2000	Average annual change	2025	Average annual change	2050
GDP per capita (US$)	1. Base	39,943	1.49%	57,813	1.32%	80,249
	2. New age structure, same total pop.	39,936	1.44%	57,040	1.19%	76,592
	3. Diff. from 1 (pure effect of pop. age structure)	-0.02%	-0.05%	-1.34%	-0.13%	-4.56%
	4. New age structure, new total population	39,925	1.41%	56,644	1.16%	75,622
	5. Diff. from 2 (pure effect of pop. size)	-0.03%	-0.03%	-0.69%	-0.02%	-1.27%
	6. Diff. from 1 (sum of 3 and 5)	-0.04%	-0.08%	-2.02%	-0.16%	-5.77%
GNP per capita (US$)	1. Base	40,228	1.52%	58,602	1.33%	81,481
	2. New age structure, same total pop.	40,221	1.46%	57,812	1.19%	77,730
	3. Diff. from 1 (pure effect of pop. age structure)	-0.02%	-0.05%	-1.35%	-0.14%	-4.60%
	4. New age structure, new total population	40,210	1.43%	57,404	1.17%	76,746
	5. Diff. from 2 (pure effect of pop. size)	-0.03%	-0.03%	-0.71%	-0.02%	-1.27%
	6. Diff. from 1 (sum of 3 and 5)	-0.04%	-0.08%	-2.04%	-0.16%	-5.81%
Net factor income from abroad per capita (US$)	1. Base	286	4.15%	789	1.80%	1,232
	2. New age structure, same total pop.	285	4.07%	773	1.56%	1,138
	3. Diff. from 1 (pure effect of pop. age structure)	-0.06%	-0.09%	-2.09%	-0.24%	-7.68%
	4. New age structure, new total population	285	4.00%	760	1.58%	1,124
	5. Diff. from 2 (pure effect of pop. size)	-0.08%	-0.06%	-1.63%	0.02%	-1.16%
	6. Diff. from 1 (sum of 3 and 5)	-0.14%	-0.15%	-3.68%	-0.22%	-8.76%
Capital-output ratio	1. Base	2.64	0.78%	3.20	0.36%	3.50
	2. New age structure, same total pop.	2.64	0.79%	3.21	0.31%	3.47
	3. Diff. from 1 (pure effect of pop. age structure)	0.02%	0.01%	0.27%	-0.05%	-0.89%
	4. New age structure, new total population	2.63	0.73%	3.16	0.27%	3.38
	5. Diff. from 2 (pure effect of pop. size)	-0.05%	-0.05%	-1.40%	-0.05%	-2.55%
	6. Diff. from 1 (sum of 3 and 5)	-0.04%	-0.04%	-1.14%	-0.09%	-3.42%
Average wage (US$)	1. Base	52,458	1.89%	83,673	1.62%	124,927
	2. New age structure, same total pop.	52,463	1.89%	83,784	1.59%	124,378
	3. Diff. from 1 (pure effect of pop. age structure)	0.01%	0.01%	0.13%	-0.02%	-0.44%
	4. New age structure, new total population	52,449	1.86%	83,203	1.57%	122,803
	5. Diff. from 2 (pure effect of pop. size)	-0.03%	-0.03%	-0.69%	-0.02%	-1.27%
	6. Diff. from 1 (sum of 3 and 5)	-0.02%	-0.02%	-0.56%	-0.05%	-1.70%
Rate of return to capital (net of indirect taxes and depreciation, %)	1. Base	5.62%		3.75%		2.99%
	2. New age structure, same total pop.	5.62%		3.72%		3.07%
	3. Diff. from 1 (pure effect of pop. age structure)	0.00%		-0.02%		0.07%
	4. New age structure, new total population	5.62%		3.85%		3.28%
	5. Diff. from 2 (pure effect of pop. size)	0.01%		0.12%		0.21%
	6. Diff. from 1 (sum of 3 and 5)	0.00%		0.10%		0.28%

Note: Differences between percents are given in percentage points.

Table A4.3.2. Baseline (CCC) versus low-mortality alternative (CLC) scenario: Saving rates (% of GDP).

		2000	2025	2050
Net savings	1. Base	7.21%	5.09%	2.63%
	2. New age structure, same total pop.	7.21%	4.75%	1.70%
	3. Diff. from 1 (pure effect of pop. age structure)	3.81%	-0.34%	-0.94%
	4. New age structure, new total population	7.22%	4.94%	2.00%
	5. Diff. from 2 (pure effect of pop. size)	0.01%	0.19%	0.30%
	6. Diff. from 1 (sum of 3 and 5)	3.82%	-0.15%	-0.64%
Households	1. Base	3.40%	0.25%	-2.08%
(adjusted for	2. New age structure, same total pop.	3.40%	-0.12%	-3.17%
change in	3. Diff. from 1 (pure effect of pop. age structure)	0.00%	-0.37%	-1.09%
pension wealth)	4. New age structure, new total population	3.40%	0.00%	-2.99%
	5. Diff. from 2 (pure effect of pop. size)	0.01%	0.12%	0.19%
	6. Diff. from 1 (sum of 3 and 5)	0.00%	-0.26%	-0.90%
Population	1. Base	6.44%	5.66%	5.37%
aged 15–59	2. New age structure, same total pop.	6.44%	5.67%	5.43%
	3. Diff. from 1 (pure effect of pop. age structure)	0.00%	0.01%	0.06%
	4. New age structure, new total population	6.45%	5.73%	5.49%
	5. Diff. from 2 (pure effect of pop. size)	0.01%	0.06%	0.06%
	6. Diff. from 1 (sum of 3 and 5)	0.01%	0.07%	0.12%
Population	1. Base	-3.04%	-5.41%	-7.45%
aged 60+	2. New age structure, same total pop.	-3.04%	-5.79%	-8.60%
	3. Diff. from 1 (pure effect of pop. age structure)	-0.01%	-0.38%	-1.15%
	4. New age structure, new total population	-3.04%	-5.73%	-8.48%
	5. Diff. from 2 (pure effect of pop. size)	0.00%	0.06%	0.13%
	6. Diff. from 1 (sum of 3 and 5)	0.00%	-0.32%	-1.03%
Firms	1. Base	4.40%	5.22%	4.98%
	2. New age structure, same total pop.	4.40%	5.19%	5.05%
	3. Diff. from 1 (pure effect of pop. age structure)	0.00%	-0.03%	0.07%
	4. New age structure, new total population	4.40%	5.28%	5.25%
	5. Diff. from 2 (pure effect of pop. size)	0.00%	0.08%	0.20%
	6. Diff. from 1 (sum of 3 and 5)	0.00%	0.05%	0.27%
Government	1. Base	-0.59%	-0.38%	-0.26%
	2. New age structure, same total pop.	-0.59%	-0.32%	-0.18%
	3. Diff. from 1 (pure effect of pop. age structure)	0.00%	0.06%	0.08%
	4. New age structure, new total population	-0.58%	-0.33%	-0.26%
	5. Diff. from 2 (pure effect of pop. size)	0.00%	-0.01%	-0.09%
	6. Diff. from 1 (sum of 3 and 5)	0.00%	0.05%	0.00%

Note: Differences between percents are given in percentage points.

Table A4.3.3. Baseline (CCC) versus low-mortality alternative (CLC) scenario: Disposable income, consumption, and savings, population aged 15–59.

		2000	Average annual change	2025	Average annual change	2050
Disposable income per capita (US$)	1. Base	29,513	1.77%	45,775	1.21%	61,819
	2. New age structure, same total pop.	29,499	1.69%	44,820	0.99%	57,274
	3. Diff. from 1 (pure effect of pop. age structure)	-0.05%	-0.08%	-2.09%	-0.22%	-7.35%
	4. New age structure, new total population	29,492	1.66%	44,539	0.97%	56,644
	5. Diff. from 2 (pure effect of pop. size)	-0.02%	-0.02%	-0.63%	-0.02%	-1.10%
	6. Diff. from 1 (sum of 3 and 5; total effect)	-0.07%	-0.11%	-2.70%	-0.24%	-8.37%
Wages (US$)	1. Base	23,526	1.68%	35,696	1.23%	48,417
	2. New age structure, same total pop.	23,514	1.59%	34,904	0.99%	44,641
	3. Diff. from 1 (pure effect of pop. age structure)	-0.05%	-0.09%	-2.22%	-0.24%	-7.80%
	4. New age structure, new total population	23,508	1.56%	34,648	0.97%	44,086
	5. Diff. from 2 (pure effect of pop. size)	-0.03%	-0.03%	-0.73%	-0.02%	-1.24%
	6. Diff. from 1 (sum of 3 and 5; total effect)	-0.08%	-0.12%	-2.94%	-0.26%	-8.95%
Entrepreneurial income, rents, dividends, interest, etc. (US$)	1. Base	3,385	-0.37%	3,086	0.22%	3,259
	2. New age structure, same total pop.	3,383	-0.52%	2,973	-0.04%	2,945
	3. Diff. from 1 (pure effect of pop. age structure)	-0.07%	-0.15%	-3.65%	-0.26%	-9.64%
	4. New age structure, new total population	3,383	-0.49%	2,990	-0.02%	2,975
	5. Diff. from 2 (pure effect of pop. size)	0.01%	0.02%	0.57%	0.02%	1.03%
	6. Diff. from 1 (sum of 3 and 5; total effect)	-0.06%	-0.12%	-3.10%	-0.24%	-8.70%
Health and long-term care benefits (US$)	1. Base	2,194	2.38%	3,952	1.37%	5,554
	2. New age structure, same total pop.	2,194	2.35%	3,917	1.24%	5,335
	3. Diff. from 1 (pure effect of pop. age structure)	-0.01%	-0.04%	-0.89%	-0.13%	-3.93%
	4. New age structure, new total population	2,193	2.32%	3,890	1.22%	5,267
	5. Diff. from 2 (pure effect of pop. size)	-0.03%	-0.03%	-0.70%	-0.02%	-1.27%
	6. Diff. from 1 (sum of 3 and 5; total effect)	-0.03%	-0.06%	-1.58%	-0.15%	-5.16%
Adjusted disposable income per capita (US$)	1. Base	31,065	1.79%	48,454	1.27%	66,419
	2. New age structure, same total pop.	31,053	1.73%	47,624	1.08%	62,344
	3. Diff. from 1 (pure effect of pop. age structure)	-0.04%	-0.07%	-1.71%	-0.19%	-6.14%
	4. New age structure, new total population	31,045	1.70%	47,332	1.06%	61,665
	5. Diff. from 2 (pure effect of pop. size)	-0.02%	-0.02%	-0.61%	-0.02%	-1.09%
	6. Diff. from 1 (sum of 3 and 5; total effect)	-0.06%	-0.09%	-2.31%	-0.21%	-7.16%
Early withdrawals from private DC pension system, per capita (US$)	1. Base	150	3.14%	325	1.42%	462
	2. New age structure, same total pop.	150	3.16%	326	1.42%	463
	3. Diff. from 1 (pure effect of pop. age structure)	0.01%	0.01%	0.34%	0.00%	0.35%
	4. New age structure, new total population	150	3.14%	325	1.40%	459
	5. Diff. from 2 (pure effect of pop. size)	0.00%	-0.01%	-0.29%	-0.02%	-0.83%
	6. Diff. from 1 (sum of 3 and 5; total effect)	0.01%	0.00%	0.05%	-0.02%	-0.48%

Note: Differences between percents are given in percentage points.

Table A4.3.3. *Continued.*

		2000	Average annual change	2025	Average annual change	2050
Consumption per capita (US$)	1. Base	27,023	1.83%	42,478	1.23%	57,726
	2. New age structure, same total pop.	27,008	1.74%	41,590	1.01%	53,466
	3. Diff. from 1 (pure effect of pop. age structure)	-0.06%	-0.08%	-2.09%	-0.22%	-7.38%
	4. New age structure, new total population	26,998	1.71%	41,279	0.99%	52,801
	5. Diff. from 2 (pure effect of pop. size)	-0.04%	-0.03%	-0.75%	-0.02%	-1.24%
	6. Diff. from 1 (sum of 3 and 5)	-0.09%	-0.11%	-2.82%	-0.24%	-8.53%
Health and long-term care (US$)	1. Base	2,742	2.38%	4,941	1.37%	6,942
	2. New age structure, same total pop.	2,742	2.35%	4,897	1.24%	6,669
	3. Diff. from 1 (pure effect of pop. age structure)	-0.01%	-0.04%	-0.89%	-0.13%	-3.93%
	4. New age structure, new total population	2,741	2.32%	4,862	1.22%	6,584
	5. Diff. from 2 (pure effect of pop. size)	-0.03%	-0.03%	-0.70%	-0.02%	-1.27%
	6. Diff. from 1 (sum of 3 and 5)	-0.03%	-0.06%	-1.58%	-0.15%	-5.16%
Other (US$)	1. Base	24,281	1.76%	37,538	1.22%	50,784
	2. New age structure, same total pop.	24,266	1.67%	36,693	0.98%	46,796
	3. Diff. from 1 (pure effect of pop. age structure)	-0.06%	-0.09%	-2.25%	-0.24%	-7.85%
	4. New age structure, new total population	24,257	1.64%	36,416	0.96%	46,216
	5. Diff. from 2 (pure effect of pop. size)	-0.04%	-0.03%	-0.75%	-0.02%	-1.24%
	6. Diff. from 1 (sum of 3 and 5)	-0.10%	-0.12%	-2.99%	-0.26%	-8.99%
Saving rate (% of disposable income, unadjusted for changes in pension wealth)	1. Base	8.44%		7.20%		6.62%
	2. New age structure, same total pop.	8.44%		7.21%		6.65%
	3. Diff. from 1 (pure effect of pop. age structure)	0.01%		0.01%		0.03%
	4. New age structure, new total population	8.46%		7.32%		6.78%
	5. Diff. from 2 (pure effect of pop. size)	0.01%		0.11%		0.14%
	6. Diff. from 1 (sum of 3 and 5)	0.02%		0.12%		0.16%
Disposable income, (billion US$)	1. Base	2,347	1.01%	3,015	0.25%	3,206
	2. New age structure, same total pop.	2,345	0.84%	2,888	-0.11%	2,808
	3. Diff. from 1 (pure effect of pop. age structure)	-0.10%	-0.17%	-4.21%	-0.36%	-12.41%
	4. New age structure, new total population	2,347	0.92%	2,953	0.03%	2,974
	5. Diff. from 2 (pure effect of pop. size)	0.06%	0.09%	2.26%	0.14%	5.92%
	6. Diff. from 1 (sum of 3 and 5; total effect)	-0.03%	-0.08%	-2.05%	-0.22%	-7.22%
Savings (billion US$, unadjusted for changes in pension wealth)	1. Base	198	0.37%	217	-0.09%	212
	2. New age structure, same total pop.	198	0.20%	208	-0.43%	187
	3. Diff. from 1 (pure effect of pop. age structure)	-0.01%	-0.17%	-4.14%	-0.34%	-12.04%
	4. New age structure, new total population	198	0.34%	216	-0.28%	202
	5. Diff. from 2 (pure effect of pop. size)	0.22%	0.14%	3.86%	0.16%	8.08%
	6. Diff. from 1 (sum of 3 and 5)	0.21%	-0.03%	-0.44%	-0.18%	-4.93%

Note: Differences between percents are given in percentage points.

Table A4.3.3. *Continued.*

		2000	Average annual change	2025	Average annual change	2050
Savings per capita (US$, unadjusted for changes in pension wealth)	1. Base	2,489	1.13%	3,297	0.87%	4,093
	2. New age structure, same total pop.	2,490	1.05%	3,231	0.66%	3,808
	3. Diff. from 1 (pure effect of pop. age structure)	0.04%	-0.08%	-2.01%	-0.21%	-6.97%
	4. New age structure, new total population	2,494	1.08%	3,261	0.66%	3,843
	5. Diff. from 2 (pure effect of pop. size)	0.13%	0.03%	0.93%	0.00%	0.92%
	6. Diff. from 1 (sum of 3 and 5)	0.17%	-0.05%	-1.10%	-0.21%	-6.11%
Adjusted disposable income (billion US$)	1. Base	2,471	1.03%	3,191	0.31%	3,445
	2. New age structure, same total pop.	2,469	0.87%	3,068	-0.02%	3,057
	3. Diff. from 1 (pure effect of pop. age structure)	-0.09%	-0.15%	-3.85%	-0.32%	-11.26%
	4. New age structure, new total population	2,470	0.96%	3,138	0.13%	3,238
	5. Diff. from 2 (pure effect of pop. size)	0.06%	0.09%	2.27%	0.14%	5.93%
	6. Diff. from 1 (sum of 3 and 5; total effect)	-0.02%	-0.07%	-1.66%	-0.18%	-5.99%
Saving rate (% of disposable income, adjusted for changes in pension wealth)	1. Base	13.01%		12.33%		13.09%
	2. New age structure, same total pop.	13.02%		12.67%		14.24%
	3. Diff. from 1 (pure effect of pop. age structure)	0.02%		0.34%		1.15%
	4. New age structure, new total population	13.04%		12.79%		14.38%
	5. Diff. from 2 (pure effect of pop. size)	0.01%		0.12%		0.13%
	6. Diff. from 1 (sum of 3 and 5)	0.03%		0.46%		1.29%
Savings (billion US$, adjusted for changes in pension wealth)	1. Base	321	0.81%	394	0.55%	451
	2. New age structure, same total pop.	322	0.76%	389	0.45%	435
	3. Diff. from 1 (pure effect of pop. age structure)	0.03%	-0.05%	-1.21%	-0.09%	-3.45%
	4. New age structure, new total population	322	0.88%	401	0.59%	465
	5. Diff. from 2 (pure effect of pop. size)	0.17%	0.12%	3.23%	0.14%	6.93%
	6. Diff. from 1 (sum of 3 and 5)	0.19%	0.07%	1.98%	0.05%	3.25%
Savings per capita (billion US$, adjusted for changes in pension wealth)	1. Base	4,041	1.58%	5,975	1.51%	8,694
	2. New age structure, same total pop.	4,044	1.61%	6,034	1.56%	8,878
	3. Diff. from 1 (pure effect of pop. age structure)	0.08%	0.04%	0.98%	0.05%	2.13%
	4. New age structure, new total population	4,048	1.62%	6,053	1.54%	8,865
	5. Diff. from 2 (pure effect of pop. size)	0.08%	0.01%	0.32%	-0.02%	-0.16%
	6. Diff. from 1 (sum of 3 and 5)	0.16%	0.05%	1.30%	0.03%	1.97%
Change in pension wealth per capita (US$)	1. Base	1,552		2,679		4,600
	2. New age structure, same total pop.	1,554		2,804		5,070
	3. Diff. from 1 (pure effect of pop. age structure)	0.14%		4.67%		10.22%
	4. New age structure, new total population	1,554		2,793		5,022
	5. Diff. from 2 (pure effect of pop. size)	-0.01%		-0.39%		-0.96%
	6. Diff. from 1 (sum of 3 and 5)	0.13%		4.26%		9.15%

Note: Differences between percents are given in percentage points.

Table A4.3.4. Baseline (CCC) versus low-mortality alternative (CLC) scenario: Disposable income, consumption, and savings, population aged 60 and older.

		2000	Average annual change	2025	Average annual change	2050
Disposable income per capita (US$)	1. Base	37,655	-0.02%	37,426	1.44%	53,556
	2. New age structure, same total pop.	37,631	-0.03%	37,350	1.38%	52,650
	3. Diff. from 1 (pure effect of pop. age structure)	-0.06%	-0.01%	-0.20%	-0.06%	-1.69%
	4. New age structure, new total population	37,635	-0.04%	37,279	1.37%	52,342
	5. Diff. from 2 (pure effect of pop. size)	0.01%	-0.01%	-0.19%	-0.02%	-0.59%
	6. Diff. from 1 (sum of 3 and 5; total effect)	-0.05%	-0.01%	-0.39%	-0.08%	-2.27%
Wages (US$)	1. Base	8,418	0.46%	9,447	1.05%	12,257
	2. New age structure, same total pop.	8,406	0.24%	8,934	0.59%	10,346
	3. Diff. from 1 (pure effect of pop. age structure)	-0.14%	-0.22%	-5.43%	-0.46%	-15.59%
	4. New age structure, new total population	8,405	0.22%	8,869	0.57%	10,217
	5. Diff. from 2 (pure effect of pop. size)	-0.01%	-0.03%	-0.72%	-0.02%	-1.24%
	6. Diff. from 1 (sum of 3 and 5; total effect)	-0.16%	-0.25%	-6.11%	-0.48%	-16.64%
Entrepreneurial income, rents, dividends, interest, etc. (US$)	1. Base	7,338	-1.16%	5,485	0.30%	5,906
	2. New age structure, same total pop.	7,326	-1.29%	5,298	0.14%	5,485
	3. Diff. from 1 (pure effect of pop. age structure)	-0.16%	-0.13%	-3.40%	-0.16%	-7.13%
	4. New age structure, new total population	7,330	-1.20%	5,414	0.23%	5,737
	5. Diff. from 2 (pure effect of pop. size)	0.05%	0.08%	2.19%	0.09%	4.59%
	6. Diff. from 1 (sum of 3 and 5; total effect)	-0.11%	-0.05%	-1.28%	-0.07%	-2.87%
Public pension benefits (US$)	1. Base	13,751	0.40%	15,201	1.68%	23,039
	2. New age structure, same total pop.	13,749	0.45%	15,376	1.68%	23,296
	3. Diff. from 1 (pure effect of pop. age structure)	-0.01%	0.05%	1.15%	0.00%	1.11%
	4. New age structure, new total population	13,749	0.43%	15,304	1.65%	23,037
	5. Diff. from 2 (pure effect of pop. size)	0.01%	-0.02%	-0.46%	-0.03%	-1.11%
	6. Diff. from 1 (sum of 3 and 5; total effect)	-0.01%	0.03%	0.68%	-0.03%	-0.01%
Private DB pension benefits (US$)	1. Base	2,806	0.08%	2,861	1.67%	4,325
	2. New age structure, same total pop.	2,806	0.12%	2,890	1.66%	4,357
	3. Diff. from 1 (pure effect of pop. age structure)	-0.02%	0.04%	1.04%	-0.01%	0.74%
	4. New age structure, new total population	2,806	0.10%	2,880	1.63%	4,312
	5. Diff. from 2 (pure effect of pop. size)	0.01%	-0.01%	-0.35%	-0.03%	-1.03%
	6. Diff. from 1 (sum of 3 and 5; total effect)	-0.01%	0.03%	0.68%	-0.04%	-0.30%
Private DC pension benefits (US$)	1. Base	233	2.13%	395	2.47%	727
	2. New age structure, same total pop.	233	2.13%	395	2.51%	734
	3. Diff. from 1 (pure effect of pop. age structure)	0.00%	0.00%	0.00%	0.04%	0.97%
	4. New age structure, new total population	233	2.13%	395	2.51%	734
	5. Diff. from 2 (pure effect of pop. size)	0.02%	0.00%	0.10%	0.00%	0.10%
	6. Diff. from 1 (sum of 3 and 5; total effect)	0.02%	0.00%	0.11%	0.04%	1.07%
Health and long-term care benefits (US$)	1. Base	6,282	1.54%	9,212	1.52%	13,431
	2. New age structure, same total pop.	6,282	1.57%	9,273	1.50%	13,462
	3. Diff. from 1 (pure effect of pop. age structure)	0.00%	0.03%	0.66%	-0.02%	0.24%
	4. New age structure, new total population	6,282	1.54%	9,209	1.48%	13,291
	5. Diff. from 2 (pure effect of pop. size)	-1.00%	-0.03%	-0.69%	-0.02%	-1.27%
	6. Diff. from 1 (sum of 3 and 5; total effect)	-1.32%	0.00%	-0.04%	-0.04%	-1.04%

Note: Differences between percents are given in percentage points.

Table A4.3.4. *Continued.*

		2000	Average annual change	2025	Average annual change	2050
Adjusted disposable income per capita (US$)	1. Base	35,020	-0.06%	34,499	1.42%	49,023
	2. New age structure, same total pop.	34,997	-0.07%	34,399	1.35%	48,102
	3. Diff. from 1 (pure effect of pop. age structure)	-0.07%	-0.01%	-0.29%	-0.07%	-1.88%
	4. New age structure, new total population	35,000	-0.08%	34,338	1.34%	47,840
	5. Diff. from 2 (pure effect of pop. size)	0.01%	-0.01%	-0.17%	-0.02%	-0.55%
	6. Diff. from 1 (sum of 3 and 5; total effect)	-0.06%	-0.02%	-0.47%	-0.08%	-2.41%
Annuity income per capita (US$)	1. Base	6,101	2.05%	10,144	2.02%	16,740
	2. New age structure, same total pop.	6,100	2.06%	10,165	2.03%	16,780
	3. Diff. from 1 (pure effect of pop. age structure)	-0.02%	0.01%	0.21%	0.00%	0.24%
	4. New age structure, new total population	6,099	2.01%	10,033	1.98%	16,382
	5. Diff. from 2 (pure effect of pop. size)	-0.01%	-0.05%	-1.29%	-0.04%	-2.37%
	6. Diff. from 1 (sum of 3 and 5; total effect)	-0.04%	-0.04%	-1.09%	-0.04%	-2.14%
Consumption per capita (US$)	1. Base	40,509	0.35%	44,216	1.56%	65,143
	2. New age structure, same total pop.	40,486	0.35%	44,207	1.51%	64,362
	3. Diff. from 1 (pure effect of pop. age structure)	-0.06%	0.00%	-0.02%	-0.05%	-1.20%
	4. New age structure, new total population	40,485	0.33%	43,982	1.49%	63,658
	5. Diff. from 2 (pure effect of pop. size)	-0.34%	-0.02%	-0.51%	-0.02%	-1.09%
	6. Diff. from 1 (sum of 3 and 5)	-6.09%	-0.02%	-0.53%	-0.07%	-2.28%
Health and long-term care (US$)	1. Base	7,853	1.54%	11,515	1.52%	16,788
	2. New age structure, same total pop.	7,853	1.57%	11,591	1.50%	16,828
	3. Diff. from 1 (pure effect of pop. age structure)	0.00%	0.03%	0.66%	-0.02%	0.24%
	4. New age structure, new total population	7,852	1.54%	11,511	1.48%	16,614
	5. Diff. from 2 (pure effect of pop. size)	-1.00%	-0.03%	-0.69%	-0.02%	-1.27%
	6. Diff. from 1 (sum of 3 and 5)	-1.32%	0.00%	-0.04%	-0.04%	-1.04%
Other (US$)	1. Base	32,656	0.01%	32,700	1.58%	48,355
	2. New age structure, same total pop.	32,633	0.00%	32,616	1.52%	47,534
	3. Diff. from 1 (pure effect of pop. age structure)	-0.07%	-0.01%	-0.26%	-0.06%	-1.70%
	4. New age structure, new total population	32,633	-0.02%	32,471	1.49%	47,044
	5. Diff. from 2 (pure effect of pop. size)	-0.18%	-0.02%	-0.44%	-0.02%	-1.03%
	6. Diff. from 1 (sum of 3 and 5)	-7.24%	-0.03%	-0.70%	-0.08%	-2.71%
Saving rate (% of disposable income, unadjusted for changes in pension wealth)	1. Base	-7.58%		-18.14%		-21.64%
	2. New age structure, same total pop.	-7.59%		-18.36%		-22.24%
	3. Diff. from 1 (pure effect of pop. age structure)	-0.01%		-0.22%		-0.61%
	4. New age structure, new total population	-7.57%		-17.98%		-21.62%
	5. Diff. from 2 (pure effect of pop. size)	0.01%		0.38%		0.62%
	6. Diff. from 1 (sum of 3 and 5)	0.01%		0.16%		0.02%
Disposable income (billion US$)	1. Base	1,040	1.33%	1,449	1.46%	2,080
	2. New age structure, same total pop.	1,042	1.50%	1,512	1.57%	2,234
	3. Diff. from 1 (pure effect of pop. age structure)	0.15%	0.17%	4.36%	0.12%	7.42%
	4. New age structure, new total population	1,040	1.33%	1,449	1.46%	2,080
	5. Diff. from 2 (pure effect of pop. size)	-0.15%	-0.17%	-4.18%	-0.12%	-6.91%
	6. Diff. from 1 (sum of 3 and 5; total effect)	0.00%	0.00%	0.00%	0.00%	0.00%

Note: Differences between percents are given in percentage points.

Table A4.3.4. *Continued.*

		2000	Average annual change	2025	Average annual change	2050
Savings	1. Base	-79	4.93%	-263	2.17%	-450
(billion US$,	2. New age structure, same total pop.	-79	5.15%	-278	2.36%	-497
unadjusted for	3. Diff. from 1 (pure effect of pop. age structure)	0.24%	0.22%	5.62%	0.18%	10.44%
changes in	4. New age structure, new total population	-79	5.18%	-279	2.47%	-514
pension wealth)	5. Diff. from 2 (pure effect of pop. size)	-0.10%	0.03%	0.59%	0.12%	3.48%
	6. Diff. from 1 (sum of 3 and 5)	0.14%	0.25%	6.24%	0.30%	14.29%
Savings per capita	1. Base	-2,854	3.53%	-6,789	2.16%	-11,587
(US$, unadjusted	2. New age structure, same total pop.	-2,854	3.57%	-6,857	2.16%	-11,711
for changes in	3. Diff. from 1 (pure effect of pop. age structure)	0.02%	0.04%	1.00%	0.00%	1.07%
pension wealth)	4. New age structure, new total population	-2,850	3.48%	-6,704	2.12%	-11,316
	5. Diff. from 2 (pure effect of pop. size)	-0.17%	-0.09%	-2.24%	-0.05%	-3.37%
	6. Diff. from 1 (sum of 3 and 5)	-0.15%	-0.05%	-1.26%	-0.04%	-2.34%
Adjusted dispos-	1. Base	968	1.30%	1,335	1.43%	1,904
able income	2. New age structure, same total pop.	969	1.46%	1,392	1.54%	2,041
(billion US$)	3. Diff. from 1 (pure effect of pop. age structure)	0.15%	0.16%	4.27%	0.11%	7.22%
	4. New age structure, new total population	970	1.57%	1,430	1.69%	2,174
	5. Diff. from 2 (pure effect of pop. size)	0.08%	0.11%	2.71%	0.15%	6.51%
	6. Diff. from 1 (sum of 3 and 5; total effect)	0.23%	0.27%	7.09%	0.26%	14.20%
Saving rate	1. Base	-15.67%		-28.16%		-32.88%
(% of disposable	2. New age structure, same total pop.	-15.68%		-28.51%		-33.80%
income, adjusted	3. Diff. from 1 (pure effect of pop. age structure)	-0.01%		-0.35%		-0.92%
for changes in	4. New age structure, new total population	-15.67%		-28.08%		-33.06%
pension wealth)	5. Diff. from 2 (pure effect of pop. size)	0.01%		0.43%		0.74%
	6. Diff. from 1 (sum of 3 and 5)	0.00%		0.08%		-0.18%
Savings	1. Base	-152	3.70%	-376	2.06%	-626
(billion US$,	2. New age structure, same total pop.	-152	3.92%	-397	2.23%	-690
adjusted for	3. Diff. from 1 (pure effect of pop. age structure)	0.22%	0.22%	5.56%	0.18%	10.21%
changes in	4. New age structure, new total population	-152	3.96%	-402	2.35%	-719
pension wealth)	5. Diff. from 2 (pure effect of pop. size)	-0.01%	0.05%	1.16%	0.12%	4.19%
	6. Diff. from 1 (sum of 3 and 5)	0.21%	0.26%	6.79%	0.30%	14.83%
Savings per capita	1. Base	-5,489	2.31%	-9,717	2.05%	-16,120
(US$, adjusted	2. New age structure, same total pop.	-5,489	2.35%	-9,809	2.04%	-16,259
for changes in	3. Diff. from 1 (pure effect of pop. age structure)	0.00%	0.04%	0.95%	0.00%	0.86%
pension wealth)	4. New age structure, new total population	-5,485	2.28%	-9,644	2.00%	-15,818
	5. Diff. from 2 (pure effect of pop. size)	-0.08%	-0.07%	-1.68%	-0.04%	-2.71%
	6. Diff. from 1 (sum of 3 and 5)	-0.08%	-0.03%	-0.75%	-0.05%	-1.87%
Change in pension	1. Base	-2,635		-2,927		-4,533
wealth per capita	2. New age structure, same total pop.	-2,635		-2,951		-4,548
(US$)	3. Diff. from 1 (pure effect of pop. age structure)	-0.02%		0.82%		0.33%
	4. New age structure, new total population	-2,635		-2,940		-4,502
	5. Diff. from 2 (pure effect of pop. size)	0.01%		-0.38%		-1.01%
	6. Diff. from 1 (sum of 3 and 5)	-0.01%		0.44%		-0.69%

Note: Differences between percents are given in percentage points.

Table A4.3.5. Baseline (CCC) versus low-mortality alternative (CLC) scenario: Distribution (%).

		2000	2025	2050
Disposable income per capita (pop. 60+ : pop. 15–59)	1. Base	127.6%	81.8%	86.6%
	2. New age structure, same total pop.	127.6%	83.3%	91.9%
	3. Diff. from 1 (pure effect of pop. age structure)	0.0%	1.6%	5.3%
	4. New age structure, new total population	127.6%	83.7%	92.4%
	5. Diff. from 2 (pure effect of pop. size)	0.0%	0.4%	0.5%
	6. Diff. from 1 (sum of 3 and 5)	0.0%	1.9%	5.8%
Consumption per capita (pop. 60+ : pop. 15–59)	1. Base	149.9%	104.1%	112.8%
	2. New age structure, same total pop.	149.9%	106.3%	120.4%
	3. Diff. from 1 (pure effect of pop. age structure)	0.0%	2.2%	7.5%
	4. New age structure, new total population	150.0%	106.5%	120.6%
	5. Diff. from 2 (pure effect of pop. size)	0.1%	0.3%	0.2%
	6. Diff. from 1 (sum of 3 and 5)	0.0%	2.5%	7.7%
Excluding health and long-term care	1. Base	134.5%	87.1%	95.2%
	2. New age structure, same total pop.	134.5%	88.9%	101.6%
	3. Diff. from 1 (pure effect of pop. age structure)	0.0%	1.8%	6.4%
	4. New age structure, new total population	134.5%	89.2%	101.8%
	5. Diff. from 2 (pure effect of pop. size)	0.1%	0.3%	0.2%
	6. Diff. from 1 (sum of 3 and 5)	0.0%	2.1%	6.6%

Note: Differences between percents are given in percentage points.

Table A4.3.6. Baseline (CCC) versus low-mortality alternative (CLC) scenario: Assets (US$).

		2000	Average annual change	2025	Average annual change	2050
Assets per capita	1. Base	99,323	2.62%	189,717	1.49%	274,916
(pop. 15–59)	2. New age structure, same total pop.	99,300	2.54%	185,912	1.22%	251,577
	3. Diff. from 1 (pure effect of pop. age structure)	-0.02%	-0.08%	-2.01%	-0.28%	-8.49%
	4. New age structure, new total population	99,207	2.43%	180,884	1.10%	237,624
	5. Diff. from 2 (pure effect of pop. size)	-0.09%	-0.11%	-2.70%	-0.12%	-5.55%
	6. Diff. from 1 (sum of 3 and 5; total effect)	-0.12%	-0.19%	-4.66%	-0.40%	-13.57%
Private DC	1. Base	5,157	3.87%	13,323	1.56%	19,622
pension system	2. New age structure, same total pop.	5,158	3.90%	13,414	1.57%	19,794
assets	3. Diff. from 1 (pure effect of pop. age structure)	0.02%	0.03%	0.68%	0.01%	0.88%
	4. New age structure, new total population	5,156	3.88%	13,355	1.55%	19,607
	5. Diff. from 2 (pure effect of pop. size)	-0.03%	-0.02%	-0.44%	-0.02%	-0.95%
	6. Diff. from 1 (sum of 3 and 5; total effect)	-0.01%	0.01%	0.24%	-0.01%	-0.08%
Private DB	1. Base	3,091	-2.70%	1,560	1.97%	2,540
pension system	2. New age structure, same total pop.	3,093	-2.64%	1,586	2.71%	3,093
assets	3. Diff. from 1 (pure effect of pop. age structure)	0.05%	0.06%	1.66%	0.74%	21.75%
	4. New age structure, new total population	3,090	-2.74%	1,544	1.85%	2,443
	5. Diff. from 2 (pure effect of pop. size)	-0.09%	-0.10%	-2.65%	-0.85%	-21.01%
	6. Diff. from 1 (sum of 3 and 5; total effect)	-0.04%	-0.04%	-1.04%	-0.12%	-3.83%
Non-pension	1. Base	91,075	2.64%	174,834	1.49%	252,753
wealth	2. New age structure, same total pop.	91,049	2.55%	170,912	1.17%	228,690
	3. Diff. from 1 (pure effect of pop. age structure)	-0.03%	-0.09%	-2.24%	-0.31%	-9.52%
	4. New age structure, new total population	90,960	2.44%	165,984	1.05%	215,574
	5. Diff. from 2 (pure effect of pop. size)	-0.10%	-0.12%	-2.88%	-0.12%	-5.74%
	6. Diff. from 1 (sum of 3 and 5; total effect)	-0.13%	-0.21%	-5.06%	-0.43%	-14.71%
Assets per capita	1. Base	202,026	1.15%	269,182	1.68%	408,315
(pop. 60+)	2. New age structure, same total pop.	201,790	1.08%	263,953	1.47%	380,398
	3. Diff. from 1 (pure effect of pop. age structure)	-0.12%	-0.07%	-1.94%	-0.21%	-6.84%
	4. New age structure, new total population	201,724	1.04%	261,040	1.45%	373,693
	5. Diff. from 2 (pure effect of pop. size)	-0.03%	-0.04%	-1.10%	-0.03%	-1.76%
	6. Diff. from 1 (sum of 3 and 5; total effect)	-0.15%	-0.12%	-3.02%	-0.24%	-8.48%
Private DC	1. Base	7,095	1.70%	10,817	2.19%	18,601
pension system	2. New age structure, same total pop.	7,089	1.65%	10,666	2.10%	17,933
assets	3. Diff. from 1 (pure effect of pop. age structure)	-0.09%	-0.05%	-1.40%	-0.09%	-3.59%
	4. New age structure, new total population	7,109	1.93%	11,465	2.44%	20,945
	5. Diff. from 2 (pure effect of pop. size)	0.28%	0.28%	7.48%	0.34%	16.79%
	6. Diff. from 1 (sum of 3 and 5; total effect)	0.19%	0.23%	5.98%	0.25%	12.60%
Private DB	1. Base	8,787	1.42%	12,490	0.39%	13,764
pension system	2. New age structure, same total pop.	8,768	1.25%	11,950	0.24%	12,688
assets	3. Diff. from 1 (pure effect of pop. age structure)	-0.22%	-0.17%	-4.32%	-0.15%	-7.81%
	4. New age structure, new total population	8,762	1.14%	11,640	0.11%	11,956
	5. Diff. from 2 (pure effect of pop. size)	-0.07%	-0.10%	-2.60%	-0.13%	-5.77%
	6. Diff. from 1 (sum of 3 and 5; total effect)	-0.29%	-0.27%	-6.81%	-0.28%	-13.13%
Non-pension	1. Base	186,144	1.12%	245,874	1.71%	375,951
wealth	2. New age structure, same total pop.	185,933	1.05%	241,336	1.50%	349,777
	3. Diff. from 1 (pure effect of pop. age structure)	-0.11%	-0.07%	-1.85%	-0.22%	-6.96%
	4. New age structure, new total population	185,853	0.99%	237,936	1.45%	340,792
	5. Diff. from 2 (pure effect of pop. size)	-0.04%	-0.06%	-1.41%	-0.05%	-2.57%
	6. Diff. from 1 (sum of 3 and 5; total effect)	-0.16%	-0.13%	-3.23%	-0.27%	-9.35%

Note: Differences between percents are given in percentage points.

Table A4.3.7. Baseline (CCC) versus low-mortality alternative (CLC) scenario: Public pension, health, and long-term care expenditure.

		2000	Average annual change	2025	Average annual change	2050
Public pension system benefits / contributions (billion US$)	1. Base	420.6	1.74%	647.3	1.69%	983.5
	2. New age structure, same total pop.	421.4	1.96%	684.6	1.86%	1,086.4
	3. Diff. from 1 (pure effect of pop. age structure)	0.20%	0.22%	5.77%	0.18%	10.46%
	4. New age structure, new total population	421.7	2.05%	701.2	2.00%	1,150.6
	5. Diff. from 2 (pure effect of pop. size)	0.08%	0.09%	2.42%	0.14%	5.91%
	6. Diff. from 1 (sum of 3 and 5; total effect)	0.28%	0.31%	8.33%	0.31%	16.99%
% of GDP	1. Base	8.42%		9.32%		11.71%
	2. New age structure, same total pop.	8.44%		9.99%		13.55%
	3. Diff. from 1 (pure effect of pop. age structure)	0.02%		0.67%		1.84%
	4. New age structure, new total population	8.44%		10.01%		13.57%
	5. Diff. from 2 (pure effect of pop. size)	0.00%		0.02%		0.02%
	6. Diff. from 1 (sum of 3 and 5; total effect)	0.02%		0.69%		1.86%
Public pension contribution rate (%)	1. Base	22.56%		25.47%		32.26%
	2. New age structure, same total pop.	22.61%		27.31%		37.32%
	3. Diff. from 1 (pure effect of pop. age structure)	0.05%		1.84%		5.06%
	4. New age structure, new total population	22.61%		27.35%		37.33%
	5. Diff. from 2 (pure effect of pop. size)	0.00%		0.04%		0.00%
	6. Diff. from 1 (sum of 3 and 5; total effect)	0.05%		1.88%		5.07%
Health system benefits / contributions (billion US$)	1. Base	261.1	2.32%	462.7	1.09%	607.1
	2. New age structure, same total pop.	261.3	2.38%	470.8	1.14%	624.6
	3. Diff. from 1 (pure effect of pop. age structure)	0.08%	0.07%	1.76%	0.04%	2.87%
	4. New age structure, new total population	261.4	2.47%	481.1	1.28%	660.4
	5. Diff. from 2 (pure effect of pop. size)	0.06%	0.09%	2.18%	0.14%	5.73%
	6. Diff. from 1 (sum of 3 and 5)	0.14%	0.15%	3.98%	0.18%	8.77%
% of GDP	1. Base	5.23%		6.66%		7.23%
	2. New age structure, same total pop.	5.23%		6.87%		7.79%
	3. Diff. from 1 (pure effect of pop. age structure)	0.00%		0.21%		0.56%
	4. New age structure, new total population	5.23%		6.87%		7.79%
	5. Diff. from 2 (pure effect of pop. size)	0.00%		0.00%		0.00%
	6. Diff. from 1 (sum of 3 and 5; total effect)	0.00%		0.21%		0.56%
Health care contribution rate (%)	1. Base	7.28%		9.47%		10.36%
	2. New age structure, same total pop.	7.29%		9.77%		11.16%
	3. Diff. from 1 (pure effect of pop. age structure)	0.01%		0.30%		0.80%
	4. New age structure, new total population	7.29%		9.76%		11.14%
	5. Diff. from 2 (pure effect of pop. size)	0.00%		-0.01%		-0.02%
	6. Diff. from 1 (sum of 3 and 5)	0.01%		0.29%		0.79%
Long-term care system contributions / benefits (billion US$)	1. Base	87.0	2.32%	154.2	1.09%	202.4
	2. New age structure, same total pop.	87.1	2.38%	156.9	1.14%	208.2
	3. Diff. from 1 (pure effect of pop. age structure)	0.08%	0.07%	1.76%	0.04%	2.87%
	4. New age structure, new total population	87.1	2.47%	160.4	1.28%	220.1
	5. Diff. from 2 (pure effect of pop. size)	0.06%	0.09%	2.18%	0.14%	5.73%
	6. Diff. from 1 (sum of 3 and 5)	0.14%	0.15%	3.98%	0.18%	8.77%
% of GDP	1. Base	1.74%		2.22%		2.41%
	2. New age structure, same total pop.	1.74%		2.25%		2.52%
	3. Diff. from 1 (pure effect of pop. age structure)	0.00%		0.03%		0.12%
	4. New age structure, new total population	1.74%		2.20%		2.39%
	5. Diff. from 2 (pure effect of pop. size)	0.00%		-0.05%		-0.14%
	6. Diff. from 1 (sum of 3 and 5)	0.00%		-0.02%		-0.02%

Note: Differences between percents are given in percentage points.

Table A4.3.7. *Continued.*

		2000	Average annual change	2025	Average annual change	2050
Long-term care	1. Base	2.43%		3.16%		3.45%
contribution rate	2. New age structure, same total pop.	2.43%		3.26%		3.72%
(%)	3. Diff. from 1 (pure effect of pop. age structure)	0.00%		0.10%		0.27%
	4. New age structure, new total population	2.43%		3.25%		3.71%
	5. Diff. from 2 (pure effect of pop. size)	0.00%		0.00%		-0.01%
	6. Diff. from 1 (sum of 3 and 5)	0.00%		0.10%		0.26%

Note: Differences between percents are given in percentage points.

Table A4.3.8. Baseline (CCC) versus low-mortality alternative (CLC) scenario: Health care expenditure.

		2000	Average annual change	2025	Average annual change	2050
Health system expenditure (US$ per capita)	1. Base	2,610	2.48%	4,812	1.65%	7,249
	2. New age structure, same total pop.	2,612	2.55%	4,897	1.70%	7,457
	3. Diff. from 1 (pure effect of pop. age structure)	0.08%	0.07%	1.76%	0.04%	2.87%
	4. New age structure, new total population	2,612	2.52%	4,863	1.67%	7,362
	5. Diff. from 2 (pure effect of pop. size)	-0.03%	-0.03%	-0.70%	-0.02%	-1.27%
	6. Diff. from 1 (sum of 3 and 5; total effect)	0.05%	0.04%	1.05%	0.02%	1.57%
Population aged 0–59	1. Base	1,680	2.34%	2,995	1.26%	4,099
	2. New age structure, same total pop.	1,680	2.30%	2,969	1.14%	3,938
	3. Diff. from 1 (pure effect of pop. age structure)	0.00%	-0.04%	-0.89%	-0.13%	-3.92%
	4. New age structure, new total population	1,679	2.28%	2,948	1.11%	3,888
	5. Diff. from 2 (pure effect of pop. size)	-0.03%	-0.03%	-0.70%	-0.02%	-1.27%
	6. Diff. from 1 (sum of 3 and 5; total effect)	-0.03%	-0.06%	-1.58%	-0.15%	-5.15%
Population aged 60+	1. Base	5,890	1.54%	8,636	1.52%	12,591
	2. New age structure, same total pop.	5,890	1.57%	8,693	1.50%	12,621
	3. Diff. from 1 (pure effect of pop. age structure)	0.00%	0.03%	0.66%	-0.02%	0.24%
	4. New age structure, new total population	5,889	1.54%	8,633	1.48%	12,461
	5. Diff. from 2 (pure effect of pop. size)	-0.01%	-0.03%	-0.69%	-0.02%	-1.27%
	6. Diff. from 1 (sum of 3 and 5; total effect)	-0.01%	0.00%	-0.04%	-0.04%	-1.04%
Health system expenditure (billion US$)	1. Base	326	2.32%	578	1.09%	759
	2. New age structure, same total pop.	327	2.38%	588	1.14%	781
	3. Diff. from 1 (pure effect of pop. age structure)	0.08%	0.07%	1.76%	0.04%	2.87%
	4. New age structure, new total population	327	2.47%	601	1.28%	825
	5. Diff. from 2 (pure effect of pop. size)	0.06%	0.09%	2.18%	0.14%	5.73%
	6. Diff. from 1 (sum of 3 and 5; total effect)	0.14%	0.15%	3.98%	0.18%	8.77%
Population aged 0–59	1. Base	164	1.61%	244	0.41%	270
	2. New age structure, same total pop.	163	1.49%	237	0.14%	245
	3. Diff. from 1 (pure effect of pop. age structure)	-0.06%	-0.12%	-3.04%	-0.26%	-9.18%
	4. New age structure, new total population	164	1.57%	242	0.28%	259
	5. Diff. from 2 (pure effect of pop. size)	0.06%	0.09%	2.18%	0.14%	5.73%
	6. Diff. from 1 (sum of 3 and 5; total effect)	0.00%	-0.04%	-0.93%	-0.13%	-3.97%
Population aged 60+	1. Base	163	2.92%	334	1.53%	489
	2. New age structure, same total pop.	163	3.12%	352	1.69%	535
	3. Diff. from 1 (pure effect of pop. age structure)	0.21%	0.20%	5.26%	0.16%	9.53%
	4. New age structure, new total population	163	3.21%	360	1.83%	566
	5. Diff. from 2 (pure effect of pop. size)	0.06%	0.09%	2.18%	0.14%	5.73%
	6. Diff. from 1 (sum of 3 and 5; total effect)	0.28%	0.29%	7.56%	0.30%	15.81%
Health system expenditure (% of GDP)	1. Base	6.53%		8.32%		9.03%
	2. New age structure, same total pop.	6.54%		8.58%		9.74%
	3. Diff. from 1 (pure effect of pop. age structure)	0.01%		0.26%		0.70%
	4. New age structure, new total population	6.54%		8.58%		9.74%
	5. Diff. from 2 (pure effect of pop. size)	0.00%		0.00%		0.00%
	6. Diff. from 1 (sum of 3 and 5; total effect)	0.01%		0.26%		0.70%

Note: Differences between percents are given in percentage points.

Table A4.3.9. Baseline (CCC) versus low-mortality alternative (CLC) scenario: Long-term care expenditure.

		2000	Average annual change	2025	Average annual change	2050
Long-term care expenditure (US$ per capita)	1. Base	870	2.48%	1,604	1.65%	2,416
	2. New age structure, same total pop.	871	2.55%	1,632	1.70%	2,486
	3. Diff. from 1 (pure effect of pop. age structure)	0.08%	0.07%	1.76%	0.04%	2.87%
	4. New age structure, new total population	870	2.52%	1,621	1.67%	2,454
	5. Diff. from 2 (pure effect of pop. size)	-0.03%	-0.03%	-0.70%	-0.02%	-1.27%
	6. Diff. from 1 (sum of 3 and 5; total effect)	0.05%	0.04%	1.05%	0.02%	1.57%
Population aged 0–59	1. Base	560	2.34%	998	1.26%	1,366
	2. New age structure, same total pop.	560	2.30%	989	1.14%	1,313
	3. Diff. from 1 (pure effect of pop. age structure)	0.00%	-0.04%	-0.89%	-0.13%	-3.92%
	4. New age structure, new total population	560	2.28%	983	1.11%	1,296
	5. Diff. from 2 (pure effect of pop. size)	-0.03%	-0.03%	-0.70%	-0.02%	-1.27%
	6. Diff. from 1 (sum of 3 and 5; total effect)	-0.03%	-0.06%	-1.58%	-0.15%	-5.15%
Population aged 60+	1. Base	1,963	1.54%	2,879	1.52%	4,197
	2. New age structure, same total pop.	1,963	1.57%	2,898	1.50%	4,207
	3. Diff. from 1 (pure effect of pop. age structure)	0.00%	0.03%	0.66%	-0.02%	0.24%
	4. New age structure, new total population	1,963	1.54%	2,878	1.48%	4,153
	5. Diff. from 2 (pure effect of pop. size)	-0.01%	-0.03%	-0.69%	-0.02%	-1.27%
	6. Diff. from 1 (sum of 3 and 5; total effect)	-0.01%	0.00%	-0.04%	-0.04%	-1.04%
Long-term care expenditure (billion US$)	1. Base	109	2.32%	193	1.09%	253
	2. New age structure, same total pop.	109	2.38%	196	1.14%	260
	3. Diff. from 1 (pure effect of pop. age structure)	0.08%	0.07%	1.76%	0.04%	2.87%
	4. New age structure, new total population	109	2.47%	200	1.28%	275
	5. Diff. from 2 (pure effect of pop. size)	0.06%	0.09%	2.18%	0.14%	5.73%
	6. Diff. from 1 (sum of 3 and 5; total effect)	0.14%	0.15%	3.98%	0.18%	8.77%
Population aged 0–59	1. Base	54	1.61%	81	0.41%	90
	2. New age structure, same total pop.	54	1.49%	79	0.14%	82
	3. Diff. from 1 (pure effect of pop. age structure)	-0.06%	-0.12%	-3.04%	-0.26%	-9.18%
	4. New age structure, new total population	54	1.57%	81	0.28%	86
	5. Diff. from 2 (pure effect of pop. size)	0.06%	0.09%	2.18%	0.14%	5.73%
	6. Diff. from 1 (sum of 3 and 5; total effect)	0.00%	-0.04%	-0.93%	-0.13%	-3.97%
Population aged 60+	1. Base	54	2.92%	111	1.53%	163
	2. New age structure, same total pop.	54	3.12%	117	1.69%	178
	3. Diff. from 1 (pure effect of pop. age structure)	0.21%	0.20%	5.26%	0.16%	9.53%
	4. New age structure, new total population	54	3.21%	120	1.83%	189
	5. Diff. from 2 (pure effect of pop. size)	0.06%	0.09%	2.18%	0.14%	5.73%
	6. Diff. from 1 (sum of 3 and 5; total effect)	0.28%	0.29%	7.56%	0.30%	15.81%
Long-term care expenditure (% of GDP)	1. Base	1.74%		2.22%		2.41%
	2. New age structure, same total pop.	1.74%		2.29%		2.60%
	3. Diff. from 1 (pure effect of pop. age structure)	0.00%		0.07%		0.19%
	4. New age structure, new total population	1.74%		2.29%		2.60%
	5. Diff. from 2 (pure effect of pop. size)	0.00%		0.00%		0.00%
	6. Diff. from 1 (sum of 3 and 5; total effect)	0.00%		0.07%		0.19%

Note: Differences between percents are given in percentage points.

Table A4.3.10. Baseline (CCC) versus low-mortality alternative (CLC) scenario: Global summary.

			2000	2025	2050
GDP per capita (US$)	Japan	Base	39,943	57,813	80,249
		Alternative	39,925	56,644	75,622
		Difference	-0.04%	-2.02%	-5.77%
	United States	Base	31,144	44,287	62,198
		Alternative	31,131	43,595	59,150
		Difference	-0.04%	-1.56%	-4.90%
	Other Industrial Countries	Base	27,791	42,710	58,591
		Alternative	27,776	41,959	55,485
		Difference	-0.05%	-1.76%	-5.30%
	LDCs	Base	2,266	3,686	5,389
		Alternative	2,265	3,636	5,206
		Difference	-0.05%	-1.34%	-3.39%
	World	Base	7,257	9,340	11,726
		Alternative	7,254	9,169	11,087
		Difference	-0.05%	-1.83%	-5.44%
GNP per capita (US$)	Japan	Base	40,228	58,602	81,481
		Alternative	40,210	57,404	76,746
		Difference	-0.04%	-2.04%	-5.81%
	United States	Base	31,233	44,433	62,456
		Alternative	31,219	43,733	59,368
		Difference	-0.04%	-1.57%	-4.94%
	Other Industrial Countries	Base	27,869	42,986	59,042
		Alternative	27,854	42,230	55,914
		Difference	-0.05%	-1.76%	-5.30%
	LDCs	Base	2,244	3,639	5,330
		Alternative	2,243	3,591	5,152
		Difference	-0.05%	-1.32%	-3.33%
Net factor income from abroad (billion US$)	Japan	Base	36	95	129
		Alternative	36	94	126
		Difference	0	-1	-3
	United States	Base	24	47	89
		Alternative	24	45	79
		Difference	0	-1	-10
	Other Industrial Countries	Base	61	212	318
		Alternative	61	212	320
		Difference	0	1	2
	LDCs	Base	-120	-353	-536
		Alternative	-120	-352	-525
		Difference	0	2	11

Note: Differences between percents are given in percentage points; LDCs = Less Developed Countries.

Table A4.3.10. *Continued.*

			2000	2025	2050
Net foreign assets (billion US$)	Japan	Base	317	670	678
		Alternative	317	661	633
		Difference	0	-9	-45
	United States	Base	49	117	528
		Alternative	49	100	418
		Difference	0	-17	-110
	Other Industrial Countries	Base	384	1,461	2,177
		Alternative	384	1,451	2,128
		Difference	0	-10	-49
	LDCs	Base	-750	-2,248	-3,383
		Alternative	-750	-2,212	-3,179
		Difference	0	36	204
Acquisition of gross foreign assets (billion US$)	Japan	Base	295	282	166
		Alternative	294	278	140
		Difference	-1	-4	-26
	United States	Base	397	597	645
		Alternative	395	575	570
		Difference	-2	-22	-76
	Other Industrial Countries	Base	1,482	1,765	1,091
		Alternative	1,477	1,736	952
		Difference	-5	-29	-139
	LDCs	Base	615	1,142	1,200
		Alternative	614	1,150	1,268
		Difference	-1	8	67
Sales of domestic assets to rest of world (billion US$)	Japan	Base	277	276	173
		Alternative	276	272	150
		Difference	-1	-4	-24
	United States	Base	402	586	616
		Alternative	401	567	547
		Difference	-2	-19	-69
	Other Industrial Countries	Base	1,452	1,714	1,080
		Alternative	1,447	1,686	944
		Difference	-4	-29	-136
	LDCs	Base	658	1,210	1,234
		Alternative	657	1,215	1,288
		Difference	-1	4	55
Change in net foreign assets (billion US$)	Japan	Base	19	6	-7
		Alternative	19	6	-9
		Difference	0	0	-3
	United States	Base	-6	11	29
		Alternative	-6	8	22
		Difference	0	-2	-7
	Other Industrial Countries	Base	30	51	11
		Alternative	30	50	8
		Difference	0	-1	-3
	LDCs	Base	-43	-68	-34
		Alternative	-43	-65	-21
		Difference	0	3	13

Note: Differences between percents are given in percentage points; LDCs = Less Developed Countries.

Afterword

The population of Japan is now declining, and the ratio of persons in the prime working ages to persons who are elderly will inexorably decline over the next half century. In a sense, this is the "unwinding" of the demographic component of the Japanese economic miracle. Looking back half a century, Japan was a poor country with a dismally overcrowded agricultural sector and an undercapitalized industrial sector producing simple consumer goods whose low quality was the butt of jokes. Japan is now one of the richest, most technologically advanced countries in the world, thanks in part to high saving rates associated with the post-war demographic transition. But the reduced youth dependency ratio that facilitated saving is now working its way up the age ladder, translating into a swollen elderly dependency ratio, with exactly the opposite effect. By the time it has run its course, the change of demographic regime will have taken about a century to work its way through the economic system.

The first two chapters of this book struck a note of fatalism, concluding that pervasive socioeconomic impacts of ageing are inevitable, especially given the extreme population ageing situation faced by Japan. Let there be no mistake, these impacts are mostly for the worse. Just as individual ageing is an imposition at the private level, and one we would all prefer to avoid, so does population ageing pose risks for society. However, the openness with which Japanese policy makers have expressed concern and their willingness to undertake measures in anticipation of the crest of the ageing phenomenon bode well for coping with the problem.

Like other transformative historical events (climate change, for example, or the HIV/AIDS epidemic), population ageing invites hyperbole. The sense of impending crisis needs to be tempered with some rough assessment of the magnitude of the impacts, and the last two chapters were occupied with providing such estimates. Unless we are being seriously misled by our model, projected demographic trends will give rise to an era of slower economic growth, reduced availability of savings, and rising social contribution rates. It may be argued that the latter can be avoided by deep structural reforms of the pension and health systems, but as we stressed in Chapter 1, resources must be transferred from the working population to the aged population one way or another. Whatever the precise nature of the claim created for the elderly, it needs to be financed by reduced consumption of the non-elderly.

In the baseline scenario that we have presented, economic growth decelerates and savings are depressed, leading us to apply the label "demographic stagnation." Disposable income of the elderly declines in the early years of the scenario due to our assumptions of increasing pensionable age and constant elderly labor force participation rates. In the long run, however, economic growth is sufficient to ensure that disposable income of *both* the young and old increases, resulting in a relatively stable intergenerational income distribution. In this sense, despite the poor growth performance, our baseline scenario is a fundamentally optimistic one. The key to this benign state of affairs is that the steady rise of payroll tax rates is more than offset by increases in wages. "Taxpayers will never put up with it," some will counter. Fine, but if not financed by wage-based taxes and social contributions, then consumption of the elderly will need to be financed in some other way, and taxpayers are unlikely to be happy with it, either.

We have tested the sensitivity of this scenario to changes in mortality and fertility rate assumptions, shifts in saving and labor force participation rates, and shocks to productivity. We made the general finding that the scenario is robust; that is, that something akin to the "demographic stagnation" picture that we describe is likely to come to pass. Inevitably, this prediction is conditional upon productivity growth. Technological progress can trump ageing, and only speculative arguments suggest that ageing can stifle technological progress.

By focusing on two alternative demographic scenarios, lower than expected fertility and lower than expected mortality, we illustrated a few propositions, some of them familiar from elsewhere and some of them relatively novel. Among the former class was the illustration that Japan's public pay-as-you-go (PAYG) financed pension system is more sensitive to mortality than fertility in the near term but more sensitive to fertility than mortality in the long term. Less familiar is the proposition, illustrated in Chapter 4, that the age distribution of income is much more sensitive to uncertainty in mortality than uncertainty in fertility, with lower than expected mortality moving the distribution in favor of the elderly. Both these findings are conditional on our assumption that demographic risks are borne by the working-age population; that is, that the response to ageing is to increase payroll tax rates, not to cut benefits.

In closing, we draw on a compelling metaphor due to John Maynard Keynes. With the depressed fertility rates of the 1930s in mind, Keynes (1937) wrote of twin demons: the Malthusian demon of population growth in excess of the job-creating capacity of the economy and the anti-Malthusian demon of demographic stagnation resulting in insufficient demand. Just as one demon is being chained up, he wrote, the other one escapes. While the precise description of the trade-off would be a bit different today, Keynes' vision of twin demographic demons is as apt, and as prescient, as it was three-quarters of a century ago. Japan tamed the Malthusian demon in the second half of the twentieth century. But in doing so, it inevitably let slip the anti-Malthusian demon, which it now must tame in the first half of the twenty-first.

References

Aaron, H.J., 1966. The social insurance paradox. *Canadian Journal of Economics and Political Science*, **32**:371–374.

Abel, A.B., 2001. Will bequests attenuate the predicted meltdown in stock prices when baby boomers retire? *Review of Economics and Statistics*, **83**(4):589–595.

Aging needs more mature attitude, *The Daily Yomiuri*, 7 January 2001, p. 6.

Alesina, A., and Perotti, R., 1997. The welfare state and competitiveness. *American Economic Review*, **87**(5):921–939.

Altonji, J.G., Hayashi, F., and Kotlikoff, L.J., 1997. Parental altruism and inter vivos transfers: Theory and evidence. *Journal of Political Economy*, **105**(6):1121–1166.

Anderson, P.M., Gustman, A.L., and Steimeier, T.L., 1999. Trends in male labor force participation and retirement: Some evidence on the role of pensions and social security in the 1970s and 1980s. *Journal of Labor Economics*, **17**(4)Part 1:757–783.

Ando, A., Morro, A., Cordoba, J.P., and Garland, G., 1995. Dynamics of demographic development and its impact on personal saving: Case of Japan. *Ricerche Economiche*, September:179–205.

Arthur, W.B., and McNicoll, G., 1977. Optimal time paths with age-dependence: A theory of population policy. *Review of Economic Studies*, **44**:111–123.

Arthur, W.B., and McNicoll, G., 1978. Samuelson, population, and intergenerational transfers. *International Economic Review*, **19**:241–246.

Atoh, M., 2001. Very low fertility change in Japan and value change hypothesis. *Review of Population and Social Policy*, **10**:1–21.

Attanasio, O.P., and DeLire, T., 2002. The effect of Individual Retirement Accounts on household consumption and national saving. *Economic Journal*, **112**(481):504–538.

Attanasio, O.P., Banks, J., Meghir, C., and Weber, G., 1999. Humps and bumps in lifetime consumption. *Journal of Business and Economic Statistics*, **17**(1):22–35.

Auerbach, A.J., and Kotlikoff, L.J., 1987. *Dynamic Fiscal Policy*. Cambridge, UK: Cambridge University Press.

Auerbach, A.J., and Kotlikoff, L.J., 1990. Tax aspects of policy towards aging populations: Canada and the United States. *National Bureau of Economic Research Working Paper No. 3405*. Cambridge, MA, USA: NBER.

213

Auerbach, A.J., Kotlikoff, L.J., Hagemann, R.P., and Nicoletti, G., 1989. The economics of aging populations: The case of four OECD countries. *OECD Economic Studies*, **12**:97–130.

Auerbach, A.J., Cai, J., and Kotlikoff, L.J., 1991. U.S. demographics and saving: Predictions of three saving models. *Carnegie-Rochester Conference Series on Public Policy*, **34**:135–56.

Bailliu, J., and Reisen, H., 1997. Do funded pensions contribute to higher aggregate savings? A cross-country analysis. *OECD Development Center Technical Paper No. 130*. Paris, France: OECD.

Bailliu, J., and Reisen, H., 2000. Do funded pensions contribute to higher aggregate savings? A cross-country analysis. In: *Pensions, Savings and Capital Flows: From Ageing to Emerging Markets*. Cheltenham, UK: Edward Elgar in association with the Organisation for Economic Co-operation and Development, pp. 113–131.

Baker, M., and Benjamin, D., 1999. Early retirement provisions and labor force behavior of older men: Evidence from Canada. *Journal of Labor Economics*, **17**(4)Part 1:724–756.

Banks, J., Blundell, R., and Tanner, S., 1998. Is there a retirement savings puzzle? *American Economic Review*, **88**(4):769–788.

Barr, N., 1992. Economic theory and the welfare state: A survey and interpretation. *Journal of Economic Literature*, **30**(3):741–803.

Barr, N., 1993. *The Economics of the Welfare State*. London, UK: Weidenfeld and Nicolson.

Barr, N., 2002. The pension puzzle: Prerequisites and policy choices in pension design. *Economic Issues*, **29**. Washington, DC, USA: International Monetary Fund.

Belan, P., and Pestieau, P., 1999. Privatizing social security: A critical assessment. *The Geneva Papers on Risk and Insurance*, **24**(1):114–130.

Bernheim, B.D., and Stark, O., 1988. Altruism within the family reconsidered: Do nice guys finish last? *American Economic Review*, **78**:1034–1045.

Bernheim, B.D., Skinner, J., and Weinberg, S., 2001. What accounts for the variation in retirement wealth among U.S. households? *American Economic Review*, **91**(4):832–857.

Blake, D., and Orszag, M., 1998. The Simple Economics of Funded and Unfunded Pension Systems. Manuscript, Department of Economics, Birkbeck College, University of London.

Blanchet, D., and Kessler, D., 1991. Optimal pension funding with demographic instability ad endogenous returns on investment. *Journal of Population Economics*, **4**:137–154.

Blanchet, D., and Kessler, D., 1992. Pension systems in transition economies: Perspectives and choices ahead. In: P. Pestieau (ed.), *Public Finance in a World of Transition*, Supplement to Public Finances/Finances Publiques, Vol. 47.

Blau, D.M., and Gilleskie, D.B., 2001. Retiree health insurance and labor force behavior of older men in the 1990s. *Review of Economics and Statistics*, **83**(1):64–80.

Blöndal, S., and Scarpetta, S., 1999. The retirement decision in OECD countries. *Economics Department Working Paper No. 202*. Paris, France: OECD.

Bloom, D.E., and Williamson, J.G., 1997. Demographic transitions, human resource development, and economic miracles in emerging Asia. In: J. Sachs and D. Bloom (eds.), *Emerging Asia*. Manila, Philippines: Asian Development Bank, Chapter 3.

Blundell, R., Meghir, C., and Smith, S., 2002. Pension incentives and the pattern of early retirement. *Economic Journal*, 112(478):C153–C170.

Boeri, T., Börsch-Supan, A., and Tabellini, G., 2002. Pension reforms and the opinions of European citizens. *American Economic Review*, 92(2):396–401.

Bohn, H., 1999. Should the social security trust fund hold equities? An intergenerational welfare analysis. *Review of Economic Dynamics*, 2(3):666–697.

Boldrin, M., Dolado, J.J., Jimeno, J.F., and Peracchi, F., 1999. The future of pensions in Europe. *Economic Policy: A European Forum*, 29:289–322.

Bolle, P., 2000. Pension reform: What the debate is all about. *International Labour Review*, 139(2):197–212.

Börsch-Supan, A., 1991. Implications of an aging population: Problems and policy questions in West Germany and the United States. *Economic Policy*, 12:104–139.

Börsch-Supan, A., 1996. The impact of population ageing on savings, investment, and growth in the OECD area. In: OECD (ed.), *Future Global Capital Shortages: Real Threat or Total Fiction?* Paris, France: OECD.

Börsch-Supan, A., 2000a. Incentive effects of social security on labor force participation: Evidence in Germany and across Europe. *Journal of Public Economics*, 78(1–2):25–49.

Börsch-Supan, A., 2000b. A model under siege: A case study of the German retirement insurance system. *Economic Journal*, 110(461):F24–F45.

Börsch-Supan, A., and Brugiavini, A., 2001. Savings: The policy debate in Europe. *Oxford Review of Economic Policy*, 17(1):116–143.

Breyer, F., and Haufler, A., 2000. Health care reform: Separating insurance from income redistribution. *International Tax and Public Finance*, 7(4–5):445–461.

Breyer, F., and Stolte, K., 2001. Demographic change, endogenous labor supply and the political feasibility of pension reform. *Journal of Population Economics*, 14(3):409–424.

Brooks, R., 2000a. What will happen to financial markets when the baby boomers retire? *International Monetary Fund Working Paper WP/00/18*. Washington, DC, USA: IMF.

Brooks, R., 2000b. Population aging and global capital flows in a parallel universe. *International Monetary Fund Working Paper WP/00/151*. Washington, DC, USA: IMF.

Brooks, R., 2002. Asset-market effects of the baby boom and social security reform. *American Economic Review*, 92(2):402–406.

Browning, E.K., 1975. Why the social insurance budget is too large in a democracy. *Economic Inquiry*, 13:373–388.

Browning, M., and Crossley, T.F., 2001. The life-cycle model of consumption and saving. *Journal of Economic Perspectives*, 15(3):3–22.

Browning, M., and Lusardi, A., 1996. Household saving: Micro theories and macro facts. *Journal of Economic Literature*, **34**(4):1797–1855.

Burtless, G., and Bosworth, B., 1998. Privatizing social security: The troubling trade-offs. *Brookings Policy Brief No. 14*. Washington, DC, USA: The Brookings Institution.

Buti, M., Franco, D., and Pench, L.R., 1997. Reconciling the welfare state with sound public finances and high employment. *European Economy* **4**(1997):7–42.

Campbell, D.W., and Watanabe, W., 2001. Household saving in Japan. *The Japanese Economic Review*, **52**(2):243–249.

Carson, E., and Kerr, L., 2001. Bust for the "baby boomers": The real midlife crisis. *Journal of Social Policy*, **6**(1):84–100.

Casamatta, G., Cremer, H., and Pestieau, P., 2000. The political economy of social security. *Scandinavian Journal of Economics*, **103**(3):503–522.

Casamatta, G., Cremer, H., and Pestieau, P., 2001. Demographic shock and social security: A political economy perspective. *International Tax and Public Finance*, **8**(4):417–431.

Chauveau, T., and Loufir, R., 1997. The future of public pensions in the seven major economies. In: D.P. Broer and J. Lassila (eds.), *Pension Policies and Public Debt in Dynamic CGE Models*. Heidelberg, Germany: Physica-Verlag.

Cichon, M., Newbrander, W., Yamabana, H., Weber, A., Normand, C., Dror, D., and Preker, A., 1999. Modelling in health care finance: A compendium of quantitative techniques for health care financing. *Quantitative Methods in Social Protection Series*. Geneva, Switzerland: International Labour Office, International Labour Organization.

Clark, R., Kreps, J., and Spengler, J., 1978. Economics of aging: A survey. *Journal of Economic Literature*, **16**:919–962.

Clark, R.L., York, E.A., and Anker, R., 1999. Economic development and labor force participation of older persons. *Population Research and Policy Review*, **18**(5):411–432.

Conesa, J.C., and Kreuger, D., 1999. Social security reform with heterogeneous agents. *Review of Economic Dynamics*, **2**(4):757–795.

Corsetti, G., and Schmidt-Hebbel, K., 1997. Pension reform and growth. In: S. Valdes-Prieto (ed.), *The Economics of Pensions: Principles, Policies, and International Experience*. Cambridge, UK: Cambridge University Press.

Costa, D.L., 1995. Pensions and retirement: Evidence from Union Army veterans. *Quarterly Journal of Economics*, **110**:297–320.

Cremer, H., and Pestieau, P., 2000. Reforming our pension system: Is it a demographic, financial or political problem? *European Economic Review*, **44**(4–6):974–983.

Crépon, B., Deniau, N., and Perez-Duarte, S., 2002. *Wages, Productivity and Worker Characteristics: A French Perspective*. Mimeo. Paris, France: INSEE.

Cubeddu, L., 2000. Intragenerational redistribution in unfunded pension systems. *IMF Staff Papers*, **47**(1):90–115.

Cutler, D.M., Poterba, J., Sheiner, L., and Summers, L.H., 1990. An ageing population: Opportunity or challenge? *Brookings Papers on Economic Activity*, **1990**(1):1–73.

Dawson, C., 2000. Defining moment. *Far Eastern Economic Review*, 27 April.

Deaton, A.S., and Paxson, C.N., 1997. The effects of economic and population growth on national saving and inequality. *Demography*, **34**(1):97–114.

Deaton, A.S., and Paxson, C.N., 2000. Growth and saving among individuals and households. *Review of Economics and Statistics*, **82**(2):212–225.

Dekle, R., 1990. Do the Japanese elderly reduce their total wealth? A new look at different data. *Journal of Japanese and International Economies*, **4**(3):309–317.

Demmel, R., and Keuschnigg, C., 2000. Funded pensions and unemployment. *Finanz-Archiv*, **57**(1):22–38.

Diamond, P.A., 1999. *What Stock Market Returns to Expect for the Future? An Issue in Brief*, Number 2, September. Boston, MA, USA: Center for Retirement Research at Boston College.

Diamond, P.A., 2000. What stock market returns to expect in the future? *Social Security Bulletin*, **63**(2):38–52.

Disney, R., 1996. *Can We Afford to Grow Older? A Perspective on the Economics of Aging*. Cambridge, MA, USA: MIT Press.

Disney, R., 2000a. Declining public pensions in an era of demographic aging: Will private provision fill the gap? *European Economic Review*, **44**(4–6):957–973.

Disney, R., 2000b. Crises in public pension programmes in OECD: What are reform options? *Economic Journal*, **110**(461):F1–F23.

Dohm, A., 2000. Gauging the labor force effects of retiring baby boomers. *Monthly Labor Review*, **123**(7):17–25.

Dutta, J., Kapur, S., and Orszag, J.M., 2000. A portfolio approach to the optimal funding of pensions. *Economics Letters*, **69**(2):201–206.

Easterlin, R.A., Schaeffer, C.M., and Macunovich, D.J., 1993. Will the baby boomers be less well off than their parents? Income, wealth, and family circumstances over the life cycle in the United States. *Population and Development Review*, **19**(3):497–522.

Elmendorf, D.W., and Sheiner, L.M., 2000. Should America save for its old age? Fiscal policy, population aging, and national saving. *Journal of Economic Perspectives*, **14**(3):57–74.

Enders, W., 1995. *Applied Econometric Time Series*. New York, NY, USA: John Wiley & Sons, Inc.

Endo, Y., and Katayama, E., 1998. Population aging and Japanese economic performance. In: B. Bosworth and G. Burtless (eds.), *Aging Societies: The Global Dimension*. Washington, DC, USA: The Brookings Institution, Chapter 5, pp. 240–265.

Ermisch, J., 1989. Intergenerational transfers in industrial countries: Effects of age distribution and economic institutions. *Journal of Population Economics*, **1**:269–284.

Ermisch, J., 1996. The demand for housing in Britain and population ageing: Microeconometric evidence. *Economica*, **63**(251):383–404.

Favreault, M., Ratcliffe, C., and Toder, E., 1999. Labor force participation of older workers: Perspective changes and potential policy responses. *National Tax Journal*, **52**(3):483–503.

Feeney, G., 1999. The demography of aging in Japan: 1950–2025. *NUPRI Research Paper Series No. 55*, February. Tokyo, Japan: Nihon University, Population Research Institute.

Fehr, H., 2000. Pension reform during demographic transition. *Scandinavian Journal of Economics*, **102**(3):419–443.

Feldstein, M., 1996. The missing piece in policy analysis: Social security reform. *American Economic Review*, **86**(2):1–14.

Feldstein, M., and Ranguelova, E., 2001. Individual risk in an investment-based social security system. *American Economic Review*, **91**(4):1116–1125.

Fenge, R., and von Weisacker, J., 2001. Compulsory savings: Efficiency and redistribution. On the interaction of means tested basic income and public pensions. *International Tax and Public Finance*, **8**(4):637–652.

Fogle, R.W., and Costa, D.L., 1997. A theory of technophysio evolution, with some implications for forecasting population, health care costs, and pension costs. *Demography*, **34**(1):49–66.

Forni, L., and Giordano, R., 2001. Funding a PAYG pension system: The case of Italy. *Fiscal Studies*, **22**(4):487–526.

Fougère, M., and Mérette, M., 1999. Population ageing and economic growth in seven OECD countries. *Economic Modelling*, **16**:411–427.

Franco, D., and Munzi, T., 1997. Ageing and fiscal policies in the European Union. *European Economy*, **4**:239–388.

Friedburg, L., 1999. The effect of old age assistance on retirement. *Journal of Public Economics*, **71**(2):213–232.

Friedman, B.M., and Warshawsky, M.J., 1990. The cost of annuities: Implications for saving behavior and bequests. *Quarterly Journal of Economics*, **105**:135–154.

Gale, W.G., 1995. The Effects of Pensions on Wealth: A Re-evaluation of Theory and Evidence. Manuscript. Washington, DC, USA: The Brookings Institution.

Gale, W.G., 1999. Privatizing social security (book review). *Journal of Economic Literature*, **37**(2):685–686.

Geanakoplos, J., Mitchell, O.S., and Zeldes, S., 1999. Social security money's worth. In: O.S. Mitchell, R.J. Myers, and H. Young (eds.), *Prospects for Social Security Reform*. Philadelphia, PA, USA: University of Pennsylvania Press.

Gokhale, J., Kotlikoff, L.J., and Sabelhaus, J., 1996. Understanding the postwar decline in U.S. saving: A cohort analysis. *Brookings Papers on Economic Activity*, pp. 315–407.

Gruber, J., and Wise, D. (eds.), 1999. *Social Security and Retirement around the World*. Chicago, IL, USA: University of Chicago Press.

Guest, R., and McDonald, I., 2001a. The impact of aging on the socially optimal rate of national saving: A comparison of Australia and Japan. *Review of Development Economics*, **5**(2):312–327.

Guest, R., and McDonald, I., 2001b. Ageing, optimal national saving and future living standards in Australia. *Economic Record*, **77**(237):117–134.

Habakkuk, H.J., 1962. *American and British Technology in the Nineteenth Century*. Cambridge, UK: Cambridge University Press.

Hackl, P., and Westlund, A.H., 1991. *Economic Structural Change Analysis and Forecasting*. Berlin, Germany: Springer-Verlag.

Hægeland, T., and Klette, T.J., 1999. Do higher wages reflect higher productivity? Education, gender and experience premiums in a matched plant-worker data set. In: J.L. Haltiwanger, J.R. Spletzer, J. Theeuwes, and K. Troske (eds.), *The Creation and Analysis of Employer-Employee Matched Data*. Amsterdam, Netherlands: North Holland.

Hamada, K., and Iwata, K., 1989. On the international ownership pattern at the turn of the twenty-first century. *European Economic Review*, **33**(5):1055–1085.

Harris, A.R., Myerson, N., and Smith, J., 2001. Social insecurity? The effects of equity investments on social security finances. *National Tax Journal*, **54**(3):645–668.

Hatta, T., and Oguchi, N., 1997. The net pension debt of the Japanese government. In: M.D. Hurd and N. Yashiro (eds.), *The Economic Effects of Aging in the United States and Japan*. National Bureau of Economic Research Conference Report, Chicago, IL, USA: University of Chicago Press, pp. 333–351.

Hayashi, F., 1991. Reply to Dekle and Summers. *Bank of Japan Monetary and Economic Studies*, **9**:79–89.

Hayashi, F., and Prescott, E., 2002. *The 1990s in Japan: A Lost Decade*, Interim Report for the Fourth International Forum of the Collaboration Projects. Tokyo, Japan: Economic and Social Research Institute, Cabinet Office, Government of Japan, pp. 1–34.

Hayashi, F., Ando, A., and Ferris, R., 1988. Life cycle and bequest savings: A study of Japanese and U.S. households based on data from the 1984 NSFIE and the 1983 survey of consumer finances. *Journal of Japanese and International Economies*, **2**:450–491.

Heller, P., 1989. Aging, savings, and pensions in the group of seven countries: 1980–2025. *Journal of Public Policy*, **9**(2):127–153.

Heller, P.S., Hemming, R., and Kohnert, P.W., 1986. Aging and social expenditure in the major industrial countries, 1980–2025. *IMF Occasional Paper No. 47*. Washington, DC, USA: International Monetary Fund.

Higgins, M., 1997. Demography, national savings, and international capital flows. *Federal Reserve Bank of New York Staff Report No. 76*. New York, USA: Federal Reserve Bank of New York.

Holzmann, R., 2000. Can Investments in Emerging Markets Help to Solve the Aging Problem? Manuscript. Washington, DC, USA: World Bank.

Horioka, C.Y., 1988. Saving for housing purchase in Japan, *Journal of Japanese and International Economies*, **2**(3):351–384.

Horioka, C.Y., 1989. Why is Japan's private savings rate so high? In: R. Sato and T. Negishi (eds.), *Developments in Japanese Economics*. Tokyo, Japan: Academic Press/Harcourt Brace Jovanovich Japan Inc., pp. 145–178.

Horioka, C.Y., 1991. The determinants of Japan's saving rate: The impact of age structure and other factors. *Economic Studies Quarterly*, **42**(3):237–253.

Horioka, C.Y., 1996. Future trends in Japan's saving rate and the implications thereof for Japan's external imbalance. In: L. Klein (ed.), *A Quest for a More Stable World Economic System: Restructuring at a Time of Cyclical Adjustment*. Boston, MA, USA: Kluwer Academic Publisher, Chapter 18, pp. 299–319.

Horioka, C.Y., 2001. Japan's public pension system in the twenty-first century. In: M. Blomstrom, B. Gagnes, and S. La Croix (eds.), *Japan's New Economy*. New York, NY, USA: Oxford University Press, pp. 99–119.

Horioka, C.Y., 2002. Are the Japanese selfish, altruistic or dynastic? *Japanese Economic Review*, **53**(1):26–54.

Horioka, C.Y., Kasuga, N., Yamazaki, K., and Watanabe, W., 1996. Do the aged dissave in Japan? Evidence from micro data. *Journal of the Japanese and International Economies*, **10**(3):295–311.

Hoynes, H.W., and McFadden, D.L., 1997. Impact of demographics on U.S. housing and nonhousing wealth. In: M.D. Hurd and N. Yashiro (eds.), *The Economic Effects of Aging in the United States and Japan*. Chicago, IL, USA: University of Chicago Press, pp. 153–194.

Hurd, M., 1990. Research on the elderly: Economic status, retirement, and consumption and saving. *Journal of Economic Literature*, **24**:565–637.

Hviding, K., and Mérette, M., 1998. Macroeconomic effect of pension reforms in the context of ageing: OLG simulations for seven OECD countries, *OECD Working Paper No. 201*. Paris, France: OECD.

Imrohoroglu, A., Imrohoroglu, S., and Joines, D.H., 1995. A life cycle analysis of social security. *Economic Theory*, **6**:83–114.

Institute of Population and Social Security Research, 1997. *Population Projections for Japan*. Tokyo, Japan: Ministry of Health, Labour and Welfare.

Itoh, T., 1996. Japan and the Asian economies: A miracle in transition. *Brookings Papers on Economic Activity*, Vol. 2, pp. 205–272.

Iwamoto, Y., 2002. Issues in medical expenditure and health policy in Japan. In: *The Economic Effect of Fewer Children and Aging and Desirable Policy Reform*, Interim Report for the Fourth International Forum of the Collaboration. Projects, Economic and Social Research Institute, Cabinet Office, Government of Japan.

Jackson, W.A., 1998. *The Political Economy of Population Ageing*. Cheltenham, UK: Edward Elgar.

James, E., 1998. New models for old-age security: Experiments, evidence, and unanswered questions. *World Bank Research Observer*, **13**(2):271–301.

Japan Aging Research Center, 1996. *Aging in Japan*. Tokyo, Japan.

Japan Institute of Labor, 2002. *National Accounts*, http://www.jil.go.jp/estatis/eshuyo/200207/e0101.htm.

Johnson, R., 2000. The effect of old-age insurance on male retirement: Evidence from historical cross-country data. *Federal Reserve Bank of Kansas City Research Working Paper: RWP 00/09*. Kansas City, MO, USA.

Karlsson, M., 2002. Comparative Analysis of Long-term Care Systems in Four Countries, Interim Report IR-02-003. Laxenburg, Austria: International Institute for Applied Systems Analysis.

Kato, R., 1998. Transition to an aging Japan: Public pension, savings and capital taxation. *Journal of the Japanese and International Economies*, 12:204–231.

Katsumata, Y., 2000. Japanese Social Security Measures to Support the Retired Aged. Manuscript. Tokyo, Japan: National Institute of Population and Social Security Research.

Kelley, A.C., and Schmidt, R.M., 2001. Economic and demographic change: A synthesis of models, findings, and perspectives. In: N. Birdsall, A.C. Kelley, and S.W. Sinding (eds.), *Population Does Matter: Demography, Poverty, and Economic Growth*. Oxford, UK: Oxford University Press.

Kenc, T., and Sayan, S., 2001. Demographic shock transmission from large to small countries: An overlapping generations CGE analysis. *Journal of Policy Modelling*, 23(2001):677–702.

Keynes, J.M., 1937. Some economic consequences of a declining population. *The Eugenics Review*, 29:13–17.

Kinsella, K., 2000. Demographic dimensions of global aging. *Journal of Family Issues*, 21(5):541–558.

Kohl, R., and O'Brian, P., 1998. The macroeconomics of ageing, pensions, and savings: A survey. *OECD Economics Department Working Paper No. 200*. Paris, France: OECD.

Kojima, H., 1995. Aging in Japan: Population policy implications. *Korea Journal of Population and Development*, 24(2):197–214, Seoul, Republic of Korea.

Kono, S., 2002. *A Study of the Speed of Population Ageing in Asia*. Paper presented at the 2002 IUSSP Regional Conference, Bangkok, Thailand, Mimeo.

Kosai, J.S., and Yashiro, N., 1998. Declining population and sustained economic growth: Can they co-exist? *JCER Discussion Paper No. 45*. Tokyo, Japan: Japan Center for Economic Research.

Kotlikoff, L.J., 1996. Simulating the privatization of social security in general equilibrium, *National Bureau of Economic Research Working Paper No. 5776*. Cambridge, MA, USA: NBER.

Kotlikoff, L.J., and Morris, J.N., 1989. How much care do the aged receive from their children? A bimodal picture of contact and assistance. In: D.A. Wise (ed.), *The Economics of Aging*, Chicago, IL, USA: University of Chicago Press, pp. 151–175.

Krueger, D., and Kubler, F., 2002. Intergenerational risk-sharing via social security when financial markets are incomplete. *American Economic Review*, 92(2):407–410.

Kune, J.B., 2001. The controversy of funding versus pay-as-you-go: What remains of the debate? *Geneva Papers on Risk and Insurance: Issues and Practice*, 26(3):418–434.

Laferrère, A., 1999. Intergenerational transmission models: A survey. *The Geneva Papers on Risk and Insurance*, **24**(1):2–26.

Lee, R.D., and Lapkoff, S.F., 1988. Intergenerational flows of time and goods: Consequences of slowing population growth. *Journal of Political Economy*, **96**:618–651.

Lee, R.D., and Miller, T., 2000. Immigration, social security, and broader fiscal impacts. *American Economic Review*, **90**(2):350–354.

Lee, R.D., and Skinner, J., 1999. Will aging baby boomers bust the federal budget? *Journal of Economic Perspectives*, **13**(1):117–140.

Lee, R.D., and Tuljapurkar, S., 1994. Stochastic population forecasts for the U.S.: Beyond high, medium and low. *Journal of the American Statistical Association*, **89**(428):1175–1189.

Lee, R.D., and Tuljapurkar, S., 1997. Death and taxes: Longer life, consumption, and social security. *Demography*, **34**(1):67–81.

Leimer, D.R., and Petri, P.A., 1981. Cohort-specific effects of social security policy. *National Tax Journal*, **24**(1):9–28.

Lewis, K.A., and Seidman, L.S., 2002. Funding social security: The transition in a life-cycle model. *Eastern Economic Journal*, **28**(2):159–180.

Lindh, T., 1999. Age structure and economic policy: The case of saving and growth. *Population Research and Policy Review*, **18**(3):261–277.

Lindh, T., and Malmberg, B., 1999. Age structure effects and growth in the OECD, 1950–1990. *Journal of Population Economics*, **12**(3):431–449.

Liu, L., Rettenmaier, A.J., and Saving, T.R., 2000. Constraints on big-bang solutions: The case of intergenerational transfers. *Journal of Institutional and Theoretical Economics*, **156**(1):270–291.

Lueth, E., 2001. Can inheritances alleviate the demographic burden? *International Monetary Fund Working Paper WP/01/97*. Washington, DC, USA: International Monetary Fund.

Lumsdaine, R.L., Stock, J.H., and Wise, D.A., 1997. Retirement incentives: The interaction between employer-provided pensions, social security, and retiree health benefits. In: M.D. Hurd and N. Yashiro (eds.), *The Economic Effects of Aging in the United States and Japan*. Chicago, IL, USA: University of Chicago Press.

Lutz, W. (ed.), 1996. *The Future Population of the World: What Can We Assume Today?* London, UK: Earthscan.

MacKellar, L., and Ermolieva, T., 1999. The IIASA Social Security Reform Project Multiregional Economic-Demographic Growth Model: Policy Background and Algebraic Structure, Interim Report IR-99-007. Laxenburg, Austria: International Institute for Applied Systems Analysis.

MacKellar, L., and McGreevey, W.P., 1999. The growth and containment of social security systems. *Development Policy Review*, **17**:5–24.

MacKellar, L., and Reisen, H., 1998. A simulation model of global pension investment. *Ageing Working Papers AWP 5.5*. Paris, France: OECD.

MacKellar, L., Ermolieva, T., and Reisen, H., 1999. Globalization, Social Security, and Intergenerational Transfers, Interim Report IR-99-056. Laxenburg, Austria: International Institute for Applied Systems Analysis.

MacKellar, L., with Ermolieva, T., Horlacher, D., and Mayhew, L., 2002. *Economic Impacts of Population Aging in Japan*, Final Report, submitted to the Daiwa Institute of Research Ltd., Tokyo, Japan.

Macunovich, D.J., 1999. The fortunes of one's birth: Relative cohort size and the youth labor market in the United States. *Journal of Population Economics*, 12(2):215–272.

Maddox, G., 1987. *Encyclopedia of Aging*. New York, NY, USA: Springer Publishing Company.

Magnussen, K.A., 1994. Old-age pensions, retirement behaviour and personal saving: A discussion of the literature. *Social and Economic Studies No. 67*. Oslo, Norway: Statistics Norway.

Mankiw, G., and Weil, D.N., 1989. The baby boom, the baby bust, and the housing market. *Regional Science and Urban Economics*, 19:235–258.

Manton, K.G., and Vaupel, J.W., 1995. Survival after the age 80 in the United States, Sweden, France, England, and Japan. *New England Journal of Medicine*, 333(18):1232–1235.

Marchand, M., Michel, P., and Pestieau, P., 1996. Intergenerational transfers in an endogenous growth model with fertility changes. *European Journal of Political Economy*, 12:33–48.

Marini, G., and Scaramozzino, P., 1999. Social security and intergenerational equity. *Journal of Economics – Zeitschrift für Nationalökonomie*, 70(1):17–35.

Martin, P., 2001. The role played by labor migration in the Asian economic miracle. In: A. Mason (ed.), *Population Change and Economic Development in East Asia: Challenges Met, Opportunities Seized*. Stanford, CA, USA: Stanford University Press, pp. 332–335.

Mason, A., and Ogawa, N., 2001. Population, labor force, saving, and Japan's future. In: M. Blomstrom, B. Gagnes, and S. La Croix (eds.), *Japan's New Economy*. Oxford, UK: Oxford University Press, pp. 48–74.

Mason, A., The, Y.-T., Ogawa, N., and Fukui, T., 1994. The intergenerational distribution of resources and income in Japan. In: J. Ermisch and N. Ogawa (eds.), *The Family, the Market, and the State in Ageing Societies*. Oxford, UK: Oxford University Press, pp. 158–197.

Masson, P., and Tryon, R., 1990. Macroeconomic effects of projected population aging in industrial countries. *IMF Staff Papers*, 37(3):453–485.

Masuda, M., and Kojima, K., 2001. Japanese social security for the elderly from a viewpoint of life cycles. *Review of Population and Social Policy*, No. 10, pp. 37–54.

Mayhew, L., 2000. *Health and Elderly Care Expenditure in an Aging World*, Research Report RR-00-21. Laxenburg, Austria: International Institute for Applied Systems Analysis.

Mayhew, L., 2001a. *Disability – Global Issues and International Perspectives*. London, UK: The Staple Inn Actuarial Society.

224   *References*

Mayhew, L., 2001b. Japan's Longevity Revolution and the Implications for Health Care Finance and Long-term Care, Interim Report IR-01-010. Laxenburg, Austria: International Institute for Applied Systems Analysis.

McGarry, K., 1999. Inter vivos transfers and intended bequests. *Journal of Public Economics*, **73**(3):321–351.

McGarry, K., and Schoeni, R.F., 1995. Transfer behavior in the health and retirement study: Measurement and redistribution of resources within the family. *Journal of Human Resources*, **30**:S184–S226.

McMorrow, K., and Roeger, W., 1999. The economic consequences of aging populations, *Economic Paper No. 138*, European Commission, Directorate General for Economic and Financial Affairs.

Meredith, G., 1995. Alternative long-run scenarios. In: *Saving Behaviour and the Asset Price "Bubble" in Japan, IMF Occasional Paper, No. 124*. Washington, DC, USA: International Monetary Fund, pp. 46–50.

Mesa-Lago, C., 2002. Myth and reality of pension reforms: The Latin American evidence. *World Development*, **30**(8):1309–1321.

Miles, D., 1999. Modelling the impact of demographic change on the economy. *Economic Journal*, **109**(452):1–36.

Miles, D., 2000. Funded and unfunded pensions: Risk, return and welfare. *CEPR Discussion Paper No. 2369*. London, UK: Centre for Economic Policy Research.

Miles, D., and Iben, A., 2000. The reform of pension systems: Winners and losers across generations in the United Kingdom and Germany. *Economica*, **67**(266):203–228.

Miles, D., and Timmerman, A., 1999. Risk sharing and transition costs in the reform of pension systems in Europe. *Economic Policy: A European Forum*, **29**:253–286.

Ministry of Health, Labour and Welfare, 2002. *Long-term Health Insurance in Japan*. Tokyo, Japan: Government of Japan. www.mhlw.go.jp/english/topics/elderly/care/2.html.

Ministry of Public Management, Home Affairs and Posts and Telecommunications, 1976–2000. *Labor Force Survey*, Tokyo, Japan: Government of Japan.

Ministry of Public Management, Home Affairs and Posts and Telecommunications, 1997. *Employment Status Survey*. Tokyo, Japan: Government of Japan.

Ministry of Public Management, Home Affairs and Posts and Telecommunications, 2001. *Statistical Handbook of Japan*. Tokyo, Japan: Government of Japan.

Ministry of Public Management, Home Affairs and Posts and Telecommunications, 2002. *Statistical Handbook of Japan*. Tokyo, Japan: Government of Japan.

Ministry of Public Management, Home Affairs and Posts and Telecommunications, 2003. *Statistical Handbook of Japan*. Tokyo, Japan: Government of Japan.

Mitchell, O., and Moore, J.F., 1998. Can Americans afford to retire? New evidence on retirement saving adequacy. *Journal of Risk and Insurance*, **66**(3):371–400.

Mitchell, O.S., and Zeldes, S.P., 1996. Social security privatization: A structure for analysis. *American Economic Review*, **86**(2):363–367.

Mulheisen, M., and Faruquee, H., 2001. Japan: Population aging and the fiscal challenge. *Finance and Development*, **38**(March):10–15.

Mulligan, C.B., 2000. Funding social security: A strategic alternative (book review). *Journal of Economic Literature*, **38**(3):659–660.

Nanjo, Z., and Kobayashi, K., 1985. Method of computing the expectation of life at old age on the basis of the principle of agreement with data. *NUPRI Research Paper Series No. 36*. Tokyo, Japan: Nihon University Population Research Institute.

National Institute of Population and Social Security Research, 1997. *The Cost of Social Security in Japan, Fiscal Year 1995*, Tokyo, Japan.

National Institute of Population and Social Security Research, 2002a. *Selected Demographic Indicators for Japan*, Tokyo, Japan, www.ipss.go.jp/English/S_D_I/Indip.html.

National Institute of Population and Social Security Research, 2002b. *Population Projections for Japan*, 2001–2050, January, Tokyo, Japan, Mimeo.

National Institute of Population and Social Security Research, 2002c. *Overview of Social Security in Japan*, Tokyo, Japan, www.ipss.go.jp/English/Jasos2002/Jasos2002.html.

Niggle, C.J., 2000. The political economy of social security reform proposals. *Journal of Economic Issues*, **34**(4):789–809.

Noguchi, Y., 1989. *Macroeconomic Implications of Population Ageing*. Paper presented at the Conference on the Economic of Aging jointly sponsored by the Japan Economic Research Center and the National Bureau of Economic Research, 8–9 September 1989, Tokyo, Japan.

O'Brien, M.J., 2000–2001. Older male labor force participation: The role of social security and hidden unemployment. *Australian Journal of Labor Economics*, **4**(3):206–223.

Ogawa, N., 1986. *Consequences of Mortality Change on Aging*, NUPRI Reprint Series No. 20, Reprinted from: Consequences of Mortality Trends and Differentials (United Nations publication, Sales No. E. 85.XIII, 3), Population Studies No. 95, Part III, Chapter XVI. Tokyo, Japan: Nihon University Population Research Institute.

Ogawa, N., 1995. *Population Change, Development and Women's Role and Status in Japan*. Bangkok, Thailand: Economic and Social Commission for Asia and the Pacific.

Ogawa, N., 2000. *"Policy Options for Meeting the Challenge of an Aging Society: The Case of Japan," Aging in Japan 2000*. Tokyo, Japan: Japan Aging Research Center, pp. 75–104.

Ogawa, N., and Clark, R., 1996. Human resource policies and older workers in Japan. *The Gerontologist*, **36**(5):627–636.

Ogawa, N., and Ermisch, J.F., 1994. Women's career development and divorce risk in Japan. *LABOUR*, **8**(2):193–219.

Ogawa, N., and Retherford, R.D., 1993a. The resumption of fertility decline in Japan, 1973–1992. *Population Development Review*, **19**(4):703–741.

Ogawa, N., and Retherford, R.D., 1993b. Care of the elderly in Japan: Changing norms and expectations. *Journal of Marriage and the Family*, **55**(3):585–597.

Ogawa, N., and Retherford, R.D., 1997. Shifting costs of caring for the elderly back to families in Japan: Will it work? *Population and Development Review*, **23**(1):59–94.

Ogawa, T., 2001. *The Long-Term Care for Older People in Japan, the Social Care Insurance Scheme (SCIS) and Marketisation of Elder Care*. Oxford, UK: Oxford Institute of Ageing, University of Oxford.

Ohtake, F., and Yamaga, H., (2002), The effects of the old age pension system for active employees on the labor supply of elderly male workers. In: *The Economic Effect of Fewer Children and Aging and Desirable Policy Reform*, Part II, Interim Report for the Fourth International Forum of the Collaboration Projects. Tokyo, Japan: Economic and Social Research Institute, Cabinet Office, Government of Japan, pp. 235–255.

Organisation for Economic Co-operation and Development, 1997. *Labor Force Statistics, 1976–1996*. Paris, France: OECD, pp. 532–586.

Orszag, P.R., and Stiglitz, J.E., 2001. Rethinking pension reform: Ten myths about social security systems. In: R. Holtzmann and J. Stiglitz (eds.), *New Ideas About Old Age Security*. Washington, DC, USA: World Bank, pp. 17–56.

Palley, T.I., 2000. Life expectancy and social security: Why indexing the payroll tax to longevity makes good economic sense. *Journal of Post Keynesian Economics*, **22**(3):507–514.

Palumbo, M.G., 1999. Uncertain medical expenses and precautionary saving near the end of the life cycle. *Review of Economic Studies*, **66**(2):395–421.

Pearson, B., 2002. Koizumi raises health insurance charges by 50 per cent. *Australian Financial Review*, **10**, February 14.

Pestieau, P., and Possen, U.M., 2000. Investing social security in the equity market: Does it make a difference? *National Tax Journal*, **53**(1):41–57.

Peterson, P.G., 1999. *Gray Dawn: How the Coming Age Wave Will Transform America—and the World*. New York, NY, USA: Times Books.

Poterba, J.M., 2001. Demographic structure and asset returns. *Review of Economics and Statistics*, **83**(4):565–584.

Poterba, J.M., Venti, S.E., and Wise, D.A., 1997. The effects of special saving programs on saving and wealth. In: M.D. Hurd and N. Yashiro (eds.), *The Economic Effects of Aging in the United States and Japan*. Chicago, IL, USA: University of Chicago Press.

Radalet, S., Sachs, J., and Lee, J.S., 1997. Economic growth in Asia, *HIID Development Discussion Paper No. 609*. Cambridge MA, USA: Harvard Institute for International Development.

Raymo, J.M., 1998. Later marriages or fewer? Changes in marital behaviour of Japanese women. *Journal of Marriage and the Family*, **60**(November):1023–1034.

Razin, A., Sadka, E., and Swangel, P., 2002. The wage gap and public sector support for social security. *American Economic Review*, **92**(2):390–395.

Reil-Held, A., 1999. Bequests and aggregate wealth accumulation in Germany. *The Geneva Papers on Risk and Insurance*, **24**(1):50–63.

Reisen, H., and Fischer, B., 1994. Pension fund investment: From ageing to emerging markets. *OECD Development Centre Policy Brief, No. 9*. Paris, France: OECD Development Centre.

Retherford, R.D., Ogawa, N., and Matsukura, R., 2001. Late marriage and less marriage in Japan. *Population and Development Review*, **27**(1):65–102.

Rios-Rull, J.-V., 2001. Population changes and capital accumulation: The aging of the baby boom. *Advances in Macroeconomics*, **1**(1):1–46.

Romer, P., 1990. Capital, labor and productivity. *Brookings Papers on Economic Activity: Microeconomics*, Washington, DC, USA: The Brookings Institution, pp. 337–367.

Roseveare, D., Leibfritz, W., Fore, D., and Wurzel, E., 1996. Ageing populations, pension systems, and government budgets: Simulations for 20 OECD countries. *OECD Economics Department Working Papers No. 168*. Paris, France: OECD.

Rust, J., and Phelan, C., 1997. How social security and medicare affect retirement behavior in a world of incomplete markets. *Econometrica*, **65**(4):781–831.

Sala-i-Martin, X., 1996. A positive theory of social security. *Journal of Economic Growth*, **1**(2):277–304.

Samuelson, P.A., 1958. An exact consumption-loan model of interest with or without the social contrivance of money. *Journal of Political Economy*, **66**:467–482.

Samwick, A.A., 2000. Is pension reform conducive to higher saving? *Review of Economics and Statistics*, **82**(2):264–272.

Schieber, S., and Shoven, J., 1994. The consequences of population aging on private pension fund saving and asset markets. *National Bureau of Economic Research Working Paper No. 4665*. Cambridge, MA, USA: NBER.

Schieber, S., and Shoven, J., 1997. The consequences of population aging on private pension fund saving and asset markets. In: M. Hurd and N. Yashiro (eds.), *The Economic Effects of Aging in the United States and Japan*. Chicago, IL, USA: University of Chicago Press, pp. 111–130.

Schneider, U., 1999. Germany's social long-term care insurance: Design, implementation and evaluation, *International Social Security Review*, **52**:2.

Siebert, H., 1997. Labour market rigidities at the root of unemployment in Europe. *Journal of Economic Perspectives*, **11**(1):191–200.

Sinn, H.-W., 2000. Why a funded pension system is useful and why it is not useful. *National Bureau of Economic Research Working Paper No. 7592*. Cambridge, MA, USA: NBER.

Skirbekk, V., 2002. Variations in Productivity over the Life Span: A Review and Some Implications, Interim Report IR-02-061. Laxenburg, Austria: International Institute for Applied Systems Analysis.

Solow, R., 1956. A contribution to the theory of economic growth. *Quarterly Journal of Economics*, **70**:65–94.

Stark, O., and Zhang, J., 2002. Counter-compensatory inter-vivos transfers and parental altruism: Compatibility and orthogonality? *Journal of Economic Behavior and Organization*, **47**(1):19–25.

Statistic Bureau of the Ministry of Public Management, Home Affairs, Posts, and Telecommunications, 2001. *Statistical Handbook of Japan 2001*, http://www.stat.go.jp.

Storesletten, K., 2000. Sustaining fiscal policy through immigration. *Journal of Political Economy*, **108**(2):300–323.

Tabellini, G., 2000. A positive theory of social security. *Scandinavian Journal of Economics*, **102**(3):523–545.

Tachibanaki, T., 1996. *Public Policies and the Japanese Economy: Savings, Investment, Unemployment, Inequality*. London, UK: Macmillan Press.

Takayama, N., 1990. How much do public pensions discourage personal saving and induce early retirement in Japan? *Hitotsubashi Journal of Economics*, **31**(2):87–103.

Takayama, N., 1992. The greying of Japan: An economic perspective on public pensions, *Economic Research Series No. 30*. Tokyo, Japan: Kinokuniya, distributed by Oxford University Press, Walton Street, Oxford, UK.

Takayama, N., 1996. Possible effects of aging on the equilibrium of public pension system in Japan. In: *European Ageing and Pension Expenditures Prospects in the Western World*, Reports and Studies 3. Brussels, Belgium: European Commission, pp. 155–194.

Takayama, N., 2001. Pension reform in Japan at the turn of the century. *Geneva Papers on Risk and Insurance: Issues and Practice*, **26**(4):565–574.

Takayama, N., 2002. Japan's never-ending social security reforms. *International Social Security Review*, **55**(4):11–22.

Takinawa, M., 2000. Mushrooming costs of Japan's aging population. *The New York Times*, December 26, C4.

Thorgerson, O., 2001. Reforming social security: Assessing the effects of alternative funding strategies. *Applied Economics*, **33**(12):1531–1540.

Thornton, J., 2001. Age structure and the personal savings rate in the United States, 1956–1995. *Southern Economic Journal*, **68**(1):166–170.

Turner, D., Giorno, C., de Serres, A., Vourc'h, A., and Richardson, P., 1998. The macroeconomic implications of ageing in a global context. *OECD Economics Department Working Paper No. 193*. Paris, France: OECD.

UK Office of Population Censuses and Statistics, 1988. *OPCS Surveys of Disability in Great Britain, Report 1: The Prevalence of Disability Among Adults*. London, UK: HMSO.

UN Population Division, 1998. *1998 Revision*. New York, NY, USA: UN.

UN Population Division, 2001a. *World Population Prospects: The 2000 Revision*. New York, NY, USA: UN.

UN Population Division, 2001b. *Replacement Migration: Is It a Solution to Declining and Ageing Populations*, Department of Economic and Social Affairs, Population Division, ST/ESA/SER.A/206. New York, NY, USA: UN.

UN Population Division, 2002. *World Population Prospects: The 2002 Revision, Vol. II: Sex and Age Distribution of the Population.* New York, NY, USA: UN.

U.S. Council of Economic Advisers, 1996. *Annex to Economic Report of the President,* Transmitted to the Congress February 1996. Washington, DC, USA: U.S. Government Printing Office.

Valdes-Prieto, S., 2000. The financial stability of notional account pensions. *Scandinavian Journal of Economics,* **102**(3):395–417.

van Dalen, H.P., 1996. Pitfalls in the economic analysis of aging. *Journal of Policy Modeling,* **18**:158–184.

van Dalen, H.P., and Henkens, K., 2002. Early-retirement reform: Can it work and will it work? *Ageing and Society,* **22**(Part 2):209–231.

van der Gaag, J., and Preker, A., 1998. Health care for aging populations: Issues and options. In: *Choices in Financing Health Care and Old Age Security,* World Bank Discussion Paper No. 392. Washington, DC, USA: World Bank

van Solinge, H., van Dalen, H., Dykstra, P., van Imroff, E., Moors, H., and van Wissen, L., 1998. Population, labour and social protection in the European Union: Dilemmas and prospects, *Netherlands Interdisciplinary Demographic Institute Report No. 52.* The Hague, Netherlands: NIDI.

Venti, S., and Wise, D.A., 1989. Aging, moving, and housing wealth. In: D. Wise (ed.), *The Economics of Aging.* Chicago, IL, USA: University of Chicago Press.

Warr, P., 1994. Age and employment. In: H. Triandis, M. Dunette, and L. Hough (eds.), *Handbook of Industrial & Organizational Psychology* (2nd edition), Vol. 4. Palo Alto, CA: Consulting Psychologist Press, pp. 485–550.

Weil, D., 1996. Intergenerational transfers, aging, and uncertainty. In: D.A. Wise (ed.), *Advances in the Economics of Aging.* Chicago, IL, USA: University of Chicago Press.

White, J., 2000. Looking in the wrong place: Why Chile provides no evidence on social security privatization. *Public Budgeting and Finance,* **20**(4):52–62.

WHO, 2000. *World Health Report 2000.* Geneva, Switzerland: World Health Organization.

Williamson, J.B., 2001. Privatizing public pension systems—lessons from Latin America. *Journal of Aging Studies,* **15**(3):285–302.

Williamson, J.G., and Higgins, M., 2001. The accumulation and demography connection in East Asia. In: A. Mason (ed.), *East Asia: Challenges Met, Opportunities Seized.* Stanford, CA, USA: Stanford University Press, pp. 123–154.

Willmore, L., 1998. Social security and the provision of retirement income. *Pensions Institute Discussion Paper PI-98-9805.* London, UK: Birkbeck College, University of London.

Wise, D., 1997. Retirement against the demographic trend: More older people living longer, working less, and saving less. *Demography,* **34**(1):83–95.

Withers, G., 2002. Population aging and the role of immigration. *The Australian Economic Review,* **35**(1):104–112.

Wolff, E.N., 1999. Wealth accumulation by age cohort in the U.S., 1962–92: The role of savings, capital gains and intergenerational transfers. *The Geneva Papers on Risk and Insurance*, **2**(1):27–49.

Wolff, E.N., 2001. Has Japan specialized in the wrong industries? In: M. Blomstrom, B. Gagnes, and S. La Croix (eds.), *Japan's New Economy*. Oxford University Press, Oxford, pp. 175–197.

Yamauchi, N., 1997. The effects of aging on national saving and asset accumulation in Japan. In: M.D. Hurd and N. Yashiro (eds.), *The Economic Effects of Aging in the United States and Japan*. Chicago, IL, USA: University of Chicago Press.

Yashiro, N., 1997. Aging of the population in Japan and its implications to the other Asian countries. *Journal of Asian Economics*, **8**(2):245–261. Greenwich, CT, USA.

Yashiro, N., 1998. The economic factors for the declining birthrate. *Review of Population and Social Policy*, **7**:129–144. Tokyo, Japan.

Yashiro, N., Oshio, T., and Matsuya, M., 1997. Macroeconomic and fiscal impacts of Japan's aging population with specific reference to pension reforms. Economic Research Institute, Economic Planning Agency, *Discussion Paper No. 78*, Tokyo, Japan, September.

Yoon, Y., and Talmain, G., 2001. Endogenous fertility, endogenous growth and the public pension system: Should we switch from a pay-as-you-go to a fully funded system? *Manchester School*, **69**(5):586–605.

Yoshikawa, H., Nishimura, K., Shirai, M., and Fukuda, S., 2002. *Aging and Economic Growth*, Interim Report for the Fourth International Forum of the Collaboration Projects, Economic and Social Research Institute, Cabinet Office, Government of Japan, pp. 1–10.

Zhang, J., and Zhang, J., 2001. Bequest motives, social security and economic growth. *Economic Inquiry*, **39**(3):453–466.

Index